Revolutionary Marxism and Social Reality in the 20th Century

REVOLUTIONARY STUDIES
Series Editor: PAUL LE BLANC

Revolutionary Marxism and Social Reality in the 20th Century

ERNEST MANDEL

Collected Essays Edited
and with an Introduction by
STEVE BLOOM

HUMANITIES PRESS
NEW JERSEY

First published in 1994 by Humanities Press International, Inc.,
Atlantic Highlands, New Jersey 07716.

© 1994 by Ernest Mandel

Library of Congress Cataloging-in-Publication Data

Mandel, Ernest.
Revolutionary Marxism and social reality in the 20th century :
collected essays of Ernest Mandel / edited and with an introduction
by Steve Bloom.
p.   cm. — (Revolutionary studies)
Includes bibliographical references and index.
ISBN 0-391-03800-1 (pbk)
1. Communism—History—20th century.   I. Bloom, Steve, 1946–
II. Title.   III. Series.
HX40.M2564   1993
320.5'32'0904—dc20   92-33943
CIP

A catalog record for this book is available from the British Library.

Printed in the United States of America

Contents

Preface

When putting together a book made up of essays that were originally written to stand on their own there are always different possibilities for organizing the material. One, obviously, is simply to put everything in chronological order. Another is by theme or subject. I have chosen to divide this book into three general categories: historical essays, the Leninist theory of organization, and other questions of Marxist program and theory. Within these broad subject areas things appear chronologically—except for the question of Leninist organization.

The reasons for separating organization from the other questions of a programmatic or theoretical nature and reversing the chronological order of the two items that appear in this section were both practical and pedagogic. There were two essays that dealt specifically with this topic. Had I put them together with the other theoretical works and divided the book into only two sections, Part I would have turned out dramatically shorter than Part II. Therefore, the three-part structure made some sense.

It was also my goal, in organizing this material, to try to make Mandel's more theoretical writings less imposing for the reader who may be unfamiliar with even basic Marxist ideas and terminology. Therefore, the shorter, more popularly written pieces appear in Part I and can begin to introduce some of these ideas and concepts. The first item in Part II then followed logically, because it was initially presented as a lecture rather than in written form and should also be more easily assimilated by those who lack any substantial previous experience with Marxism. Reading it before the second, longer piece—which looks exhaustively at the philosophical and theoretical basis for Lenin's ideas on party organization—may help provide a transition between the more easily accessible materials in Part I and the longer, more abstract articles.

When editing older writing for republication—things that date from before the early 1970s when we all became conscious (as a result of the second wave of feminism) about the inherent sexist bias in Western languages—one can be faced with a dilemma: What to do about the use of the masculine form to refer to the entire human species? In the present volume this arises especially in "Trotsky: The Man and His Work," first published in 1947. I have chosen not to alter the way things appeared in the original English publication on this point, and ask the reader to keep in

mind that, where it appears, the use of such terms as "he" and "mankind"
to refer to all humanity stems from a universal literary tendency at the time
the material was written. In later works, Mandel himself corrects this—
reflecting his commitment to the complete equality of women in language
as well as in society as a whole (a general theme he repeats throughout the
essays in this book).

   Notes which are not by Mandel will indicate their source, being identified
as either a "translators' note" or "editor's note."

STEVE BLOOM

Introduction

The earliest essay in this book was published in 1947. The latest appeared in 1990. This spans more than four decades of work and dedication by Ernest Mandel to the Fourth International and to revolutionary Marxism. The beginnings of his activity in the world Trotskyist movement go back even further—to the anti-Nazi struggle in Europe during World War II and before.

It is rare, to say the least, for young revolutionary militants to maintain their consciousness and commitment for so long, to become, we might say, old revolutionary militants. Most often, youthful enthusiasm succumbs to the innumerable material pressures that bear down in our society, or to cynicism and demoralization as a result of the difficulties of the struggle, or else it falls victim to the murderous repression which is so often inflicted on those who fight for the liberation of humanity.

This ordinarily rapid turnover of individuals is something for which our movement pays a substantial price. An activist with even a decade's experience in building a revolutionary organization will inevitably have gained considerable practical knowledge. If we combine that practical knowledge with a little theoretical and programmatic understanding gained through basic educational work, or through dealing with specific problems of the class struggle as they arise, it is easy to see how difficult it can be to replace a lost cadre with a new recruit. More is involved than a question of how many people belong to the revolutionary organization. We also have to ask how much collective consciousness and experience these people represent.

This general problem is important to keep in mind when reading these pages—not, in particular, as a personal tribute to Ernest Mandel for continuing in his seventh decade of life as an active revolutionary leader. Rather, it is significant because it helps us to appreciate that behind these essays lies a truly profound commitment to the cause of working people, to studying—and contributing to—the program and theory of social change, as well as a considerable depth of experience during more than half a century of struggle.

It is a well-known fact that for years Mandel has been acknowledged as the foremost Marxist economist in the world. But his experience and expertise are not limited to economics, as the broad range of subjects covered by this book clearly demonstrates. They range from an assessment of Rosa Luxemburg's role in the social-democratic movement during the early part of this century to a series of discussions about Marxist theory as it applies in today's world—with a great deal of territory covered in between. Yet, despite this variety of topics, there remain a number of things that tie all of the materials in this volume together.

As with any good Marxist, Mandel displays a genuine consistency of method. Works such as his can, in many ways, serve as the best kind of introductory textbook to historical materialism—because they illustrate how the dialectic of social development can be consciously understood and applied in life, used by human beings to better understand the reality in which we exist and to provide real insight into how that reality might be changed. This is, in many respects, a far better way to *begin* studying the Marxist method than with abstract discussions of differing philosophical views—though going on to the further study of theoretical and philosophical questions in their own right will certainly lead any activist to a better appreciation of the way things work in society, and therefore an increased ability to analyze and act to change them.

This last point has particular relevance as we read this volume. There is something in particular that stands out: how much the attention Mandel has paid during his lifetime to a general study of theory and philosophy can be brought to bear to improve our concrete collective understanding of real problems in the real world. Young activists are often impatient with this truth. They would like to think that their elemental, quite profound, and thoroughly justified outrage at social injustice ought to be enough to bring this system of exploitation and oppression crumbling down. But a long and bitter experience in the workers' movement proves that this is not true. If, therefore, only a small proportion of those who read this book are inspired to go on to a more in-depth study of the general methodology and philosophy of revolutionary Marxism which Mandel relies on for his analysis, it will have served its purpose well.

One is also bound to notice many specific themes that Mandel returns to again and again (presented here in no particular order): those aspects of program and activity which differentiate revolutionists from reformists; the real practicality of a revolutionary perspective in the 20th century and the completely utopian nature of any outlook that hopes to solve the problems of humanity by reforming capitalism; the absolute necessity for the revolutionary movement to recognize historical truth and present reality in all of its aspects—even (or especially) if this may sometimes make things less comfortable for those with their own ideological axe to grind; the key role played by democracy within the revolutionary party and in the mass movement as a whole; the combined dialectic of international and national struggles in the process of the proletarian revolution; the complex interrelationship between what Marxists call the objective and subjective factors in the maturation of the revolutionary process; the central revolutionary role of the working class, which at the same time cannot be used as an excuse for rejecting the importance of other forms of struggle; and much more.

Time will not verify all of the conjunctural, or even historical prognoses made by Mandel in these works. I was particularly struck, for example, when reading his projection, in "The Marxist Case for Revolution Today," about how future developments in the Soviet Union were likely to unfold. Comparing this to the reality that has developed in that country—even in the short period of time since this article was written—provides a stark contrast. (I make this statement with the full realization that events in the ex-U.S.S.R. during the next months and years may be just as full of sharp turns and surprises as the recent past has been, conceivably even forcing a revision of what I have said before these words find their way into print.)

But such discrepancies should not upset us too much. After all, every Marxist who has ever put pen to paper has made similar errors. This is true because any prediction we might try to make based on our theoretical knowledge is inevitably a conditional one—that is, it is conditioned by the reality which exists at the moment we make our prediction, and it is based on the limitations of our knowledge about what that reality is and the social forces that are acting upon it. We constantly discover that conditions change in unexpected ways, and in no small part this is because our appreciation of them was incomplete, failing to take into account certain factors that were working beneath the surface, hidden from view. Mandel himself in "Reasons for Founding the Fourth International and Why They Remain Valid Today" discusses this general problem as it affected prognoses made by Trotsky before his death in 1940—about what was likely to happen in the aftermath of World War II.

It would be false, however, to conclude, from problems such as this, that the Marxist method itself is invalid, or to reject the importance of continuing to make general projections that can serve as guidelines in our day-to-day activity. As with any science, Marxism advances by a process of formulating ideas about the real world and then proceeding to test them against reality as it unfolds—learning more about both our theory and reality in the process. We can then strive to improve our theories in order to take account of things that we did not know before.

Only if one conceives of Marxism in the form advocated by its most caricatured proponents—as a church, with a high priest or council of elders which has, always has had, and always will have all of the answers to all of the questions, revealed either through scripture or some omniscient power—can we believe that specific errors of prognosis about particular events in the class struggle can invalidate our basic method. One might just as well decide—on the grounds that death sometimes occurs in patients as a result of complications unforeseen by their doctors—that all of medicine is a fraud.

Marxism is not a church, which is why it can legitimately lay claim to being a science—though it is certainly one that is even less precise, we might say more of an art, than medicine. I can proclaim with absolute certainty that other Marxists, just as committed as Mandel to the cause of working-class liberation, will find specific points in these pages with which they do not agree. (I can be certain of this, in part, because I myself find a number of such points.)

That is all to the good. Because not only does our science advance through testing its knowledge against reality, but we also have the trait in common with other sciences that Marxism moves forward through the active theoretical (even polemical) struggle between individuals with different interpretations of reality. Once again, there can never be any one person with all of the answers. We will come to the truth through a collective effort, or we will not find it at all.

What is required, then, is for the reader of this work, or any Marxist writing for that matter, to keep critical faculties intact. Nothing said here should be accepted on faith. Once that is fully understood, there is a great deal to be learned from the specific ideas, and from the general approach to the world, that Ernest Mandel develops in these pages.

PART I
Historical Essays

1

Trotsky: The Man and His Work

"Lenin is the reflection, the image of the [Russian] working class, not only in its proletarian present, but also in its still more recent proletarian past. . . . He absorbed from the national *milieu* all that he needed for accomplishing the greatest revolutionary action in all history. . . ." Thus Trotsky characterized the founder of Bolshevism, and it is thus that Lenin appears today. Lenin and Bolshevism could not have been born except as an outgrowth of the whole of Russia's ancient past: an imperialism that combined the defects of autocracy with its own special defects and developed so as not to breed the illusion of pacifist evolution that gripped the workers' aristocracy of the Western countries. There wasn't a trace of fatalistic passivity in Lenin, and it could not have been otherwise; the leader of the Russian revolution from his youth was oriented toward action. In fact, Lenin's life is a most striking example of the concentration of all the forces of a personality toward a realization of the historical objective of the class. The leaders of the Western working-class movement were unable to view Lenin before 1914 as anything but an incomprehensible trouble-maker; after 1914, for the most part, they hated him as an implacable enemy.

Trotsky was different. In spite of a childhood spent on a farm he was influenced not so much by the peasant forces of his people as by the living forces of the imperialist world's great capitals, to which his first two emigrations took him: London, Berlin, Vienna, Paris, Madrid, New York. Of all the great Russian revolutionists he was without doubt the most "European," the one who absorbed Western civilization most thoroughly, who impregnated it with that revolutionary dynamism which existed intact within the Russian working class, and thus succeeded in giving it its highest expression in this century.

This article appeared in the theoretical magazine of the Socialist Workers' Party in the U.S.A., *Fourth International*, Vol. 8, no. 7 (New York, July-August 1947), p. 205.

With Lenin, action is the natural expression of his being and, starting from the concrete, inscribes itself on a body of ideas from which it remains inseparable. With Trotsky, action is the natural fulfillment of thought which seizes the concrete on the wing without ever letting it go. There is here only a shade of difference, but it is this nuance which gives a finished maturity to their collaboration beginning in 1917.

These two giants did not live the simple life of legendary heroes. "Only incurable philistines imagine Lenin as a saint who never made a mistake," said Trotsky on this subject. Their faults and errors are closely linked with their profound natures. There is in Lenin, in his writings of 1905, in his ideas before 1917 on the nature of the Russian revolution, a reticence to leave the realm of the immediate, to push to its end the concept of the proletariat as the motivating force of the revolution. For Lenin, not to exclude in advance the possibility of a revolutionary alliance between the proletarian party and an eventual party resting on the peasantry meant not to eliminate in advance the most immediate, direct, and least hazardous way of achieving the overthrow of the autocracy.[1] This error, however, remains at all times within the framework of his revolutionary temperament. He could never have anything in common with Menshevism, which, likewise characterizing the Russian revolution as being confined at first to the boundaries of the bourgeois revolution, surrendered leadership of the historic process to the "liberal" bourgeoisie (nonexistent, said Trotsky, and events proved him to be right!). Lenin's will, rigorously turned toward the solution of every "theoretical" problem, was still too hidebound to be able to conceive of the immediate conquest of power by the proletariat. Twelve years later, when Trotsky's theory was realized,[2] thanks to the leadership of Lenin, he did not hesitate for a single instant to make the necessary turn in ideas as in action. But did he not say at the decisive moment that "this gave him vertigo"?

Trotsky, for his part, standing politically at the opposite pole from Menshevism, was for a long time led astray by a too-great confidence in the possibilities of uniting divergent political currents by purely intellectual persuasion.[3] It is true that with a stroke of genius he formulated, while still very young, his concept of the permanent revolution, which served as a key to understanding most of the revolutions of the 20th century, thus distinguishing himself not only from other Russian revolutionists but also from those of all Europe. Nevertheless, he remained too attached to the "traditional" and inadequate organizational forms of Western social democracy to understand the necessity for the split which appeared so brutal in the eyes of the European leaders of the workers' movement. The application of Bolshevik organizational methods was necessary for all Europe; even Lenin himself had not yet grasped this. Trotsky, who all his life had a horror of fatalism and could not rest content with the empty hopes of the German leaders, who thought that the process of "evolution" would "automatically" eliminate the "extravagances" of Lenin, nevertheless struggled in practice for organizational reconciliation. That is why he permitted himself to embark on the notorious "August bloc," which was entirely hostile to his political concepts. This is the explanation for the paradox that Lenin, guided by his fierce will to achieve his goal, long remained an admirer of Kautsky, although the first in his own party to break sharply with the organizational concepts of centrism. Trotsky, whose more profound knowledge of the European working-class movement enabled him to understand long before Lenin the bankruptcy of Kautskyan ideology, remained for many years the defender of centrist[4] organizational principles in Russia.

But it is characteristic of truly great men to have a quality which permits them, at decisive moments, to go beyond their own particular limitations, to raise themselves to the height of the burning tasks which history presents to their class. This transformation was brought about "naturally," without any clashes or internal conflicts, both in Lenin and Trotsky, in 1917. The same Lenin who all his life clung with superhuman obstinacy to political principles once they were adopted, abandoned from the first day of the Russian revolution his formula of the "democratic dictatorship of the proletariat and peasantry," which was "by-passed by events," as he said, and became the fiercest partisan of the struggle for the dictatorship of the proletariat. Trotsky, the "conciliator," understood, at the same moment and with the same quickness, that "unity" between the Bolsheviks and Mensheviks "was no longer possible" (irony of history, it was Stalin who drove him to that) and thus became, in Lenin's own words, "the best Bolshevik." Only the revolution itself was able to bring about this twofold transformation with a minimum of difficulty, because both of these men, true revolutionists that they were, felt and understood that the revolution was necessary to open the way to the victory of their class.

Trotsky has often been accused of having been too ambitious, too "personal" in his attitude toward the party, too haughty in his attitude toward the comrades. These accusations are absurd. Lenin, who possessed a psychological insight of rare quality, had a clearer vision when he revealed the weakness as a "too pronounced attraction" on Trotsky's part "toward the administrative side of things." But even the elderly Angelica Balabanov, who too often simply takes tidbits of corridor gossip and transforms them into the motive forces of history, made this penetrating remark: during the Revolution, at the very moment when the crowd was bearing him on their shoulders, Trotsky was able to efface more than ever before the pronounced "personal" traits of his character. Never was the arrogance of the "leader" more foreign to him than when all the threads for unleashing the revolution were gathered together in his hands. "With his natural tact," said Angelica, he knew how to impose the severest self-criticism when that was most necessary, and when it is nevertheless most difficult for the majority of mortals. It is here that we see the real strength of character which is at the base of every great action.

There was nothing in Trotsky of that vulgar "Marxism" which thinks it can read the historical process in statistics just as the palm-reader reads the future in the lines of the hand. Going far beyond "economics" or "sociology" as separate studies, he sought to capture *human reality* in all its aspects. That is why he was without question one of the greatest historians who has ever lived, the one who succeeded more than any other in that "integrated resurrection of the past" which has only been dreamed of since the time of Michelet.[5] With his penetrating eye he encompasses, in a moment, the great movements of the masses and the personalities of political leaders, the price of bread and the tone of the literary gazettes, the movements on the stock exchange, as well as piquant anecdotes overheard in the salons. His powerful brain is like an immense crucible in which are remolded once again all the constituent elements of history. The subjects treated in his works range from philosophy, through political economy, applied economics, sociology, political polemics, history, biography, military technique, to journalistic essay and art criticism. How sum up a work so vast? Is it simply political journalism? Or is it "applied Marxism"? It is that, but it is much more besides. It is a tremendous and continuous effort to understand and interpret man in his entirety, in order to be able to preside over his transformation. It is an unceasing effort to subject all phases of human activity to conscious criticism, so that they may be transformed under the direction of man's critical consciousness.

UNIVERSAL INTERESTS

Although he had universal interests, Trotsky was at the opposite pole from dilettantism and eclecticism. This universality of interests, in order to be real and effective, requires their fundamental unity, their integration in a concept of the world which never stops "becoming," but which remains no less a unity, and which at the same time possesses precise outlines. More preoccupied than any other contemporary thinker with the many-sidedness of human reality, Trotsky is precise and careful in his documentation to the point of pedantry, and at the same time broad in his perspectives, capable of breaking away from the immediate in order to grasp the fundamental direction of events. Starting from the reality of the thousand and one aspects of human activity which are observed directly, he traces with the hands of a magician-sculptor a majestic panorama in which the essential outlines stand out with perfect clarity.

The leitmotif which links all his works is the materialist conception of history. This leitmotif he employs with a mastery that is unequalled; sometimes going from the "essential reality," which is the class struggle, to the most "far-removed" manifestations of intellectual life; sometimes digging the soil, with a science confident of itself, in order to probe the profound class roots of political and ideological phenomena. To each of these tasks he brought too much passion to be able to tolerate a negligent, superficial, or *blasé* attitude toward Marxist theory. It was for him an indispensable key to the understanding of history. Thanks to this key he always made history live for us in his works. He was at one and the same time its severest critic and its most eloquent herald. But he was able to be both of these only because he understood history so well.

There is in Trotsky a complete unity of theory and practice, of thought and action. Lenin poured on the renegade Kautsky the indignation of the proletariat toward one who is a traitor to their interests and their struggle for emancipation. Trotsky castigated with his contempt and bitter irony Kautsky's thinking, which was in decay because it was divorced from action, a practice which was truly corrupt because it was divorced from principle. This unity between his own thought and action was most clearly revealed in revolutionary strategy and attains its highest form in the *military* strategy of the victorious proletariat. The revolutionary leader shoulders an overwhelming responsibility when he finds himself at the head of the masses; the military chief has the same responsibility, plus the added responsibility for the very short lives of the thousands of soldiers who battle under him. Apart from the cynics, the morally deranged, or the luminaries, who are mentally deranged, men, in the face of such responsibilities, remain for the most part exposed to their doubts, their convictions, their wills, their capacity for making decisions. Trotsky, the outstanding military leader, possessed the additional resources of Trotsky, the revolutionary leader of the proletariat. Just as he understood how to feel the pulse of history, so with a penetrating glance he could take up a military map and determine the decisive place where all efforts should be concentrated. The resolution, the power, the steel-sharpness of his actions sprang from a clear understanding and an unshakable conviction in the justice of the cause of the proletariat. Addressing the Red Army soldiers was for him the same as speaking in September 1917 in the *Cirque Moderne* in Petrograd. Directing the work of the staff office of the Southeastern front was only the logical continuation of his direction of the Revolutionary Military Committee; and this, in turn, logically flowed from his work on the Central Committee of the Party.

One would seek in vain in his speeches to the Army, or in his attitude at the front, for a trace of the saber-rattler's arrogance or of that sinister "military spirit" which betrays an absurd discipline, a sterile routine, and a bureaucratic approach, the whole combined with a "strategy" which makes sport of men as it does of the cheapest material. As against all the usual generals—Stalin's present marshals included—who see no other means of preserving the cohesion of their troops than by appealing to their lowest instincts and by the threat of the knout, Trotsky never ceased to appeal to the revolutionary consciousness of the oppressed. To pseudo-revolutionary romanticism, with its opposition to centralized coordination in battle—only the counterbalance to bourgeois discipline—he counterposed the conscious and voluntary discipline of the proletariat. On this subject he declared 20 years later: "Even during the civil war I tried within the army—even in the midst of campaigns—to give full opportunity to the Communists to discuss all military decisions. I have even discussed these decisions with the soldiers and, as I have explained in my autobiography, even with deserters." Who could reproach him for not always being able to realize this completely, since it was necessary to improvise everything in the midst of a world of enemies—and many enemies that he even had to utilize? The essential consideration is that unity of thought and action involves a *comprehension* of the dialectical interaction between means and ends which guides every true revolutionist in his acts, by his desire above all to achieve the raising of the consciousness of his own class.

Soldier of Revolution

This soldier of the Revolution differed very much from the image drawn of him not only by his enemies but also by some of his admirers. The Hungarian White Guards in a celebrated caricature have represented him as a red lion, seated on a gigantic pyramid of skulls. On the other side, Karl Mayer tells us that at bottom he had a certain gentleness, whose origin undoubtedly was an intelligence which seemed capable of understanding everything. This gentleness is seen again in his last words, where, after expressing his confidence in the victory of our movement, he adds that all his life he has struggled for a society which would be free of all violence.

And how could it be otherwise? In the heart of every true Marxist is a belief in man, without which all revolutionary activity is devoid of meaning. Throughout the last 20 years of his life, years of battling in retreat, of struggle against infamy, calumny, and the growing degradation of humanity, he maintained that unshaken faith, without being ensnared by illusions, and retained his magnificent clear-sightedness until the end. He liked to repeat that man's climb from the semi-ape stage has been long and arduous, but that nevertheless no little progress has been achieved. And how well he knew how to scorn professional pessimists who are always trying to avenge themselves on humanity for their own illusions. All life ends in death, he said, but statistics continue to prove that men do not for this reason stop coming into the world. . . .

At the foundation of all human activity there is, in reality, an indestructible optimism which is only another expression of the instinct of preservation. Marx's favorite adage was the Latin one: "Nil humani a me alienum puto" (Nothing human can be alien to me). Trotsky understood that a revolutionary leader must be a man among men, and through his best works there runs the thread of this optimism, which is only an attachment to life, and which will always constitute a supplementary attractive force for all healthy men: "To love life with open eyes, with a critical spirit which never surrenders, without illusions, never embellishing it, but always taking it as it is, for whatever it may have to offer us and even more for what it may sometime become—that is an achievement of the highest order!" This achievement he realized better than any other.

But his faith in man has nothing of the mystic or irrational in it. It is only the highest form of consciousness. To love man is to grasp the alienation in one's own nature; it means to rebel against the social inequality which has produced this frustration; it means to struggle for man's integration into a classless society. In Trotsky there is not only complete unity of thought and action, but also of thought and feeling. The sharp sword of aggressive reasoning is animated by the fire of artistic sensibility; and this formidable combination imparts to his speeches and writings, at one and the same time, that majestic cadence and that menacing spirit of warning which characterizes the multitudes in their march toward the revolution! The workers who heard him immediately felt his complete communion with them, and they instinctively put confidence in him because they felt that he not only defended their interests but also that he hated, loved, struggled, suffered, and rejoiced with them. Trotsky did not idealize the proletariat, but he understood it perfectly, for he knew that none can lead the workers to victory without understanding them, and that no one will ever completely understand them without truly uniting with them.

His whole past and his whole character thus predestined him to become the standard-bearer of the opposition against the nascent bureaucracy in the U.S.S.R. Even when he was living at the Kremlin, the thick stone walls never separated him from the life of the masses. Even while in power, his ear was attuned to all the expressions of humor, criticism, and dissatisfaction of the workers. With that conspicuous gift for generalization characteristic of him, he was able, beginning with 1923, to discern underneath that murmur of dissatisfaction the beginning of a gigantic realignment of historic forces. In this realignment of forces, his place was predestined. How he must have scorned those who ceased to be conscious builders of history in order to become transmission belts for hostile social forces. And how pitiful must have appeared to him the conservatism of those who satisfied their ambitions by driving to their offices in a limousine! His own "ambition" embraced a vaster purpose: the revolutionary emancipation of the world proletariat! When the political orientation of the Kremlin began to deviate from that aim, he parted company with it in the same natural manner with which, all his life, he had known how to attune his actions to his convictions. "The error" with which so many superficial critics reproached him, of having "hesitated" to "struggle for power" in 1923, is in reality an additional expression of that inherent quality; never to act contrary to his convictions. The usurpation of power by the bureaucracy was by itself an indication for the Left Opposition of the ebbing forces of the Revolution. To struggle "for power" in a period of the passivity of the masses is the work of adventurers and standard-bearers of reaction—even if these people occasionally hide themselves in the folds of history's revolutionary flag. For those who conceive of "power" only as deriving from the revolutionary assault of the *masses*, the tasks in the period of reaction were clearly those of preserving the revolutionary traditions, of maintaining contact among the advanced elements of the party, of analyzing the developments of Thermidor[6] and thus preparing the future revolutionary wave on the world arena as well as in the U.S.S.R. These are the tasks which the Left Opposition, and the world cadres of the Fourth International which have sprung from it, have without respite tried to accomplish under Trotsky's leadership.

Thus was Trotsky: every one of his acts was completely conscious! Replying to a question of the French novelist Tatayans, who was questioning him regarding his "idea on happiness," Trotsky replied: To think—to write—to realize one's ideas—. It is thus that he lived in his hotel rooms in Paris, in the salons of the Kremlin, in the semi-prisons of his third emigration, and in that sunny field where death finally felled him. Indifferent to the vicissitudes of the material conditions of life, his genius ripened, his thought clarified, his style was enriched and simplified along a straight line. His life in itself is thus a monument of conscience, a monument to the future man, the man who will be set completely free of material servitude, and who will no longer live alienated from his own nature.

AUTHENTIC MARXISM

Marx denied that he was a "Marxist," and Lenin scorned the word "Leninist." He merely considered himself a "consistent revolutionary Marxist." In his turn, Trotsky in his works has carefully placed the term Trotskyism between quotation marks and for years characterized it as the designation on the part of Stalinist bureaucrats for Bolshevism. As one cannot doubt the authentic Marxist character of Leninism, so little can one doubt, after an objective examination, the authentic Leninist character of Trotskyism. Moreover, just as Leninism possesses no less its own physiognomy and constitutes a definite stage in the development and enrichment of Marxism, so Trotskyism appears today with its own specific traits, as a broadening of the teaching of Marx, Engels, and Lenin. Trotskyism is the *Marxism of our epoch*, and that is true in a most profound sense.

The chief merit of Trotsky from the point of view of the history of ideas consists in this: he has literally preserved Marxism in the midst of a general recession in the workers' movement and of a complete degeneration of the traditional parties and ideologies. Without yielding an inch, he has preserved the Leninist heritage, on the theoretical as well as the tactical planes, against the enveloping movements of the epigones of Lenin and the scribes of Stalin. With the same tenacity he defended this heritage against the feeble yet incessant frontal attacks of reformism and centrism.

The ideological decline of the great traditional movements was much more rapid and profound than their organizational decomposition. In its turn, European social democracy's actual break in *practice* with class politics, in 1914, preceded its complete *theoretical* rupture with revolutionary Marxism. German Social Democracy adopted a party program that was officially "reformist" only in 1921 (program of Gorlitz) and definitively so only in 1925 (Heidelberg program). But one can state without exaggeration that beginning with 1914, the Social Democracy ceased paying any attention to theory. The rare "theoretical" writings which appeared after this date consist entirely of empirical rationalizations for successive phases of party "tactics." "The ideological efforts" of the degenerated Social Democracy consisted of an occasional attempt to "justify" theoretically the criminal passivity of their leaders, confronted with the decay of capitalism, their cynical rejection of all revolutionary activity, their avowed incorporation into bourgeois "democracy," their cowardice before the attacks of the bourgeoisie, and their bad conscience with regard to the rebels in their own ranks. The result was a mixture of mechanistic fatalism and evolutionary cretinism. Hilferding "foresaw" several months before the outbreak of the 1929 crisis a "long period" of soaring capitalist prosperity!—which left the reader only the choice between ennui and pity.

The ideological decay of the Stalinist bureaucracy came about with still more overwhelming rapidity. "Theory" became the abject servant of a "tactic" which was inspired by the appetites of the bureaucrats, just as in the Middle Ages philosophy was the servant of theology, a necessary covering for the temporal power of the Church. Never had it fallen so low, from the height of Lenin's genius down to the heavy feet of the professional apologists of the Great Leader. The servility of the Stalinist "theoreticians," whose only function consisted of garnishing with "classical" quotations the spicy dishes which the too-famous cook prepared for the proletariat of Russia and the entire world, robs them of all esteem, even that of their own masters.

But this complete ideological impotence is armed with the most powerful material apparatus that history has ever known, and the quantity of inept and lying books, mass-produced, combined with opportune raids by the G.P.U., is a social reality which has proven devastatingly strong. Theory becomes a power when it takes hold of the masses, Marx said. The lie has been proven a no less terrible power in the hands of an unscrupulous apparatus, so long as the masses do not surge back upon the political stage.

One trembles at the thought of what would have happened had Trotsky died in 1923. Of course, Marxism, the expression of contemporary social reality and its internal dynamics, would have been preserved by others. Tens, later hundreds and thousands of young theoreticians and tacticians of five continents would have striven to arrive by common effort at a Marxist conception of events. But the balance of these efforts, in proportion to the positive results attained, would have witnessed a striking amount of wasted effort and lost time. Within his own person, Trotsky filled the gap created in the history of the working-class movement by the disappearance of one whole generation, which was corrupted and physically broken by Stalinism, demoralized by the dismal succession of defeats, and annihilated by the mounting waves of reaction and fascism. The polemical works of those who had materially "vanquished" Trotskyism have passed into oblivion. Was it not because the authors themselves were for the most part executed as "Trotskyists"? But the works of Trotsky dating from this period continue to be studied by thousands of young workers and intellectuals throughout the world, because these works alone represent the Marxist tradition in this black period in the history of humanity. The education of new revolutionary Marxist cadres is possible only thanks to the works of Trotsky. In preserving Marxism during the years of retreat and reaction, he has built the springboard for the ascending period which is just beginning. In the face of Stalinist victories, Trotsky used to rely upon the verdict of history. Seven years after his death, this verdict is already clear in the sphere of ideas—as Trotsky never doubted that it would be!

Like any method of investigation and systemization of the facts of experience, Marxism can be maintained only on condition that it be continually *enriched*. Any attempt to fall back defensively on "tradition," without any effort to pass new developments which are continually taking place through the sieve of the materialist dialectic, is certain to bring about a fatal ossification of the theory and to end in its certain death. Trotsky's represents the only serious effort to interpret in the light of Marxism those disconcerting phenomena of the last three decades, namely: the development of fascism, the usurpation of power in the U.S.S.R. by the bureaucracy, the zigzag evolution of the soviet economy, the monstrously accelerated decay of the capitalist world, and the general crisis in the revolutionary leadership of the proletariat. Lenin had advanced and enriched the heritage of Marx by his study of imperialism, of the world war, and of the first revolutionary wave. His work is Marxism in the epoch of the rise of imperialism and of the October revolution. On Trotsky has fallen the heavy task of enriching the heritage of Marx and Lenin in the epoch of reaction and triumphant counter-revolution. He has thus continued the tradition with the same implacable clarity, the same breadth of vision, the same sharpness of analysis possessed by those who preceded him.

The instinct to preserve privileges, except in the case of individuals who consciously break with this, imparts to thought a narrow and insurmountable framework, against which every effort at "objective" social study comes to grief. The dynamism of revolutionary proletarian thought lies precisely in its "emancipation" from every social privilege; its "material interests" coincide with a "disinterestedness" from the social point of view. But the workers' bureaucracies, both reformist and Stalinist, have in their turn become privileged and conservative social forces in contemporary society. Just as they have debased ideology in general to the level of serving their material greeds, so have they rendered their own thought sterile and impotent for the new investigations which history is constantly demanding. The betrayals of the traditional leaderships during the Spanish Civil War, which were historic expressions of their own material interests as opposed to those of the world proletariat, took the form of a total incapacity to *understand* the significance of fascism, the decay of capitalism, and the revolutionary strategy of the proletariat that could vanquish these additional obstacles. It is not by chance, then, that for two decades not a single work has appeared by a Stalinist or reformist "theoretician," except as an isolated or secondary phenomenon. All the enrichments of Marxism in the field of history, sociology, the study of art, literature, or psychology are in works by the disciples of Trotsky or by those who have been educated in his spirit. Certainly, the period of reaction, which has barely ended, is not favorable for the flowering of a large generation of Marxists. This generation is only beginning to knock at the door. Nevertheless, there is an interest in theory which is to be found in the ranks of the sympathizers or partisans of the Fourth International. They make an effort to study the most pressing ideological problems—the materialist conception of important aspects of history not yet clarified; the relationship between Marxism and psychology; the investigation of the subjective factor in history; the study of the materialist dialectic; the attempt to elaborate a materialist conception of art and literary criticism. All these efforts, begun by young theoreticians in France and China, in India and the United States, in Argentina and Palestine, have been done under the signs of the works of Leon Trotsky. In these works themselves is to be found an endless treasure of fertile ideas and outlines of new methods of investigation. An entire generation will be required to elaborate on the suggestions interspersed through his works. This generation will work and succeed only thanks to the school which was built by his efforts.

But the preservation of Marxism and its enrichment through the study of the new phenomena of our epoch—that alone does not demarcate the place which Trotsky occupies in the development of Marxist thought. There is an essential part of Marxism which could not have been systematized before his time.

Marx's work in its entirety is only the scientific interpretation of the world and of the tendencies inherent in its transformation. As for the conscious realization of this transformation and the actual proletarian revolution, of that he was able to leave us only general considerations and numerous isolated remarks, but no systematic study. On the contrary, the tenacity with which he resisted the elaboration of any "advance plan," the formulation of any "general rule," arose precisely from his clear understanding that the detailed study of proletarian strategy and tactics for the conquest of power must be based on a broad *revolutionary experience*. He lived to see only the initial effort of the Paris Commune in this scheme of ideas. That is why he had to leave to his successors the task of completing Marxism, in this sense.

Lenin, for his part, made a tremendous effort to state precisely and demarcate the role of the *subjective factor*: the importance of the party, the formation of the vanguard, its relationship with the class. These efforts, combined with a precise and systematic *tactic of struggle*, which was principled, realistic, and revolutionary, are considered by us today, and deservedly, to have a universal application; Lenin, however, at least up to 1914, limited his vision to the Russian Social Democracy. Beginning with the downfall of the Second International, however, his field of action rapidly broadened. He became the educator of the whole world proletariat. His writings on the strategy of *revolutionary defeatism*, on the building of revolutionary parties, on the tactics of the united front, on national and colonial questions, as well as the Russian revolution, constitute the most precious teaching that the proletariat possesses for the elaboration of a revolutionary policy. Nevertheless, Lenin's experience was limited to the Russian revolution and to the first stage of the German revolution. Subsequent experience has shown that the general study of the subjective factor, of the role and policy of the revolutionary party—which constitutes Lenin's contribution to contemporary Marxism—has to be completed by a special study of the *internal laws of the development of the proletarian revolution*, of the mechanism of revolution, and of the tactic of the revolutionary party with a view to the conquest of power. This indispensable complement to Marxism, this "science of revolution" in the double sense of the word, could be systematically elaborated only on the basis of a wider revolutionary experience than that of 1917. Trotsky made a brilliant beginning in *Lessons of October* and *The Communist International after Lenin*. He has more precisely elaborated it to the point where it now exists in exact outline form, in his *Permanent Revolution*, his *History of the Russian Revolution*, and his writings on the subject of Germany, France, and Spain between 1930 and 1938. The substance of this historically important work is found in the programmatic writings of the Fourth International. These represent not only the heritage of Marx and Lenin, the teachings of the *Communist Manifesto*, of *Capital*, of *What Is to Be Done?*, *Imperialism*, and the *First Four Congresses of the Communist International*, but also of 30 years of proletarian victories and defeats in an epoch when the world was constantly swinging between revolution and counter-revolution.

Lenin educated three generations of Russian worker-militants in the art of building the revolutionary party and the principled development of its political tactics. But only in 1917 did he arrive at a clear understanding of the dictatorship of the proletariat. Most of the leaders of the Bolshevik Party were unable for their part to assimilate the lessons of October 1917. No more did the revolutionary militants who came to the Comintern in 1919 have an understanding of these lessons on the basis of their own individual experience, heavily handicapped as they were by the "peaceful" development of the prewar years, their isolation during hostilities, the too rapid and tumultuous unfolding of the postwar revolutionary wave. The subsequent development of this vanguard was completely blocked by the degeneration of the Third International, beginning with 1923—the most nefarious crime of Stalinism against the world proletariat. In place of a selection of a revolutionary leadership on the basis of its political maturity, there occurred a reverse selection, on the basis of servility and obedience to the Kremlin. When the Trotskyists were excluded from the C.I., everything had to be started all over again. The building of a new revolutionary vanguard was begun, one that was capable of acting in accordance with the lessons of the October victory and the subsequent defeats. It was to this task that Trotsky devoted most of his time. It is the accomplishment of this task which will have the greatest influence on the future course of history.

This building of a new revolutionary vanguard was undertaken under the most difficult conditions, at a time when the world working-class movement was dragged into a long series of defeats. Thus, of necessity it was a movement "against the current." Around the *living Marxism*, personified by Trotsky, were gathered above all those elements who had not been discouraged by the defeats. These were always the most fearless, but were not always the best. Those who, because of their more intimate ties with the proletariat, reflected the illusions and discouragements of the class did not enter our ranks. Those who never succeeded in integrating themselves in the mass movement came with less hesitation to the small handful of outcasts. The education of this vanguard too often took the form of a literary and academic exercise, for the only real school of revolutionary strategy is in active participation in the *revolutionary* movement of the *masses*. The vanguard, due to its isolation, developed a number of defects characteristic of a whole period of recession: excessive factionalism, sectarianism, and presumptuousness of the intellectual with its inevitable corollary, professional proletarianism. Work was directed inward and political discussions, indispensable to any healthy organization, took on a too abstract character, rarely consisting of a critical review of tactical concepts in the light of their *concrete* application to the workers' struggle. Moreover, in Europe as well as in the U.S.S.R. and the Far East, fascist, Stalinist, and imperialist terror implacably mowed down the most courageous and capable of our cadres, thus destroying at each turn the *continuity* in education and experience of this new vanguard. All these factors, which expressed themselves differently in different countries, can be summed up thus: *Since a genuine revolutionary vanguard can be built only in close contact with the activity of the class, and a genuine revolutionary policy can only be elaborated in contact and under the critical eye of the masses*, we possessed in most countries at the close of the period of retreat only groups of cadres, only skeleton organizations. But the first test, that of the war, has shown how effective was this necessary preparation. Some people may have deserted; here and there human material may have shown itself to be too weak; new groups of revolutionists have had to take up the torch in not a few countries, *but everywhere the basic policy was formulated, a common line was elaborated, the same method of organization was applied*, thanks to the program, tradition, and the cadres which Trotsky had created in the years before the war. On the basis of the program he elaborated are gathered together all those who desire to build genuine revolutionary parties. The tradition which he first began in the history of the working-class movement is that of a genuine world leadership which is more than merely the sum total of the national leaderships or the authority of one organization leading in its wake all the others. Thereby, one of the essential causes of early Comintern weakness might have been avoided and supplementary guarantees provided for the harmonious development of our movement.

At the time that the Fourth International was founded, Trotsky predicted that it would count millions of partisans within ten years. Sarcastic critics maliciously enjoy citing this prognosis and asking where these millions are. But historic predictions are not payable on a certain date like bills. The historic process has developed more slowly than Trotsky anticipated but it has developed along the same line. In countries like France, India, the United States, and Bolivia we count tens of thousands of workers and poor peasants who sympathize with our ideas, and in the world arena there are already, without doubt, several hundreds of thousands. These remain few enough compared with the forces necessary to bring our work to fruition, but it is even now an impressive army compared to our feeble forces of 1938. The first important wave of workers' struggles in France was sufficient for organs as diverse, but equally hostile to our movement, as the Stalinist *L'Umanità* and Henry Luce's *Time* magazine, to discover "Trotsky's shadow" projecting itself upon events. This alone is sufficient to imbue us with confidence.

We very strongly doubt that we shall meet our critics again in the next stage!

SLOWER TEMPO

All of us have erred in our immediate perspectives; in drawing too-mechanical analogies with 1918. We were not sufficiently impregnated with Trotsky's fundamental concept that we had to "prepare for long years, if not decades, of wars, uprisings, brief interludes of peace, new wars and new insurrections." It is now clear, however, that we are not passing through a brief period, analogous to that of 1918–23, in which the revolutionary energy of the proletariat was rapidly exhausted by the extreme violence and the rapid succession of decisive struggles. Such a period can no longer be repeated in Europe, because the bourgeoisie is incomparably weaker and its economy incomparably more shaken; and decisive actions on the part of the proletariat have been impossible because it started from a much lower level of consciousness and organization than that of 1918; it did not have behind it 30 years of progress, making it confident of its own forces, but instead 25 years of continual defeats, which have left a dangerous heritage of skepticism and discouragement. This paradox must be understood, that the rhythm will be slower in the stage of the atomic bomb than when airplanes first began to drop bombs. But it will be precisely this slower rhythm of development which "will provide the young revolutionary party with opportunities of testing itself, of accumulating experience and of maturing." We no longer have the living brain of Trotsky, who with his incomparable clarity of thought would have made it easier to discover, under the surface of an apparently calm sea, the powerful currents which are already proclaiming the next tempest. But we have his method as a guide and his teachings on the subject of the nature of our epoch, which permit us to repeat confidently today what he himself said in the past:

History is a powerful machine in the service of our ideas. It works with merciless deliberation and insensibility, but it does work! We believe in it. It is only in those instants when its greedy mechanism absorbs the very hot blood of our hearts that we have the urge to cry out: "This thing you are doing, do it more quickly!"

Notes

1. *Editor's note*—Before his famous "April Theses" in 1917, Lenin believed that a "democratic dictatorship of the proletariat and the peasantry" was the kind of government that would immediately follow an anti-tsarist revolution in Russia. He accepted the idea, traditional among Marxists at the time, that a genuine proletarian revolution was impossible there because of the economic backwardness of the country. This meant a very limited industrial base, a small working class, etc. The revolution, at least in its initial stages, would undertake strictly bourgeois-democratic tasks to pave the way for a real development of capitalism, which in turn would pave the way for a proletarian revolution. But Lenin also understood—unlike the Menshevik wing of the Russian Social-Democratic movement—that the Russian bourgeoisie was too weak and indecisive to lead such a revolution. Therefore, Lenin asserted, it would be up to the workers and peasants to carry through a radical restructuring of Russian society along bourgeois-democratic lines.

2. *Editor's note*—This is a reference to Trotsky's theory of "permanent revolution." Like Lenin, Trotsky understood that the workers and peasants, not the "liberal bourgeoisie," would have to be the driving force of a revolution in Russia. But Trotsky insisted that once they had begun such a process the masses would not be willing to stop at the limits of a strictly "bourgeois-democratic" revolution. They would inevitably try to drive ahead to their full liberation, and this was antithetical to continued domination of the economy by a capitalist class. The proletariat, unlike the peasantry, had a viable alternative political and economic program to that of the bourgeoisie, and therefore was in a position to lead the worker-peasant alliance even though it was numerically much much weaker. The economic backwardness of Russia and the small size of its working class represented real problems, but they could be overcome through a spread of the Russian revolution westward, to the more industrialized countries of Europe—which could then aid in the development of the Russian economy.

3. *Editor's note*—During the years before the 1917 revolution, Trotsky refused to join either the Bolshevik or the Menshivik faction in the Russian Social-Democratic Labor Party. He insisted that there were no principled differences that justified the split in the movement, and tried to undertake initiatives to reunify its two main wings.

4. *Editor's note*—The term "centrism" refers to political currents which, while to the left of outright reformism, nevertheless lack an adequate theoretical understanding or commitment to independent working-class political action. This makes it impossible for them to act in a genuinely revolutionary way. Centrist groups tend to vacillate between revolutionary and reformist positions.

5. *Editor's note*—Jules Michelet (1798–1874) was a French writer and historian who championed the cause of the poor and the oppressed.

6. *Editor's note*—Trotsky used the term "Thermidor" to draw an analogy between the French revolution and the development of the Stalinist bureaucracy in Russia. In both cases, he asserted, a partial counter-revolution had placed individuals in power whose personal interests and political goals were completely contrary to the original aims of the masses in establishing the revolutionary order. But in neither case did this process go so far as to overturn the social gains of the revolution. (That is, feudal rule was not restored in France, and capitalism was not restored in Russia.)

2

Solzhenitsyn's Assault on Stalinism . . . and on the October Revolution

Aleksandr Solzhenitsyn. *The Gulag Archipelago* (New York: Harper & Row, 1974). 660 pp.

The Gulag Archipelago testifies to a threefold tragedy. First, the tragedy of the Stalinist purges that struck at millions of Soviet citizens, among them the majority of the old cadres of the Bolshevik Party, who were innocent of the crimes they were charged with. Second, the tragedy of a present-day generation of rebel intellectuals in the Soviet Union whose experience with Stalinism has led them to reject Leninism and Marxism and who are thus incapable of understanding the causes of Stalinist repression, the present reality of the Soviet Union, or the solutions required by the crisis of Soviet society. And third, the personal tragedy of a writer of exceptional talent who, because of his inability to understand the origins and character of the evil he is confronted with, has come to reactionary conclusions that, to some extent, even adopt the theories with which Stalin and his executioners justified their crimes in the past—the same theories that are used to justify the repression that is once again striking political oppositionists in the U.S.S.R.

STALIN'S WORLD OF CONCENTRATION CAMPS

The first subject of *The Gulag Archipelago* is the world of forced labor camps created by Stalin and the G.P.U. During Stalin's reign the inmates of these

This book review appeared in *Intercontinental Press*, Vol. 12, no. 29 (New York, July 29, 1974), p. 1051. It had been translated from a French text published in the Paris-based magazine *Inprecor*. Both journals were published to present the viewpoint of the Fourth International.

camps numbered in the millions, the overwhelming majority of them deported, if not executed, in obvious violation of Soviet legality. They were railroaded to the camps by a whole range of monstrous arbitrary procedures: torture, total suppression of all the rights guaranteed by the Soviet constitution, use of secret decrees that themselves violated the constitution and the penal code.

Solzhenitsyn has assembled a mass of testimony about the conditions under which the great Stalinist purges took place. He especially denounces the direct responsibility for these crimes borne by the team around Stalin. Not just the Berias and Yezhovs but also the Kaganoviches and the Molotovs, the men whose complicity accounts for the reluctance of so many bureaucratic dignitaries to press ahead, after the Twentieth Congress of the Soviet Communist Party, with the plan of bringing all Stalin's crimes to light.[1]

Solzhenitsyn recounts in detail the condemnations and deportations of those categories of citizens: all the personnel of the East China railway, all the Korean Communist refugees in the U.S.S.R., most of the old fighters of the Austrian Schutzbund, most of the former members of the Lettish Red Guard—who had played such an important role in the victory of the October revolution and the creation of the Red Army.

To be sure, those (in the West!) who have been able to read Leon Trotsky's books *The Revolution Betrayed* and *The Crimes of Stalin*, or the book on the Soviet labor camps by the Mensheviks Dallin and Nikolayevsky, will not learn anything basically new from *The Gulag Archipelago*. But they will appreciate the series of vignettes through which the great novelist Solzhenitsyn sketches the personalities he met in prison and in the camps: the old revolutionary worker Anatoly Ilyich Fastenko; chief technician S—vs, prototype of the careerist bureaucrat; M. P. Yakobovich, the old Menshevik, later a Bolshevik and victim of the first witch-hunt trial (the dry run for the future Moscow trials); M. D. Ryumin, the vice-minister of state security, who in the realm of depravity surpassed even the sinister Abakumov, Stalin's right-hand man, and who seems to have been the organizer of the "doctors' plot," which was intended to set off a massive new purge that was just barely averted by the death of the tyrant. These unforgettable sketches, which join those of *The First Circle* and *One Day in the Life of Ivan Denisovich*, are no doubt the most valuable part of *The Gulag Archipelago*.

The book also contains details on the tortures used by the G.P.U. to extract confessions from the accused. Here Solzhenitsyn generally confirms Trotsky's conclusion that lack of a political outlook independent of Stalinism (that is, the political capitulation of Stalin's unfortunate victims before the bureaucratic dictatorship) was the real basis of the confessions.

One of the rare sensational revelations of *The Gulag Archipelago* is that there were some trials that turned out badly for the bureaucracy, trials in which the accused retracted their confessions and turned the accusations not only against the torturers themselves but also against Stalin's policies, which were often responsible for the "crimes" the prisoners were accused of. Such was the case in the trial of the communist leaders in the small village of Kadyj in the district of Ivanov.

The general impression that emerges from this important part of *The Gulag Archipelago* is a thorough condemnation of institutionalized repression as a system of government, for that was the objective character of the Stalinist purges. A regime based neither on the political support of the laboring masses nor on the satisfaction of their material needs must resort to terror, which becomes the main state institution. That is the most striking aspect of the Stalinist world of concentration camps, and not the supposed "economic" contribution that prison labor is said to have made to the industrialization of the U.S.S.R.

Those who blindly denied the reality of that terror or who still deny it today do not contribute one iota to "defending the cause of communism." On the contrary, they cover up foul crimes *against* communism and *against* the Soviet working class, crimes that are all the more pernicious in that they have discredited and continue to discredit the cause of communism in the eyes of a not inconsiderable section of the world proletariat.

DID STALIN ONLY CONTINUE WHAT LENIN AND TROTSKY HAD STARTED?

If there were nothing in *The Gulag Archipelago* except a denunciation of Stalin's crimes sprinkled with a few observations on the old theme that "Leninism is at bottom responsible for the crimes of Stalin," it would be enough merely to defend Solzhenitsyn against the bureaucracy's repression while regretting his ideological confusion.

But the reality is otherwise. In *The Gulag Archipelago*, Solzhenitsyn *systematically* attempts to demonstrate with facts and figures that institutionalized terror began at the time of the October revolution. This is the second central theme of the book, and it is scarcely less developed than the first one. Presented with a mass of evidence and in the impassioned language of an author whose literary talent need not be demonstrated, an author who presents himself to millions of readers adorned with the halo of a victim of contemptible persecution, this theme will have a deep influence on the people of the capitalist countries as well as those of the bureaucratized workers states.

The dialectical interplay between Solzhenitsyn and the Soviet bureaucracy on this point immediately asserts itself as fundamentally counter-revolutionary. Incapable of answering Solzhenitsyn's arguments, the Kremlin bolsters the credibility of the novelist's thesis by heaping slanders and lies upon him and by expelling him from his country, thus facilitating his efforts to drag Bolshevism, Marxism, and the workers' movement through the mud. And the circle is closed when the Kremlin uses Solzhenitsyn's reactionary ideology to "prove" that the opposition in the U.S.S.R. is counter-revolutionary and that, after all, freedom of expression has to be "controlled" in order to avoid the appearance of "two, three, many Solzhenitsyns"—with or without talent.

It would take a long book to refute in detail Solzhenitsyn's slanders of the October revolution. We hope that a revolutionary Marxist militant will write such a book. That would confirm once again who are the real heirs and continuators of Bolshevism. Here we can deal only with the most essential points.

First, let's look at the facts. Here the moralist Solzhenitsyn begins with an enormous fraud. In dozens of pages he lays out a detailed description of the Red terror. *But not a word about the White terror that came first and that led to the Bolsheviks' response!*

Not a word about the *generosity* of the revolutionists in October, November, and December 1917, when they freed most, if not all, of their prisoners; like General Kaledin, for example, who quickly responded by unleashing a wave of terror and assassinations against the proletariat in power! Not a word about the thousands of communists, commissars, and soldiers traitorously murdered throughout a country put to the torch and drowned in blood with the air of reestablishing the rule of the landlords and capitalists. Not a word about the armed attacks of Bolshevik leaders—not imaginary attacks, like the ones the victims of the Moscow trials were accused of, but real ones like the assassination of Volodarsky and the attempted assassination of Lenin! Not a word about the intervention of foreign armies, about the invasion of Soviet territory on seven different fronts! Solzhenitsyn the "moralist" and "nationalist" is singularly reduced in stature by presenting such a one-sided analysis.

And further on the level of facts: Solzhenitsyn tries to prove too much, and he winds up proving nothing. In trying to draw a parallel between the "absence of law and legality" during the early years of the revolution and a similar absence under Stalin, Solzhenitsyn cites a series of court speeches by the Bolshevik Commissar of Justice, Krylenko. But what does this "evidence" prove? That under Lenin and Trotsky, there were no confessions extracted under torture, that the accused were able to defend themselves freely—and not without chance of success—that these trials were hardly witch-hunt trials, but rather revolutionary ones, doubtlessly sometimes based on circumstantial and insufficient evidence, as is always the case in a revolutionary period, but a thousand miles removed from the caricatures of justice staged by Stalin.

Two trials cited by Solzhenitsyn himself perfectly illustrate the basic difference between the Bolshevik revolution and the Stalinist counter-revolution.

V. V. Oldenberger, an old apolitical engineer who was chief technician of the Moscow waterworks, was persecuted by a Communist cell that wanted to remove him because he was so apolitical. He was driven to suicide. Solzhenitsyn waxes indignant about the corrupt, ignoble, Communist plotters in this factory. It's not until you read to the end of Solzhenitsyn's account that you find out that the trial he is talking about was organized by the Soviet state *to defend Oldenberger*, a trial organized *against* the communist cell that had persecuted him, a trial that ended by *sentencing* his persecutors, a trial that proved that the workers in the plant had been able to freely elect Oldenberger to the Soviet *against* the unanimous pressure of the communist cell.

The second trial involved a Tolstoyan, a determined opponent of bearing arms who was condemned to death at the height of the civil war for conscientious objection. That trial ended in an even more dramatic fashion. The soldiers assigned to guard the condemned man justifiably considered the verdict monstrous. So they organized a general assembly in the barracks and sent a motion to the city soviet demanding that the verdict be overturned. And they won!

So we have workers who can *elect* an apolitical technician to the soviet despite the opposition of a communist cell composed of members who were at best ultrasectarians and at worst totally corrupted careerists. We have soldiers who revolt against the verdict of a court, organize a general assembly, interfere in the "great affairs of state," and save the life of their prisoner. Solzhenitsyn—without realizing it—is describing the real difference between an era of revolution and an era of counter-revolution. Let him cite similar examples from the Stalin era to prove that basically it was the same under Lenin and under Stalin!

No Leninist worthy of the name would be so obstinate as to deny today that the Soviet regime made mistakes both in matters of repression and in political decisions. And how could it be otherwise with leaders who had the formidable honor of being the first in history to construct a state in the service of the workers and all the exploited, on the scale of a vast country, in the face of bloody and ferocious attacks from powerful enemies, and who had to do it without being able to rely on precedents, instead developing their theories as they went along?

Today we know it was a mistake to step up the repression when the civil war was over, that it was a mistake to suppress all the other Soviet parties in 1921 and thereby institutionalize one-party rule, and that it was a mistake to ban factions within this party. All these measures were conceived at the time as temporary and taken in response to immediate difficulties. They were characterized by an overestimation of the immediate danger posed by the counter-revolution, which actually had been beaten and dispersed, and by an underestimation of the demoralizing consequences they would have for the consciousness and activity of the proletariat—in a political climate characterized more and more by administrative repression and less and less by the conscious participation of the masses. These measures facilitated the political expropriation of the proletariat, the strangulation of internal democracy in the Bolshevik Party, and the establishment of the bureaucracy's dictatorship. But all this could not have been known with certainty at the time. We know it today. And the Fourth International has drawn all the necessary programmatic conclusions.

But those who denounce the Bolsheviks today have to look at what real alternatives existed at the time. They have to take account of the terrible responsibility of the German Social Democracy (that is, Menshevism), which, by drowning the German revolution in blood, paved the way first for Stalin and then for Hitler. They have to consider the fate that awaited the workers and peasants in Germany, where the revolution was not defended mercilessly and effectively. The thousands of victims of Horthy's White terror in Hungary—to cite just one example—would have been nothing compared to the hundreds of thousands of workers and peasants who would have been massacred in Russia had the White terror been victorious. That rather seems to speak in favor of the justice of the Bolsheviks.

THE SCAPEGOAT OF IDEOLOGY

Solzhenitsyn is on even weaker ground when he moves from the realm of facts to the realm of ideology. In seeking an explanation for the Stalinist terror, all he manages to come up with is an attack on ideology, or rather contemporary ideological fanaticism. Under 20th-century conditions, he claims, inquisitionists, conquistadors, colonizers, fascists, Jacobins, and—obviously—Marxists would all be transformed into the murderers of millions of their contemporaries.

The first thing that is striking about this little list is that it is, to say the least, incomplete. Why has Solzhenitsyn forgotten religious fanaticism? Religious wars have "caused" the death of millions of people throughout history. And what about nationalism and the ideology of "defense of the fatherland" in the imperialist countries, which in the First World War alone "caused" more deaths than the entire Stalinist terror? Is Solzhenitsyn's forgetfulness perhaps a result of the fact that he is an advocate of these two ideologies, religion and nationalism?

What is also striking is the extremely superficial character of Solzhenitsyn's explanation. Why has the same "ideology" produced murderous fanaticism in some epochs and liberal and peaceful tolerance in others? Is it really for "ideological" reasons? Or is it rather because definite and tangible material interests were at work?

Solzhenitsyn likes to "count up" the victims of the Stalinist purges and compare the total to the tally rung up by tsarist and fascist repression. But these "quantitative" comparisons can be extended. What "ideology" was it that "fanaticized" the semi-illiterate book-burners in Chile, who in the space of a few days killed 20,000 people and imprisoned 40,000 others? These are figures that on the scale of the U.S.S.R. would amount to 600,000 murdered and 1.2 million deported! In the space of a few days! Stalin would be green with envy. Were the book-burners motivated by "ideological fanaticism" or by the desire to defend private property and the eternal values of "free enterprise" and capitalist exploitation?

And what about the famous "crusade" that Franco organized in 1936 to "reconquer" the country that had "fallen into the hands of the reds"—a crusade that resulted in the murder of more than a million Spaniards by "nationalist troops"? On the scale of the U.S.S.R. that would be the equivalent of 9 million dead, if we were to play Solzhenitsyn's numbers game. Was it really some sort of "ideology" that could have provoked such a frightful massacre? Wasn't it rather an attempt—at any price, even the price of rivers of blood—to prevent the establishment of a workers' and poor peasants' regime on the Iberian peninsula?

It is only Marxism that can explain and account for the successive periods of barbarism and civilization throughout human history. When a class is firmly in power, sure of itself and its future, when its strength is increasing and social contradictions are temporarily easing, then it can afford the luxury of ruling through relatively peaceful and civilized means. (Except for moments when its power is suddenly challenged; then we have the massacres of the Communards by the Versaillais, even in the 19th century, so "civilized" and peaceful in comparison to our own "barbaric" epoch.) But when a ruling class is in decline, when its power is crumbling, when its regime is torn by deeper and deeper contradictions, then barbarism comes to the surface again and the reality of class domination appears in its bloodiest form.

Our epoch is the epoch of the death agony of the capitalist system. The longer this death agony is prolonged, the more features of barbarism, bloody repression, and contempt for human life will proliferate. In this historic sense, Stalin is a product of capitalism, just as much as Hitler,

Auschwitz, Hiroshima, and the bombing and defoliation of Vietnam. He is not the product of Soviet society or the October revolution.

In a narrower and more immediate sense, Stalinist terror is the product of the victory of political counter-revolution in the Soviet Union. The fact that Stalin had to exterminate a whole generation of revolutionists who had led the October revolution and erected the Soviet state is in itself sufficient to refute the identity Solzhenitsyn arbitrarily establishes between the executioner and his victims. This political counter-revolution in turn represents definite material and social interests: those of a privileged bureaucratic layer that, while basing itself on the new property relations created by the socialist revolution, defends its own monopoly of economic and political control as well as the immense advantages that it draws from the prevailing conditions of prolonged scarcity.

By rejecting Marxism, Solzhenitsyn and those who think like him render themselves incapable of explaining the events that have so deeply affected them. Trotsky was fond of quoting Spinoza: "Do not laugh, do not cry, but understand." Solzhenitsyn laughs bitterly and cries a great deal. But he doesn't understand very much.

MORALISTIC POLITICS CAUGHT IN ITS OWN TRAP

The contradictions in Solzhenitsyn's thought—consequences of his rejection of Marxism—come through in a most striking fashion when the moralist is forced to abandon even the most elementary moral considerations when he deals with the Marxists of our epoch, especially Trotsky and the Trotskyists. In order to justify his claim that Stalin was the continuator and not the gravedigger of Bolshevism, Solzhenitsyn tries to demonstrate that all the Bolsheviks aided Stalin, capitulated before him, collaborated in his crimes, and were accomplices in his frame-up trials.

Beginning from the correct observation that those who *politically capitulated* before Stalin were logically led to act in this way (because, as Solzhenitsyn puts it, "politics without moral foundation leads inevitably to covering up any crime"), Solzhenitsyn concludes that *all* Communists were politically defenseless against Stalin and collaborated in the terror of the 1930s and 1940s. He even goes so far as to say that Trotsky himself would have confessed to anything the G.P.U. required had he fallen into Stalin's hands. This because Trotsky also lacked an "independent outlook" and an ideology really independent of Stalinism! Besides, he supposedly had no experience with physical and mental tortures that would have made him able to resist the G.P.U.

There is not the slightest evidence to support such allegations. They represent only a dredged-up version, scarcely even amended or edited, of Stalinist slanders of Trotskyism.

To claim that no Communist tendency had an ideological basis independent of Stalinist terror and that all Communists therefore were fated to capitulate before the terror is to sweep away the 15 years of determined battle waged against the Soviet bureaucracy first by the Left Opposition and later by the movement for the Fourth International, a battle that was waged on a coherent theoretical and political basis that has been brilliantly confirmed by history. It is to insult the memory of thousands of militants—Trotskyists and others—who refused to capitulate, refused to become accomplices in the parodies of justice, and who paid with their lives for their loyalty to their principles, demonstrating courage and strength of character unparalleled in history.

To say that Leon Trotsky did not prove his capacity to stand up to personal trials is to forget that he continued his struggle against Stalinism in spite of the G.P.U.'s assassination of his children, his secretaries, and his closest co-workers, to forget that he continued this opposition without faltering after the first assassination attempt by the G.P.U., knowing that at any moment he was likely to be assassinated by Stalin's agents.

To claim, as Solzhenitsyn does, that Trotskyists in the labor camps behaved in a secretarian manner and were incapable of waging hunger strikes for prolonged periods in order to win a series of demands is to insult the memory of the heroes, who numbered more than a thousand, who launched an *18-week-long* hunger strike around a five-point program defending the rights of all political prisoners just at the height of the Stalinist terror.

It is easy to understand why Solzhenitsyn, a determined opponent of revolutionary Marxism, would follow in Stalin's footsteps in wanting to erase from history the decisive contribution Trotskyism made to the struggle against the dictatorship of the Soviet bureaucracy. This is only an attempt to break down any continuity between the October revolution and the present political tasks posed in the Soviet Union. But the immoral methods that Solzhenitsyn has to use to try to prove his point illustrate once again the dead end of any political outlook that claims to be based on absolute moral precepts, a dead end that leads the advocates of such outlooks to trample on their own principles.

Historical Justification of the October Revolution

Solzhenitsyn tries to reduce all Soviet reality to the Stalinist and post-Stalinist terror. This reality is supposed to have resulted from a revolution that should never have taken place: "Russia was not ripe for revolution," he writes.

But what was it ripe for? For tsarist barbarism? For eternal famine, poverty, and illiteracy? By challenging the legitimacy of the October revolution—and the legitimacy of revolution in all relatively underdeveloped countries as well—Solzhenitsyn reveals yet another contradiction in moralistic politics. Should we weep only for the dead assassinated by terror? What about the deaths caused by inhumane socioeconomic regimes, the tens of millions who died of hunger during the great famines in India and prerevolutionary China? Is this any less deplorable? Are those deaths merely products of blind fate before which we must powerlessly bow?

The results of the October revolution cannot be reduced to the misdeeds of the bureaucracy and its terrorist repression. There are other results of the October revolution too: the transformation in just a few decades of a vast backward country into the world's second industrial power, a country in which illiteracy has been eradicated, in which the number of doctors and the number of new books published (including translations!) is among the highest in the world, in which the infant mortality rate is lower than it is in Britain. Those who fight against arbitrary police repression in the U.S.S.R. by claiming that it is the inevitable result of the October socialist revolution cannot help but overlook this other aspect of Soviet reality, which has created exactly the material basis for a flowering of real Soviet democracy if the power of the bureaucracy is overthrown.

Neither Marx, Lenin, nor Trotsky ever believed it would be possible to build a real socialist, classless society in one country alone, still less an economically underdeveloped country. The imperialist epoch is especially characterized by a twofold phenomenon: on the one hand the international domination of capital restricts and distorts the development of the backward countries, and on the other hand revolutionary movements themselves tend more and more to become international. Solzhenitsyn regrets this and calls upon the Soviet leaders (!) to abandon "communist messianism," something from which they have hardly suffered. But the slightest bit of moral feeling for the misery in the world today and the catastrophes that threaten humanity leads instead to the conclusion that it is necessary to redouble efforts to bring about the victory of the world socialist revolution, which would incidentally also contribute to the elimination of arbitrary police repression in the bureaucratized workers' states, that is, to the victory of the political revolution in these countries.

THE DILEMMA OF THE INTELLECTUAL OPPOSITION IN THE U.S.S.R.

Like the work of any great novelist, *The Gulag Archipelago* reflects not only a social situation as a whole but also the thought of a particular social layer. Solzhenitsyn represents the wing of the opposition intelligentsia in the Soviet Union that has reacted to the crimes of Stalin by breaking with Lenin and Marx. The importance and breadth of this layer, even among Soviet youth, must not be underestimated. Its very existence constitutes yet another condemnation of the political regime that rules in the U.S.S.R.

Here is a society that calls itself socialist, that claims to have eradicated "antagonistic social contradictions," that represents itself as the "most united society in the world," in which generations of intellectuals born after the revolution are developing in a manner ever more hostile to Marxism! This development can only be encouraged by an "ideological struggle" waged against it by the falsifiers of Marxism, whose "arguments" in the end come down to suppression of writings, deportations, banishments, or internment of oppositionists in insane asylums!

But—an irony of history!—trenchant enemies of Stalinism like Solzhenitsyn and his friends, people who reject Leninism on the grounds that it was responsible for Stalinism, remain to a large extent *prisoners of Stalinist ideology*. In large measure they move in the universe of myths with which Stalin excused and justified his crimes.

These myths are reflected not only in the anti–Trotskyist slanders taken directly from the cookbook of the General Secretary. They are also reflected in the way this wing of the intellectual opposition approaches the problems of present-day Soviet society and their solution. For there is yet a third theme in *The Gulag Archipelago*, one that is less obvious and explicit than the two we have been discussing, but is no less integral to the Solzhenitsyn's thought. That theme is *the inability of the working class to manage the state and the economy*. It must be stated clearly: This theme reflects an intellectual arrogance common to technocrats and bureaucrats.

It is in a passage devoted to the 1930 trial of the members of the so-called Industrial Party that this notion of Solzhenitsyn's comes through most clearly. In this passage we read that it was logical for the technicians to try to impose discipline in the workplace! That it is logical for those who "are capable of rationally organizing their activity" to stand at the head of society! That it is logical for politics to be partially determined by the exigencies of technology!

The whole technocrat credo, as well as the rejection of direct workers' power and of soviet power that it implies, has been and remains one of the ideological bases of Stalinism. It is no accident that the same notion is found among Solzhenitsyn and his friends. What unites them with the bureaucracy is that both share a refusal to accept the possibility of workers exercising power; they share the same basic isolation from the life-style, thought, aspirations, and ideals of the working class.

In this sense, after all is said and done, Solzhenitsyn remains an ideological prisoner of the bureaucracy, an advocate, at bottom, of an authoritarian political regime—but one without excessive repression. His is the voice of an enlightened authoritarianism that rejects soviet democracy as fundamentally evil and utopian. His political action is oriented not toward the masses but toward individual protest and "open letters" to the Kremlin.

Once we understand the social character of Solzhenitsyn's work we

cannot but agree with the position taken both by the new Leninists in the
U.S.S.R. and by the revolutionary Marxists in the capitalist countries: to
support the movement for democratic rights in the U.S.S.R. One would
have to completely misconstrue the socio-political relationship of forces in
the Soviet Union to believe that currents like Solzhenitsyn's, cut off from
the living forces of a proletariat that represents the absolute majority of the
active population, could seriously threaten the economic foundations of
society and initiate a movement for the restoration of capitalism.

What encourages the rebirth of anti-worker, anti-rationalist, anti-
Marxist, and Slavophile tendencies is the repressive and conformist lead
weight that bears down on Soviet society and fosters political and ideological dynamism among the masses.

The best antidote to these reactionary ideologies—and in the long run,
the *only* effective antidote—is the rebirth of critical political consciousness
among the masses, which will win them to Marxism. All those who
encourage such a rebirth are working toward defending and strengthening
the socioeconomic foundations of the U.S.S.R. All those who perpetuate
the absence of public political debate and differentiation can only encourage
obscurantism and hostility to Marxism, which appears as a state religion.

In the Soviet intellectual opposition there are many wings and tendencies,
united only by the common struggle against Stalin's crimes and for the real
reconquest of civil rights that are formally guaranteed; that is, for an
application of the Soviet constitution. The left wing of this opposition, of
which Major General Pyotr Grigorenko is the most stirring symbol, is
composed of surviving old Bolsheviks, militant Leninists who by their
exemplary courage are defending and rehabilitating Leninism in the eyes of
Soviet youth. What a windfall it is for the Kremlin to be able to denounce
the anti-socialist ideology of Solzhenitsyn (while of course not daring to
publish his books in the U.S.S.R.)! And how much more thankless is the
bureaucracy's job in suppressing oppositionists who claim allegiance to
Marx and Lenin!

At a time when the international bourgeoisie wants to concentrate attention on *The Gulag Archipelago* in order to divert attention from its own
crimes and to whip up hostility to communism, we must redouble our
efforts to free Grigorenko, Yakhimovich, and their comrades from the
torturers and to defend the rights not only of the Solzhenitsyns but also of
the Marxist and Leninist oppositionists to freely speak, discuss, publish, and
organize in the U.S.S.R.!

Note

1. *Editor's note*—At the Twentieth Congress of the Soviet Communist Party in 1956, Nikita Khrushchev made a famous speech in which he exposed a small portion of Stalin's crimes. This caused shock waves throughout the Soviet Union and the world—in Communist parties that identified with the Kremlin bureaucracy.

3

Rosa Luxemburg and German Social Democracy

The real place of Rosa Luxemburg has still to be located precisely in the history of the revolutionary movement. The disintegration of the Stalinist monolith has meant that, while many have acknowledged her merits, they have hastened to add that "she belongs to the pre-1914 epoch."[1] Those writers who pigeon-hole her in this fashion create an impediment for themselves by approaching the history of the workers' movement with essentially subjective criteria. In this way the merits of Rosa Luxemburg become—depending on the whim of the author in question—her uncompromising defense of Marxism against the revisionism of Eduard Bernstein, her deep attachment to the principles of mass action and spontaneity, or even her defense of workers' democracy against Bolshevik "excesses."

The difficulty disappears as soon as we approach the history of the workers' movement with objective criteria and apply the golden rule of historical materialism to Marxism itself: in the final analysis it is material existence which determines consciousness and not the reverse. We must start from the changing social reality in order to interpret the modifications which have taken place in the thought of the international workers' movement, including successive contributions which have enriched or impoverished Marxism itself. With this method, Rosa Luxemburg's part in the evolution of the workers' movement before 1914 (if not before 1919), instead of appearing atomized and fragmented, retains its unity. Only through such a method rather than the empirical approaches of narrative history and specialized research is the crucial importance of her theoretical and practical activity fully revealed.

This article appeared in the theoretical magazine of the International Marxist Group in Great Britain, *International*, Vol. 3, no. 4 (London, Summer 1977), p. 6.

"THE TRIED AND TESTED TACTIC" IN CRISIS

For 30 years the tactics of German Social Democracy, "die alte bewährte Taktik" ("the tried and tested tactic"), had completely dominated the international proletarian movement. In fact, apart from the splendid isolation of the Paris Commune and the experiences of certain, mainly anarchist, sections of the international workers' movement, the history of the class struggle had borne the social-democratic stamp for half a century. Its influence was so preponderant that even those like Lenin and the Bolsheviks, who had broken in practice with this tradition at a national level, continued to regard the German model religiously as a model which was universally applicable.

"The tried and tested tactic" had a first-class pedigree. During the last 15 years of his life, despite significant vacillations,[2] Frederick Engels had become its champion even to the extent of making it a veritable deed in his "political testament": the "Introduction" that he wrote in 1895 to the new German edition of Karl Marx's *The Class Struggles in France 1848–50*. The most famous extracts from this "Introduction" were cited innumerable times in every European language between 1895 and 1914. And it was this path which social democracy followed from 1918 to 1929, when the world economic crisis and the crisis of social democracy itself combined to put an end to this sterile exercise:

> Everywhere the German example of utilizing the suffrage, of winning all the posts accessible to us, has been imitated. Everywhere the spontaneous unleashing of the attack has retreated into the background. . . . The two million voters whom it sends to the ballot box, together with the young men and women who stand behind . . . them as non-voters, form the most numerous, most compact mass, the decisive "shock force" of the international proletarian army. This mass already supplies over a fourth of the recorded votes. . . . Its growth proceeds as spontaneously, as steadily, as irresistibly, and at the same time as tranquilly as a natural process. All government interventions have proved powerless against it. We can count even today on two and a quarter million voters. If it continues in this fashion, by the end of the century we shall conquer the greater part of the middle section of society, petty bourgeois and small peasants, and grow into the decisive power in the land, before which *all other powers will have to bow, whether they like it or not. To keep the growth going without interruption until of itself it gets beyond the control of the ruling governmental system, not to fritter away this daily increasing shock force in advance guard fighting, but to keep it intact until the decisive day, that is our main task.*[3]

Of course, we now know that the German Social Democratic leaders had scandalously censored Engels's text and had twisted its meaning, removing everything that remained fundamentally revolutionary in the words of this old fighter and lifelong companion of Marx.[4] But all that is by the way. The quotation is authentic. It completely justifies "the tried and tested tactic": recruit as many members as possible, educate as many workers as possible, gain as many votes as possible in elections, and put new social legislation on the statute book (above all the reduction of the working week)—everything else will follow automatically: "All other powers will have [sic] to bow before us"; our growth is "irresistible"; we must "keep our shock force intact until the decisive day" [sic].

Even more convincing than the blessing of the venerable authority of international socialism was the verdict of the facts. The facts gave credence to Bebel, Vandervelde, Victor Adler, and the other pragmatists who were content to plod this path, thereafter elevated to the status of holy writ. At each election the votes grew. If sometimes there was an unexpected reversal (the "Hottentot elections" in Germany in 1907)[5] it was followed by a particularly brilliant riposte: the Reichstag elections in 1912, when the German Social Democracy won a third of the votes. The workers' organizations were continually gathering strength, extending into every sphere of social life and becoming bastions of what was truly a "counter society," stimulating a sustained development of class consciousness. There were wage rises, there was increasing legislation to protect the workers, and poverty was declining (even if it had not disappeared entirely). The tide seemed so irresistible that not only the faithful but even their adversaries were heady with it.

But, as always, consciousness lagged behind reality. All this "irresistible tide" amounted to was a reflection of the international capitalist boom, a secular reduction in the "industrial reserve army" in Europe, notably through emigration, and the increasing super-exploitation of the colonial and semi-colonial countries by imperialism. By the beginning of the 20th century the resources that had fuelled this temporary easing of socio-economic contradictions in the West were beginning to run out. Thenceforth the intensification and not the lessening of social contradictions was on the agenda. Waiting to take the stage was not an epoch of peaceful progress but an epoch of imperialist wars, national liberation struggles, and civil war. The long period of amelioration would be followed by 20 years when real wages stagnated or even fell. The epoch of evolution was at an end; the epoch of revolutions was about to begin.

In this new epoch "the tried and tested tactic" lost all justification; from an organizational principle it was to be transformed into a death trap for the European working class. The vast majority of contemporaries did not grasp this before August 4, 1914. Even Lenin had not understood it for the countries which lay to the west of the tsarist empire; Trotsky was hesitant. Rosa Luxemburg's merit was that she was the first to grasp clearly and systematically the necessity for a fundamental change in the strategy and tactics of the workers' movement in the West, confronted by a changed objective situation: the dawning of the imperialist epoch.[6]

THE ROOTS OF LUXEMBURG'S FIGHT
AGAINST "THE TRIED AND TESTED TACTIC"

Of course, the new objective situation had been partially grasped by the most far-sighted Marxists at the end of the 19th century. The phenomenon of the extension of colonial empires and the beginnings of imperialism, insofar as it was the expression of the political expansion of big capital, had been analyzed. Hilferding had erected that remarkable monument, *Finance Capital*. He recorded the appearance of cartels, trusts, and monopolies (used by the revisionists to claim that capitalism would become more and more organized and thus its contradictions less acute; there really is nothing new under the sun). After the International's Stuttgart Conference (1907) the suspicions of Lenin, the Polish, Dutch, Belgian, and Italian left regarding Kautsky's concessions to the revisionists increased, especially on the question of the fight against imperialist war. Electoral opportunism and "tactical" blocs with the liberal bourgeoisie of this or that region or national group (such as the Baden group in Germany,[7] the majority of the Belgian Workers' Party, the followers of Jaurès in France, etc.) came under heavy fire. However, all this criticism remained partial and fragmented, and, above all, "the tried and tested tactic" was not scrapped in favor of a new system of strategy and tactics. On the contrary, it was treated with more reverence than ever before.

From 1900 to 1914 Rosa Luxemburg was the only socialist west of Russia to strike out in a new direction. This exceptional achievement was not just the result of her undeniable genius, her clarity of thought, and her unflinching devotion to the cause of socialism and the international working class. It can be explained above all by the historical and geographical, that is to say social, conditions in which her theory and practice were nurtured and developed.

Her unique position as a leader of *two* social democratic parties (the German and Polish parties) placed her at a vantage point for understanding the two contradictory tendencies in international social democracy. On the one hand there was the dangerous slide into bureaucratic routinism which was becoming ever more pronounced in Germany, and on the other hand there was the rise of new forms and methods of struggle in the tsarist empire. She was therefore able to perform for the tactics of the workers' movement the same audacious operation that Trotsky had performed for revolutionary perspectives. No longer did the most "advanced" countries necessarily show the "backward" ones the image of their own future. On the contrary, the workers of the "backward" countries (Russia and Poland) were showing the Western countries the urgent tactical modifications that had to be adopted.

Naturally, this too had been foreseen by certain Marxists. As early as 1896, Parvus had published a long study in the *Neue Zeit* in which he envisaged the use of "a mass political strike" as a weapon against the threat of a coup to suppress universal suffrage.[8] This study was itself inspired by a resolution Kautsky had submitted to the 10th Session of the Socialist Congress in Zurich (1893) on the appropriate response to threats to universal suffrage. Engels had broached the same question in the past, but all these had been isolated forays which led to no strategic or tactical changes.

Rosa Luxemburg was also helped by an in-depth study of the two political crises which had shaken Western Europe toward the end of the century: the Dreyfus affair in France[9] and the general strike for universal suffrage in Belgium (1902). From this twofold experience she developed a deep hatred of parliamentary cretinism. Furthermore, she developed a growing conviction that "the tried and tested tactic" would fail at "the decisive hour" if the masses were not trained well in advance *in the politics of extra-parliamentary action* as well as routine electoralism and purely economic strikes. However, it was above all the experience of the Russian revolution of 1905 that enabled Luxemburg to integrate her scattered criticisms into a systematic critique of "the tried and tested tactic." With hindsight we can say that it was undoubtedly 1905 which marked the end of the essentially progressive role of international social democracy and ushered in the prolonged phase of vacillation in which formerly progressive traits were increasingly combined with reactionary influences. These steadily grew in strength until they brought the party to the disaster of August 1914.

To grasp the importance of the Russian revolution of 1905 we must bear in mind that it was the first mass revolutionary upheaval which Europe had witnessed since the days of the Paris Commune: that is, for 34 years! It was therefore perfectly natural that such a passionate revolutionary as Rosa Luxemburg should carefully study every detail of the explosion and all its particular characteristics in order to draw out the central lessons of 1905 for the coming upheavals in Europe. In this she merely followed in the footsteps of Marx and Engels, who performed exactly the same examination for the upheavals of 1848 and the Paris Commune.

One aspect of the 1905 revolution in particular was decisive in precipitating the development of a new strategy and new tactics for international social democracy, counterposed to "the tried and tested tactic" of the S.P.D. For decades the debate between the anarchists and syndicalists on the one hand and the social democrats on the other had been caught in a false polarization which counterposed the supporters of *minority direct action* to those who supported *mass, organized action*, which meant in practice "peaceful," "legalistic" work (in the electoral arena or the trade unions). However, the revolution of 1905 produced a combination of events which neither side had foreseen. The year 1905 saw direct action by the masses, yet these masses, far from wallowing happily in a pristine state of spontaneous and unorganized innocence, organized themselves precisely through their experience of mass action in order to prepare themselves for even more audacious actions in the future.

Thus, even though revolutionary syndicalism had for many years counterposed the "myth" of the general strike[10] to social-democratic electoralism, and even though it was at this very moment that a general strike was victorious in Europe for the first time, both Lenin and Rosa Luxemburg grasped a fact that had not been understood in the West: 1905 sounded the death-knell of revolutionary syndicalism in Russia! They should have added, of course—and Lenin understood this only after 1914—that the eclipse of revolutionary syndicalism in Russia could only be explained by the fact that, far from opposing the mass strike or trying to curb it in any way, the Russian and Polish Social Democrats (or at least their most radical wings) had become enthusiastic organizers and propagandists for the mass strike and had thus definitively overcome the old dichotomy: "gradual action—revolutionary action."[11]

Rosa Luxemburg was dazzled by the experience of the 1905 revolution, an experience which had struck a chord in the hearts of workers in several countries to the west of the tsarist empire—beginning with Austria, where it provoked a general strike that won universal suffrage. The last 14 years of her life thus became a sustained effort to teach this one fundamental lesson to the German proletariat: it is necessary to abandon gradualism, it is necessary to prepare for mass revolutionary struggles which are once again on the agenda. The outbreak of the First World War, of the Russian revolution of 1917, and of the German revolution of 1918 all confirmed the accuracy of the estimation she had made in 1905.

On the first of February 1905 she wrote:

But for international social democracy, too, the uprising of the Russian proletariat constitutes something profoundly new which we must feel with every fibre of our being. All of us, whatever pretensions we have to a mastery of dialectics, remain incorrigible metaphysicians, obsessed by the immanence of everything within our everyday experience. . . . It is only in the volcanic explosion of the revolution that we perceive what swift and earth-shattering results the young mole has achieved and just how happily it is undermining the very ground under the feet of European bourgeois society. Gauging the political maturity and revolutionary energy of the working class through electoral statistics and the membership of local branches is like trying to measure Mont Blanc with a ruler!

She continued on the first of May:

This is the main point to grasp: we must understand and assimilate the fact that the actuality of a revolution in the Tsarist Empire will provoke a colossal acceleration in the tempo of the international class struggle so that even in the heartlands of "old Europe" we will face in the not too distant future revolutionary situations and entirely new tactical problems.

Finally, in a confrontation with reformist syndicalists like Robert Schmidt at the Jena Congress on September 22, 1905, she cried out indignantly:

So far you have sat here and heard many speeches delivered on the political mass strike. Doesn't it make you feel like putting your head in your hands and asking yourself: are we really living in the year of the glorious Russian revolution or is it still decades away? Every day you can read the accounts of the revolution in the papers, every day you can read the dispatches, and yet you obviously have neither eyes to see nor ears to hear. . . . Doesn't Robert Schmidt see that the moment predicted by our great teachers Marx and Engels has actually arrived? The moment when evolution becomes revolution! We have the Russian revolution right in front of our eyes. We would be fools if we didn't learn anything from it.[12]

Looking back we know that she was right. Just as the victory of the Russian revolution in 1917 would have been infinitely more difficult without the experience of 1905 and the tremendous revolutionary apprenticeship that it represented for tens of thousands of Russian worker cadres, so the victory of the German revolution of 1918–19 would have been far easier had the German workers experienced prerevolutionary or revolutionary mass political struggles before 1914. You can't learn to swim without getting your feet wet, and the masses cannot attain revolutionary consciousness without the experience of revolutionary actions. Even if it was impossible to imitate the 1905 revolution in Germany between 1905 and 1914, it was at least perfectly possible to transform completely the daily routine of social democracy, to reorientate it toward an ever more revolutionary mode of intervention and cadre formation, and thus to prepare the masses for the inevitable confrontation with the bourgeoisie and its state apparatus. By refusing to strike out on a new course and by clinging to increasingly unreal formulas about the "inevitable" victory of socialism, the "inevitable" retreat of the bourgeoisie and its state in the face of "the calm and tranquil strength" of the workers, the leaders of the S.P.D. during these decisive years sowed the dragons' teeth which sprang up as armed warriors in 1914, 1919, and 1933—as the German workers reaped the bitter harvests of defeat.

THE DEBATE ON THE MASS STRIKE

It is in this context that we must examine the debate on the mass strike which unfolded in the S.P.D. after 1905. The main stages of the debate were marked by: the Jena Conference of 1905 (in a certain sense the most "gauchiste" conference before 1914, obviously due to the pressure of the Russian revolution); the Mannheim Conference of 1906; the publication in that same year of two pamphlets, one by Kautsky and one by Rosa, both addressed to the problem of the "mass strike"; the 1910 debate between Rosa and Kautsky; and finally the debate between Kautsky and Pannekoek.[13]

We can review the essential points of the debate, even if rather schematically, in the following way. Having fought the idea of a general strike as a "general stupidity" ("Generalstreik ist Generalunsinn") for decades under the pretext that one must first organize the vast majority of workers before such a strike could be successful, the S.P.D. leaders were shaken by the Belgian General Strike of 1902–03, but approached any revision of their "quietist" conceptions very hesitantly.[14] In 1905, at the Jena Conference, a clash broke out between the union leaders and the leaders of the S.P.D. during which the unionists went so far as to suggest that the supporters of the general strike should depart for Russia or Poland posthaste to put their ideas into practice.[15] With reluctance, but not without vigor, Bebel entered the arena and attacked the union leaders, admitting the possibility of a mass political strike "in principle." However, a compromise was hammered out between the conferences of Jena and Mannheim. At Mannheim (1906) peace was restored in the central apparatus. Thereafter only the union chiefs were to be considered "competent" to "proclaim" strike action, including a mass political strike—after they had weighed up all the problems of "organization," the funds available, the "balance of forces," etc. After the untoward intervention of an actual revolution in Russia, the S.P.D. leaders heaved a sigh of relief and returned to the familiar and well-trodden paths of "the tried and tested tactic."

Throughout all this Rosa Luxemburg was, of course, furiously chomping at the bit. She was just waiting for the most propitious moment to strike a decisive blow for her new strategy and tactics. The moment dawned with the elections to the Prussian Diet in 1910, when agitation for universal suffrage was launched. The masses were demanding action and Rosa organized a dozen mass meetings aided by thousands of workers and militants. A police ban on the meetings led to skirmishes, and finally a central demonstration of 200,000 was organized in Traptow Park, Berlin. But the S.P.D. leadership hated these "disturbances" like the plague, and concentrated on preparing the best possible intervention in the 1912 elections. Consequently the agitation was stifled at birth and this time it was Kautsky

himself, the "guardian of orthodoxy," who took up the cudgels and led the
theoretical and political struggle of the apparatus against the left. He produced countless pedantic articles and pamphlets which reveal, above all else,
a complete failure to grasp the dynamic of the mass movement.[16]

At first sight a reversal of alliances had occurred. At the turn of the
century, Luxemburg and Kautsky (the left and the center) had blocked with
the apparatus of the party around Bebel and Singer against the revisionist
minority led by Bernstein. In 1906, at the Mannheim Conference, the trade
union apparatus went over to the revisionist camp and the Bebel-Kautsky-
Luxemburg alliance seemed stronger than ever. How, then, should we
account for the sudden reversal in this system of alliances which took place
within the space of four years (1906–10)? In fact, the social and political
realities of the problem differed decisively from their appearance. Bebel and
the party apparatus were just as much enamored of "the tried and tested
tactic" in 1900 as in 1910. They were fundamentally conservative, that is to
say *supporters of the status quo in the heart of the workers' movement itself* (without
having lost for all that their socialist convictions and even passions, but
having relegated these to the distant future). Bernstein and the revisionists
threatened to upset the delicate equilibrium between "the tried and tested
tactic" (that is, the daily reformist practice), socialist propaganda, the hopes
and faith of the masses in socialism, the unity of the party, and the unity
between the masses and the party. For that reason Bebel and the apparatus
opposed him—for essentially conservative reasons—so as not to upset the
apple cart.

However, the revolution of 1905 and the impact of imperialism on
relations between the classes in Germany itself aggravated the tensions in
the heart of the workers' movement. When the possibility of a split
emerged after the Jena Conference, Bebel, Ebert, and Scheidemann showed
that they preferred the unity of the apparatus to unity with radicalizing
workers—that is how they interpreted "the primacy of organization."
From that moment on, the whole of the party apparatus broke with the left,
because it was now the left which was demanding that "the tried and tested
tactic" be jettisoned, not only in theory but also—horror of horrors—in
practice. The die was cast.

The only question which remained open for a time was what position
Kautsky would take. Would he side with the party apparatus against the
left, or with the left against the apparatus? After the 1905 revolution he
momentarily leaned to the left, yet a significant incident decided his fate. In
1908 Kautsky wrote his pamphlet *The Road to Power*. In it he examined
precisely the question that had been left unanswered since Engels's famous
preface of 1895: How does one pass *from winning the majority of the working
masses to socialism* (by means of "the tried and tested tactic") *to the conquest of*

political power itself? His formulas were moderate and did not imply any systematic revolutionary agitation. The question of the abolition of the monarchy was not posed (instead he modestly referred to "the democratizations of the Empire and its component states"). But even so there were too many "dangerous phrases" in the pamphlet for the small-minded, conservative, and bureaucratized *Parteivorstand*. The possibility of "revolution" was mentioned; it was even suggested that "nobody should be so naive as to imagine that we will pass imperceptibly and peacefully from a militarist state . . . to democracy." This was "dangerous phrasemongering." It might even "provoke a law-suit." And so the *Parteivorstand* decided to turn the pamphlet back into pulp.[17]

A tragicomedy ensued which decided the fate of Kautsky as a revolutionary and a theoretician. He appealed to the Control Commission of the party, which found in his favor. But Bebel remained unmoved. Kautsky then agreed to submit to party censorship and to *sanitize the text himself*. He censored anything that might prove controversial and thus rendered the pamphlet completely innocuous, emerging from the whole affair as a completely spineless individual with no strength of character. Even in this episode one can see the seeds of his future break with Rosa Luxemburg, his centrism, his role as an apparatchik in the 1910–12 debate, his base capitulation in 1914, and so on.

It is no accident that the acid test for Kautsky, as for all centrists, was the question of the struggle for power and the reintegration of revolution into a strategy founded entirely upon a daily reformist routine. Effectively, this had been the decisive question for international social democracy since 1905.

An analysis of the first draft of *The Road to Power* reveals that elements of centrism were present even before the bureaucratic axe fell. For although Kautsky perceptively analyzed those factors leading to increasing class contradictions (imperialism, militarism, reduced economic expansion, etc.), his fundamental philosophy was still that of "the tried and tested tactic": industrialization and the concentration of capital are working for us, our rise is irresistible unless something unforeseen occurs. . . . Such was Kautsky's reasoning, and the idea of abandoning passive fatalism was only entertained for those instances when "our enemies commit a foolish mistake"—a coup d'état or a world war. After all, matters had not progressed one inch since 1896, when Parvus first formulated the problem.

Revolutionary strikes and mass explosions were of no importance in Kautsky's *The Road to Power*. Even the Russian revolution was only invoked to show that it opened an era of revolutions in the East (which was correct), and that because of inter-imperialist conflicts the revolutionary period in the East would have profound effects on conditions in the West (which was also correct) and would undoubtedly exacerbate the tensions and increase the instability of bourgeois society. But no connections were made between the objective effects of the Russian upheaval in creating instability and *the effects of the revolution on the activity of the proletarian masses of Western Europe*. Political initiative, the subjective factor, the active element—these go completely by the board. "Await your enemy's mistake, prepare for zero hour by purely organizational means, *be careful to leave the initiative to the enemy*"— that is the sum total of the centrist wisdom of Kautsky in a nutshell! Later this was to be rendered still more profound by the Austro-Marxists—whose catastrophic failure did not burst upon the world until 1934!

Rosa Luxemburg's superiority is clearly revealed in every aspect of this crucial debate. To the dull rote of statistics with which Kautsky justified his thesis that "the revolution can never break out prematurely," she counterposed a profound understanding of the immaturity of conditions which *each and every* proletarian revolution will know in its birth-pangs:

> These "premature" advances of the proletariat constitute in themselves a very important factor which will create the political conditions for the final victory, because the proletariat cannot attain the degree of political maturity necessary to accomplish the final overthrow unless it is tempered in the flames of long and stubborn struggles.[18]

Luxemburg had written this as early as 1900, and it was here that she began to formulate the first elements of a theory of the *subjective conditions* necessary for a revolutionary victory, while Kautsky was still obsessed by an examination of purely *objective conditions*, to the extent of denying the very existence of the problems raised by Luxemburg! With her deep sympathy for the life and aspirations of the masses, her sensitivity to the moods of the masses and the dynamics of mass action, she was able to raise, as early as the debate of 1910, the crucial problem of proletarian strategy in the 20th century: the futility of expecting an uninterrupted rise in the combativity of the masses and the fact that if they were frustrated by a lack of results and a lack of leadership they would relapse into passivity.[19]

When Kautsky asserted that the success of a general strike "capable of stopping all the factories" depended on the preliminary organization of *all* the workers, he pushed the "primacy of organization" to an absurd point. History has shown that in this debate he was wrong and Rosa Luxemburg was right. We have known numerous general strikes that have succeeded in paralyzing the entire economic and social fabric of a modern nation, despite the fact that only a minority of workers were organized. May 1968 in France is only the latest confirmation of an old experience.

If Luxemburg is guilty of a "theory of spontaneity" (something far from proven) it certainly cannot be found in her judgments on the inevitability of mass, spontaneous initiatives during revolutionary upheavals (she was 100 percent right on this point), nor in some illusion that these spontaneous initiatives would be sufficient for revolutionary victory, nor even that such initiatives in and of themselves would produce the organization which would lead the revolution to victory. She was never guilty of the infantile misconceptions so dear to today's spontaneists.

What gave the "mass political strike" such an exceptional place in Rosa Luxemburg's outlook was that she saw in it *the essential means to educate and prepare the masses for the coming revolutionary conflicts* (better still: to educate them and create the conditions which would enable them to *perfect their education through self-activity*). Although she had not elaborated a strategy of transitional demands, she did draw the following conclusions from the sum of past experiences: that it was necessary to break with the daily practice of electoral struggles, economic strikes, and abstract propaganda "for socialism." For her the mass political strike was the essential means to break out of that ghetto.

Confrontation with the state apparatus, raising the political consciousness of the masses, revolutionary apprenticeship . . . all this was seen from a clearly revolutionary perspective which anticipated revolutionary crises in a relatively short period of time. If it was Lenin who founded Bolshevism on the conviction of the actuality of the Russian revolution, if it was he who extended this notion to the rest of Europe only after August 4, 1914, then it was Rosa Luxemburg who merits the distinction of first conceiving a socialist strategy based on the same imminence of revolution in the West itself, directly after the first Russian revolution of 1905.

When Kautsky argued against Luxemburg that "spontaneous movements of the organized masses are always unpredictable" and for this reason dangerous for a "revolutionary party," he revealed the mentality of a petty bureaucrat, who imagines that a "revolution" will run according to a carefully worked-out schedule. Rosa Luxemburg was a thousand times right to stress in opposition to this view that a revolutionary party, like Russian and Polish Social Democracy in 1905, distinguished itself precisely by its ability to understand and grasp what was progressive in this unavoidable and healthy mass spontaneity—in order to link its energy to the revolutionary goals that the party had formulated and embodied in its organization.[20] It took all the dogged conservatism of the Stalinist bureaucracy to dredge up again against Luxemburg the unfounded accusation that her analysis of the revolutionary processes in 1905 placed "too much emphasis" on the spontaneity of the masses and "not enough on the role of the party."[21]

The fact that she had a realistic—and unfortunately prophetic—vision of the role that the bureaucracy in the workers' movement could play in such a revolutionary crisis comes out in her speech to the Jena Conference in September 1905:

Previous revolutions, and especially those of 1848, have shown that in the course of revolutionary situations it is not the masses who must be curbed, but the parliamentary tribunes, to stop them betraying the masses.[22]

After the bitter experiences of 1906–10 she was even more precise when she returned to the same subject in 1910:

If the revolutionary situation comes to full bloom, if the waves of struggles are very advanced, then the leaders of the party will find no effective brake and the masses will simply push aside those leaders who stand in the path of the storm. This could happen one day in Germany. But I do not believe that in the interests of social democracy it is necessary or desirable to move in this direction.[23]

THE UNITY OF THE WORK OF ROSA LUXEMBURG

In the context of Luxemburg's "grand design"—to lead Social Democracy to abandon "the tried and tested tactic" and to prepare for the revolutionary struggles which she judged imminent—the totality of her activity acquires an undeniable unity.

Her analysis of imperialism not only corresponds to autonomous theoretical preoccupations, although these preoccupations were real.[24] She was aiming to uncover, in all its aspects, one of the main causes of the worsening contradictions in the capitalist world and in German society in particular. Similarly, internationalism was not simply a more-or-less Platonic theme for propaganda, but was thought of as a function of two requirements: the increasing internationalization of strikes and the preparation of the working class for the struggle against the coming imperialist war. The internationalist campaign which Rosa Luxemburg waged for 20 years in international social democracy was guided by a revolutionary perspective and a strategic alternative, like her campaign for the "mass political strike" and her profound analysis of imperialism.

The same is true for her anti-militarist and anti-monarchist campaigns. Contrary to a widely held belief, sometimes even repeated by sympathetic commentators,[25] Rosa Luxemburg's anti-militarist campaign was not only a function of her "hatred" (or her "fear" of the war) but was the result of a precise understanding that the bourgeois state had to be smashed for a socialist revolution to be victorious. As early as 1899 she wrote in the *Leipziger Volkszeitung*:

The power and domination of the bourgeois state as well as the bourgeois class is concentrated in militarism. Likewise social democracy is the only political party which fights militarism for principled reasons.

So this principled struggle against militarism belongs to the very *nature* of social democracy. To abandon the fight against the militarist system would simply lead in practice to the abandonment of the struggle against the existing social order.[26]

In *Reform or Revolution* one year later, as part of her comments on compulsory military service, she succinctly repeats that, if this prepares the material basis for the arming of the people, it does it "under the guise of modern militarism, which expresses in a most striking manner the domination of the people by the militarist state, the class nature of the state." These crystal-clear formulas demonstrate the immense gulf that separated her not only from the rambling of Bernstein but also from the lawyer's phrases of Kautsky on the "democratization [*sic*] of the Empire."

We can therefore immediately understand the terrible anger that must have gripped Rosa Luxemburg when she saw those very reformists who had blamed her for "risking the workers' blood" with her "adventurist tactics"[27] themselves spill the blood of the workers after August 1914 on a scale a thousand times greater—not for their own cause but for that of their exploiters. This indignation was what inspired her bitter verdicts on the S.P.D.: "Social democracy is nothing but a stinking corpse"; "the German Social Democrats are the greatest and most infamous criminals that have ever lived on earth."[28]

So what, then, is the verdict of history on Rosa Luxemburg? She was to all intents and purposes wrong in her mutual appreciation of the Bolsheviks and Mensheviks in Russia. She had simultaneously fought against Lenin's "ultra-centralism" while tolerating Leo Jogisches' iron regime in her own underground Polish Workers Party. She was inclined to set too much store by the vanguard's assimilation of socialist doctrine, and thus underestimated the need to forge working-class cadres really capable of guiding those broad masses who would politicize and enter the historic stage only on the day of the revolution. For the same reason she devoted no resources to building a tendency or an *organized* left faction within the S.P.D. after 1907 (the formation of a new party was of course impossible until the treachery of the S.P.D. leadership had been irremediably demonstrated to the masses by manifest betrayals of an historic scope). The young Spartakusbund and later the K.P.D. were to pay a terrible price for this failure to use the intervening decade to build a real leadership team; they were forced to undertake this task in the midst of the revolution.

Yet all these problems existed in the context of that great struggle which had dominated her life. Rosa Luxemburg was actually in Germany, and as such she developed an increasing scorn and suspicion for the social democratic apparatus of time-servers and functionaries whose crimes she

perceived far earlier and far more clearly than did Lenin. Not until 1914 did
Lenin adopt her conclusions on German Social Democracy. Only then did
he deduce the fundamental historic lesson of the tragedy—that to ensure
victory it was completely insufficient merely to have built a "powerful
organization." What was needed was an organization whose program and
whose daily use of it to intervene in the class struggle would make sure that,
on the day of the revolution, the party would be the driving force of the
proletariat and not its bureaucratic hangman. Not until 1918 did Rosa
Luxemburg in turn reach Lenin's conclusions. It was then that she grasped
the need to build an organization of the revolutionary vanguard and firmly
understood that it was not sufficient to have unbounded confidence in the
creativity of the masses or in their spontaneous ability to jettison social
democratic bureaucrats, who had finally nailed their counter-revolutionary
colors to the mast.

All in all, contemporary revolutionary Marxism owes a tremendous debt
to Rosa Luxemburg. She was the first Marxist to have defined and begun to
resolve the central problems of revolutionary Marxist strategy and tactics,
which alone can ensure the victory of the proletarian revolution in the
imperialist heartlands.

Notes

1. This is particularly the judgment of J. P. Nettl, who has written the fullest
   biography to date (*Rosa Luxemburg*, London: Oxford University Press, 1966).
   Nettl combines a wealth of detail and an often impressive judgment on partial
   events with a complete lack of comprehension of the general problems of
   proletarian strategy, the mass movement, and revolutionary perspectives; precisely the problems that preoccupied Rosa Luxemburg throughout her life.
2. Therefore, when the danger of war was posed for the first time in the 1890s,
   Engels asserted that, in the event of a war, social democracy would be forced to
   take power, and expressed the fear that this could end disastrously. In the same
   letter to Bebel he expressed his conviction that, "we would be in power by the
   end of the century" (letter to Bebel, October 24, 1891). In a previous letter (May
   1, 1891) he attacked Bebel's plan to censor the publication of the *Critique of the
   Gotha Programme* and denounced the attack on the freedom of criticism and
   discussion within the party (August Bebel, *Briefwechsel mit Friedrich Engels*
   [Paris: Mouton & Co., 1965], pp. 417, 465.)
3. Engels, *Selected Writings*, ed. W. O. Henderson, pp. 294–296. Our emphasis.
   Translators' note—In seeking the source of this quotation most easily accessible to
   the English audience we turned to the Pelican edition of Engels's writings edited
   by Henderson. This has probably been one of the most widely read translations
   of Engles to appear in English. Yet even in the 1967 edition a translation is used
   which dates from 1937 and was made by E. Burns. This translation completely

omits a crucial passage: "Everywhere the spontaneous unleashing of the attack has *retreated* into the background." Obviously, Ernest Mandel is too generous to the reformists—even in 1937 it was still necessary to falsify and bowdlerize this "old fighter and companion of Marx."

4. Engels wrote to Kautsky in 1895: "I see an extract from my 'Introduction' has appeared in *Vorwarts* today, reprinted without my knowledge and laid out in such a manner that I appear as nothing more than a peaceable lover of legality at all costs. I therefore desire all the more that an uncut version of the 'Introduction' be published in the *Neue Zeit* so that this shameful impression is wiped out."

   Using the pretext of threats of legal sanctions, Bebel and Kautsky refused to comply. Engels let himself be coaxed and did not insist on a complete reproduction of the "Introduction." This only happened after 1918 through the good offices of another International—the Comintern.

5. *Translators' note*—The so-called Hottentot elections of 1907 resulted in an unexpected setback for the S.P.D. As the election followed several years of unprecedented rise in the living standards of the masses and the institution of social legislation, it was generally expected that the S.P.D. would increase its vote. However, when Imperial Chancellor Bulow dissolved the Reichstag he did so as a maneuver to discipline the Catholic "Center Party" and create a parliamentary bloc which would govern without reliance on the "Center." The chosen battleground proved to be the question of guerilla activity in South West Africa; although the ostensible target of Bulow's campaign was the Center Party, his violently xenophobic campaign was in reality launched against the S.P.D.

   As so often in European history, the socialist movement crashed on the rocks of the chauvinism and patriotism inspired in the working class by the bourgeois demagogues, and the S.P.D. suffered a major reverse, declining from 81 to 53 seats. However, although this was seen as a clear defeat for the S.P.D., the underlying strength of German Social Democracy was clearly revealed by the fact that it actually increased its vote by 240,000—that it lost seats was more a result of the anti-socialist coalition and the vagaries of the German electoral process than any real decline in mass support. This is an important point to remember, as the sacred question of the "balance of forces" was to be one of the major reasons given by the union bureaucracy for refusing to organize a thoroughgoing resistance to the government in the following years.

6. Trotsky had almost echoed Rosa Luxemburg's opinion in *Results and Prospects* (1906), emphasizing the increasingly conservative character of social democracy. However, because of the conciliatory position he adopted on the faction fight in the R.S.D.L.P., he came closer to Kautsky in 1908 and supported him against Luxemburg in the debate on the "mass political strike." Lenin took a very cautious attitude on the conflict between Luxemburg and Kautsky in 1910, attempting to stop a bloc developing between Kautsky and the Mensheviks. In his article "Two Worlds" he asserted that the differences between the Marxists (among whom he numbered not only Luxemburg and Kautsky, but also Bebel) were only tactical and, moreover, in the final analysis minor. He praised the "caution" of Bebel and justified his thesis that it was preferable to leave the enemy the initiative in starting the war. (Lenin, *Collected Works*, Vol. XVI [Moscow: Progress Publishers, 1978], pp. 305–313.)

7. *Translator's note*—To understand the degeneration of German Social Democracy it is necessary to grasp the differential conditions which operated through-

out 19th and 20th century Germany. The situation in South Germany was very
different from that in Prussia, and power was based on an alliance of conservative landowners and liberal professional classes who presented a very different
image from the Junker-dominated and militaristic Prussian state. Hence from
the beginning of the 20th century the Baden Social Democratic group used
Parliament not merely as a propaganda tribune but also blocked with the liberals
against the Catholic "Center Party" to promote certain social reforms. From
that moment on reformist degeneration spread rapidly; the deputies soon re-
nounced even the traditional social democratic gesture of defiance and ceased to
vote against the budget.

8. The article was entitled "Staatsstreich und politischer Massenstreike," first
   published in *Neue Zeit*, reproduced in the anthology *Die Massenstreikdebatte*,
   published by Europäische Verlagsanstalt (Frankfurt 1970, pp. 46–95).

9. *Editor's note*—Alfred Dreyfus, a captain in the French Army, was court-
   martialed in 1894 on a charge of treason, falsely convicted, stripped of his rank,
   and imprisoned on Devil's Island. Antisemitism played a prominent role in the
   campaign against him. The writer Émile Zola led a campaign against the
   injustice, as part of which, in 1898, he wrote his famous article, "J'accuse."
   Dreyfus was ultimately exonerated.

10. *Translators' note*—The concept of the general strike as a "myth" was mainly the
    work of Georges Sorel, major theorist of revolutionary syndicalism. His book
    Reflections on Violence (1906) defined the mythical quality of the general strike,
    "the myth in which Socialism is wholly comprised, i.e., a body of images
    capable of invoking instinctively all the sentiments which correspond to the
    different manifestations of the war undertaken by Socialism against modern
    society." Thus the general strike does not divert the working class into the
    avenues of social reform but actualizes the "cleavage" between the classes,
    transforming individual conflicts into pure class war. The general strike becomes
    the moment of proletarian transformation into the class-for-itself, and conse-
    quently has this central mythical quality which encloses "all the strongest
    inclinations of a people, of a party, or of a class." Consequently, a clear
    counterposition was made by Sorel between the revolutionary act and the
    "middle class" reformism of social democracy. See Sorel, *Reflections on Violence*
    (New York: Collier Books, 1950), pp. 124–126 and 133–135.

11. As early as *Reform or Revolution*, Rosa Luxemburg had written: "It fell to
    Bernstein to consider it possible that the farmyard of the bourgeois parliament
    would be called upon to bring about the most incredible social transformation in
    history—the passage from capitalist to socialist society."

    Her critique of parliamentarianism and her analysis of the decline of the
    bourgeois parliament written in 1900 retains a freshness and a relevance which
    no other Marxist writing in Western Europe before 1914 possesses. In the same
    vein Luxemburg explained the increasing strength of revolutionary syndicalism
    in France as a result of the illusions of the French working class in "Jauressist"
    parliamentarianism. (See her article published in the *Sächsische Arbeiterzeitung* of
    December 5 and 6, 1905—Rosa Luxemburg, *Ausgewählte Reden und Schriften*,
    Vol. 1 [Berlin: Dietz Verlag, 1955], p. 196.)

12. These quotations are from an article published in the *Neue Zeit* ("Nach dem
    ersten Akt"), in the *Sächsische Arbeiterzeitung* ("Im Feuerscheine der Revolu-
    tion") and from her speech at the Jena Congress (see Rosa Luxemburg, *Ausge-
    wählte Reden und Schriften*, Vol. II [Berlin: Dietz Verlag, 1955], pp. 220–221,
    234–235, and 244).

13. A good summary of this debate is given by Antonia Grunenberg in her Introduction to *Die Massenstreikdebatte* (pp. 5–44).
14. For example, in the article "The Lessons of the Miners' Strike" ("Die Lehren des Bergerbeiterstreik") which appeared in the *Neue Zeit* in 1903.
15. Rosa Luxemburg, Speech at the Jena Congress, September 21, 1905 (*Ausgewählte Reden und Schriften*, Vol. II, pp. 240–241).
16. See in particular his article "What Next" (*Neue Zeit*, 1910), with its distinctions between "pre-emptive defensive strikes" and "strikes of aggression" (a distinction which originates from the book by Henriette Roland-Horst on the mass strike), "economic" and "political" strikes, "strategy of attrition" versus "strategy of overthrow," etc. (*Die Massenstreikdebatte*, pp. 96–121).

    Translators' note—For the most recent resumé of this whole debate in English, see Perry Anderson, "The Antinomies of Antonio Gramsci," in *New Left Review* 100 (November 1976–January 1977), pp. 61–66.
17. See the edition of *The Road to Power* published by Editions Anthropos (Paris, 1969), with an introduction and an appendix of correspondence which throw some light on this sad affair.
18. Rosa Luxemburg, *Ausgewählte Reden und Schriften*, Vol. II, p. 136.
19. Ibid., pp. 325–326, 330. These are extracts from an article published in *Dortmunder Arbeiterzeitung*, entitled "Was Weiter?"
20. It is simply a slander, spread by the Stalinists and "innocently" repeated by today's spontaneists, that Rosa Luxemburg attributed "all the merits" of the 1905 revolution to the "unorganized masses" without mentioning the role of the R.S.D.L.P. Here is just one quotation which proves the opposite: "And even if, in the first moments, the leadership of the uprising fell into the hands of chance leaders, even if the uprising was apparently bedeviled by all sorts of illusions and traditions, the uprising is nothing but the result of the enormous amount of political education spread deep inside the Russian working class by the underground agitation of the men and women of Russian Social Democracy. . . . In Russia, as in the rest of the world, the cause of liberty and social progress is in the hands of the conscious proletariat." (February 8, 1905, in *Die Gleichheit*—*Ausgewählte Reden und Schriften*, Vol. I, p. 216).
21. See the biography of Rosa Luxemburg by Fred Oeissner, (Berlin: Dietz Verlag, 1951)—especially pp. 50–53.
22. *Ausgewählte Reden und Schriften*, Vol. I, p. 245.
23. "Theorie und Praxis" (*Neue Zeit*, 1910), reproduced in *Die Massenstreikdebatte*, p. 231.
24. Rosa herself remarked that while writing her "Introduction to Political Economy" she had difficulty demonstrating the impediments to the realization of surplus-value. Hence her project to write "The Accumulation of Capital."
25. Notably Antonia Grunenberg in her introduction to *Die Massenstreikdebatte* (p. 43), where she maintains that Pannekoek was diametrically opposed to both Luxemburg and Kautsky in formulating strategic conceptions on the conquest of power, posing the question of the struggle against bourgeois state power.
26. *Ausgewählte Reden und Schriften*, Vol. I, p. 47.
27. Ibid., p. 245.
28. Speech on the program delivered to the founding conference of the K.P.D. (*Der Gründungsparteitag der KPD* [Frankfurt: Europäische Verlagsanstalt, 1969], p. 194). In particular her hackles were raised when, after the 1918 Armistice, S.P.D. leaders tried to use German soldiers against the Russian revolution in the Baltic countries.

4

Trotsky's Economic Ideas
and the Soviet Union Today

As the bureaucratic U.S.S.R. sinks into chaos, the economic platform of
Trotsky and the Left Opposition emerges as an indispensable guide to the
relaunching of a socialist project. This explains why for the liberals the
"neo-Bolsheviks" are today the main enemy.

The disgraceful slanders hurled by Stalin and the neo-Stalinists against
Leon Trotsky are today unanimously rejected in the U.S.S.R. On the eve of
the 50th anniversary of his assassination the government daily *Izvestia*
solemnly recognized that Lev Davidovich was a great and honest revolutionary, one of the principal founders and leaders of the Soviet state. Other
newspapers have revealed that at two points during 1922 Lenin had proposed that Trotsky be vice president of the Council of People's Commissars
and his designated successor in case of sickness or death.

But this is not to say that this rehabilitation of the founder of our
movement signals an approval of his political platform, which was opposed
to that of Stalin. On the contrary. The media and social science circles in the
U.S.S.R. are dominated today by neo-social democratic and neo-liberal
tendencies hostile to Leninism, to Marxism, and to the October revolution.
For these currents, Trotsky remains an ideological adversary, Trotskyism a
political enemy.

What is at stake, however, is an undeniable historical figure and tradition
in the Soviet Union. It is difficult to deny that Stalin considered them as his
number one enemy. As Stalin is hated by the immense majority of the Soviet
people, it is necessary that the current ideologues work to prevent this hatred
from translating automatically into a certain sympathy concerning Trotsky.

This article appeared in the *Bulletin in Defense of Marxism*, no. 84 (New York, Fourth
Internationalist Tendency, April 1991), p. 24. It had been translated from a French article,
under the title "L'alternative economique," that had appeared in a special magazine supplement
of the newspaper *Rouge*, published by the Ligue Communiste Revolutionaire in France.

The solution which they have generally opted for is that of raising a new set of slanders, less inflammatory than those of the Stalinists and neo-Stalinists, but founded just as much on open historical falsifications.

It is an historical irony that Trotsky is reproached today not for having been a counter-revolutionary but for having been an ultraleft "revolutionary fanatic." He is not reproached for having been an adversary of Lenin but for having been, in 1917 and later, the damned soul and "inspirer" of Lenin. Trotsky, the "bloody" incarnation of the October revolution (a Jew and a "cosmopolitan" imbued with "European culture" to boot), is the prime target of the neo-fascists and the neo-Black Hundreds who are sometimes openly allied with the neo-Stalinists. According to all the "democratic" opponents of the October revolution, Trotsky, the "dogmatic utopian" of "the historical mission of the working class," was the great leader of the "deviation" of Russian history from 1918 on.

AN OPPONENT OF THE NEP?

Within this cacophony the debate around economic alternatives occupies a key place. Trotsky is said to have been an opponent of the N.E.P. (New Economic Policy), the partisan of "superindustrialization," a fierce enemy of the private peasant, and the father of the "command economy." Stalin only applied Trotsky's economic program. The anti-Trotskyists in the U.S.S.R. today say that the struggle between Stalin and Trotsky was simply a struggle for power between two despots.

This interpretation of the debate which swept the U.S.S.R. from 1923 through 1928 all the way to 1934 involves a confusion between two distinct points of departure by Trotsky and the Left Opposition (not counting the capitulationists after 1929): the long-term analytical approach on the one hand and the political approach operating in the immediate and medium term on the other. This confusion is the fruit of a deliberate lie, of ignorance, or of a lack of understanding about these questions.

In opposing the Stalinist theory that socialism could be achieved in one country, Trotsky affirmed his belief that, considering the nature of imperialism, whether socialism or capitalism would end up victorious in the Soviet Union could only be approached on an international scale. It was impossible to establish a true classless society of the "freely associated producers" in Russia, because this required a median level of labor productivity superior to that of the most advanced capitalist countries, but also in permanent conflict with the world capitalist market. The weight of this antagonism would end up by crushing the chances for socialism in the U.S.S.R. through military or economic pressure if the revolution did not spread to the "advanced industrial nations." This analysis of long-term trends certainly also had short-term implications. It underscored the dangers of a lagging development of industry which risked promoting an alliance between private Russian agriculture and the world capitalist market—a rupture of the worker-peasant alliance. To fight the dangers of capitalist restoration, it stressed the necessity of limiting the private accumulation of capital and of raising the productivity of state industry, which would permit the sale of products at a lower price. This necessitated a more rapid development of industry.

Therefore, contrary to the legend of Stalinist-Bukharinist origin, and developed in the 1960s by George Lukacs, Trotsky did not draw adventurist-defeatist conclusions from this analysis, which history has now confirmed in a striking way precisely on the economic plane. It in no way reduced the middle-term destiny of the Soviet Union to the dilemma of either a revolutionary war and territorial expansion or an inevitable retreat toward capitalism. On the contrary, he advanced the idea of a steady consolidation of the gains of the socialist revolution while waiting for the ripening of the objective and subjective conditions for revolutionary victories in the advanced countries. In other words, he proposed that the U.S.S.R. enter the road of beginning to build socialism in a realistic and prudent manner without fanfare or illusions.

This "Trotskyist" alternative was based on the dialectic of economic logic and on the dynamic of social forces. Trotsky's analysis remains unmatched among 20th-century Marxists. The acceleration of the rhythm of industrialization must proceed through the steady transfer of the social surplus toward the productive socialized sector of the economy, that is to say, essentially at the expense of the middle bourgeoisie (kulaks and N.E.P.-men) and at the expense of the bureaucracy, by a radical reduction of unproductive expenditures.

A reinforcement of the social weight of the proletariat and the poor peasantry in society (as well as a fraction of the middle peasantry ready to participate) had to be realized through the raising of their standard of living and an improvement of their working conditions: the elimination of unemployment; the leading role of workers in factory management; the recruitment of the working peasantry to production cooperatives founded from the start on mechanized labor in order to guarantee to its members returns higher than they had known as individual producers.

These proposals were marked by an internal coherence that is still impressive today. The building of the first large tractor factory in 1923 would have assured the "voluntary participation of the poor peasants in the state farms." It would have freed the towns from the danger of being blackmailed by reductions in deliveries from the rich peasants by preventing the concentration of the agricultural surplus in their hands. It would have allowed the continued raising of real wages that had proceeded until 1926–27. It would have provided the U.S.S.R. with a powerful arms industry in order to defend itself from an eventual military attack over a ten-year rather than a five-year period.

At the same time this economic road, proposed to the Comintern and to the Communist parties, would permit them to take full advantage of revolutionary situations like those which occurred between 1923 and 1937 in Germany, Great Britain, Spain, and France.

Far from being "Trotskyism without Trotsky," Stalinist economic policy from 1928 on was the antithesis of that advanced by the opposition. Full-scale industrialization was accompanied by a lowering, not a raising, of real wages, by a catastrophic deterioration, not an improvement of labor conditions. Administrative expenses were not reduced but colossally increased, absorbing the major part of what had been taken from worker consumption. This was the monstrous deadweight of the bureaucracy and its absolute power over society. If the rise in production could not be supported by the interests and consciousness of the producers, it must be realized by force and general control. In place of "soviets everywhere" the reality was police control and red tape everywhere.

The forced collectivization of agriculture was the antithesis of the voluntary participation advocated by the opposition, consistent with Lenin's "cooperative plan." It led to desperate resistance by the peasants, notably the massive slaughter of livestock. It was accompanied by a systematic underdevelopment of investments, in agriculture as much as in the service sector (stockpiling, transportation, distribution), and a fluctuating price policy. It was thus the source of misery in the countryside and poverty in the towns for decades.

AGAINST THE COMMAND ECONOMY

As soon as Stalin's policies became clear, Trotsky, Rakovsky, and the Left Opposition denounced the forced collectivization of agriculture, the total suppression of the N.E.P., "superindustrialization," the attacks against real wages and peasant incomes, and the deepening of social inequality. To identify the opposition with these policies, to hold that they inspired them, amounts therefore to a pure and simple lie. To identify the thesis of Preobrazhensky-Trotsky, according to which *in the long term* an extension of private appropriation of the social surplus and market mechanisms would make capitalist restoration inevitable, with Stalin's policy of a *short- and medium-term* elimination of these mechanisms is a falsification of the economic orientation of Trotsky and the Left Opposition. Several quotations will suffice to demonstrate this.

THE OPPOSITION SPEAKS

Khristian Rakovsky, V. Kossior, N. Muralov, and V. Kasparova wrote in the declaration of 1930:

> The decree that abolished the NEP and the kulaks as a class is . . . an economic absurdity. . . . No charter, no decree can abolish the contradictions that still operate in the economy and in everyday life. . . . Attempts to ignore this economic truth . . . have led to the use of violence, breaking with the party's program, with the fundamental principles of Marxism, and show contempt for Lenin's most basic warnings concerning collectivization, the middle peasantry, and the NEP.

On October 22, 1932, Trotsky continued in his article "The Soviet Economy in Danger":

> If a universal mind existed, of the kind that projected itself into the scientific fancy of Laplace—a mind that could register simultaneously all the processes of nature and society, that could measure the dynamics of their motion, that could forecast the results of their interactions—such a mind, of course, could *a priori* draw up a faultless and exhaustive economic plan, beginning with the number of acres of wheat down to the last button for a vest. The bureaucracy often imagines that just such a mind is at its disposal; that is why it so easily frees itself from the control of the market and of Soviet democracy. But, in reality, the bureaucracy errs frightfully in its estimate of its spiritual resources. . . .
>
> The innumerable living participants in the economy—state and private, collective and individual—must serve notice of their needs and of their relative strength not only through the statistical determinations of plan commissions but by the direct pressure of supply and demand. The plan is checked and, to a considerable degree, realized through the market. The regulation of the market itself must depend upon the tendencies that are brought out through its mechanism. The blueprints produced by the departments must demonstrate their economic efficacy through commercial calculation. The system of the transitional economy is unthinkable without the control of the ruble. This presupposes, in its turn, that the ruble is at par. Without a firm monetary unit, commercial accounting can only increase the chaos.[1]

He followed up on this in *The Revolution Betrayed*:

> While the growth of industry and the bringing of agriculture into the sphere of state planning vastly complicates the tasks of leadership, bringing to the front the problem of *quality*, bureaucratism destroys the creative initiative and the feeling of responsibility without which there is not, and cannot be, qualitative progress. The ulcers of bureaucratism are perhaps not so obvious in the big industries, but they are devouring,

together with the cooperatives, the light- and food-producing industries, the collective farms, the small local industries—that is, all those branches of economy which stand nearest to the people. . . .

It is possible to build gigantic factories according to a ready-made Western pattern by bureaucratic command—although, to be sure, at triple the normal cost. But the farther you go, the more the economy runs into the problem of quality, which slips out of the hands of a bureaucracy like a shadow. The Soviet products are as though branded with the gray label of indifference. Under a nationalized economy, *quality* demands a democracy of producers and consumers, freedom of criticism and initiative—conditions incompatible with a totalitarian regime of fear, lies, and flattery.[2]

THREE ORIENTATIONS

There were three distinct currents of economic policy in the C.P.S.U. between 1928 and 1934—assuming the supporters of Bukharin continued as such after 1933, which is not at all certain.

Stalin's line was founded on the forced collectivization of agriculture and superindustrialization at the expense of the workers and peasants, and ultracentralized and ultradisproportionate planning (or rather semiplanning).

Bukharin's line was based on the "peaceful coexistence" of the private and socialized economy, the former being charged with providing for the latter, whose expansion would remain sharply limited.

The opposition's line foresaw a more rapid expansion of the socialized sector than Bukharin's plan, but much less rapid and certainly more balanced than Stalin's. It called for the reduction of unproductive expenses like those appropriated by the bureaucracy, as well as the improvement of the lives of workers and working peasants.

These three currents clearly reflected the pressure of different social forces. But it must be remembered that, at least during the period 1930–33, the differences between the concrete proposals of the opposition and those of the Bukharinists were much less clear than with those of Stalin. What characterized the economic program of the opposition more than anything else was the unity and clarity of its economic positions on the one hand and its political and social positions on the other: soviet democracy, satisfaction of the material demands of the producers, the struggle against inequality and bureaucratic privileges.

In 1932, also in "The Soviet Economy in Danger," Trotsky declared that:

The struggle between living interests, as the fundamental factor of planning, leads us into the domain of *politics*, which is concentrated

economics. The instruments of the social groups in Soviet society are/
should be: the Soviets, the trade unions, the cooperatives, and in first
place the ruling party. Only through the interaction of these three
elements—state planning, the market, and Soviet democracy—can the
correct direction of the economy in the transitional epoch be attained.[3]

This last sentence deserves to be underlined. And in *The Revolution
Betrayed*, Trotsky held that:

A restoration of the right of criticism and a genuine freedom of elections
are necessary conditions for the further development of the country. This
assumes a revival of freedom of Soviet parties, beginning with the party
of Bolsheviks, and a resurrection of the trade unions. The bringing of
democracy into industry means a radical revision of plans in the interests
of the toilers. Free discussion of economic problems will decrease the
overhead expense of bureaucratic mistakes and zigzags. Expensive
playthings—palaces of the Soviets, new theaters, show-off subways—
will be crowded out in favor of workers' dwellings. "Bourgeois norms
of distribution" will be confined within the limits of strict necessity, and,
in step with the growth of social wealth, will give way to socialist
equality.[4]

These lines, written 55 years ago, retain a burning relevance in today's
U.S.S.R. Once again, we find three fundamentally different currents of
economic policy:

- The first is to maintain bureaucratic control over the economy at the price
of important economic reforms.
- The second aims at developing an important private sector with en-
couragement given to the primitive accumulation of capital.
- The third is a neo-socialist defense of the immediate interests of the
workers (full employment, increased buying power, social services) and
of the reduction of social injustices and inequalities.

The second tendency, in contradiction to that of Bukharin and his comrades, who were honest communists, is essentially anti-communist and
anti-socialist. The third is not Trotskyist. But it must increasingly borrow
from the ideas of revolutionary Marxism, regardless of the vocabulary it
chooses, in order for it to join hands with the real independent workers'
movement currently reviving in the U.S.S.R.

NEW SLANDERS

It is noteworthy that a pro-capitalist and liberal opponent of Bolshevism,
Leonid Radzikhovski, writing in the September 9, 1990 issue of *Moscow
News*, accuses both neo-Stalinists like Nina Andreyevna, and Comrade

Buzgalin, spokesman of the "Marxist Platform" in the C.P.S.U., of being inspired by Trotsky's ideas—putting them in the same bag in the best Stalinist tradition. "Neo-Bolsheviks" are thus all "neo-Trotskyists."

However, the same Radzikhovski had to recognize that, "Thanks to his Marxist analysis, Trotsky discovered the principal evil in Soviet society: The struggle of a new aristocracy, of the bureaucracy against the popular masses who brought it to power. . . . Trotsky also developed in the 1930s a program for reorganizing the Soviet Union that involved democratization, self-management, openness, and even the market." Exactly. But to accuse the new Soviet socialist left of wanting to "defend the bureaucratic system against capitalism" is a gross slander. Like Trotsky, the true "neo-Bolsheviks" fight on two fronts: against the bureaucracy and against the rising middle bourgeoisie. That is consistent with the workers' material interests.

The supreme contradiction that the neo-liberals face is the following: How can the majority of citizens be prevented from defending their own interests while the sacred right of every individual is proclaimed? In the name of what principle? Could it be, in the best Stalinist tradition, that the people must be made to be happy in spite of and against itself by the use of force?

Notes

1. Trotsky, "The Soviet Economy in Danger," *Writings of Leon Trotsky, 1932* (New York: Pathfinder Press, 1973), pp. 273–274.
2. Trotsky, *The Revolution Betrayed* (New York: Pioneer Publishers, 1937), pp. 275–276.
3. Trotsky, "The Soviet Economy in Danger," p. 275.
4. Trotsky, *The Revolution Betrayed*, p. 289.

PART II
Leninist Organization

5

Vanguard Parties

To approach the problem of parties, party-building, and the necessity of the revolutionary vanguard party is to point to the peculiarities of a socialist revolution (or, if you do not like the word "revolution," a socialist transformation of bourgeois society). The socialist revolution is going to be the first revolution in the history of mankind which tries to reshape society in a conscious way according to a plan. It does not go into all the details, of course, which depend on concrete conditions and on the changing material infrastructure of society. But at the very least it is based on a plan of what a classless society has to be and how you can get there. It is also the first revolution in history which needs a high level of activity and of self-organization of the whole toiling population, that is to say, the overwhelming majority of men and women in society. It is from these two key features of a socialist revolution that you can immediately draw a series of conclusions.

You cannot have a spontaneous socialist revolution. You cannot make a socialist revolution without really trying. And you cannot have a socialist revolution commandeered from the top, ordered around by some omniscient leader or group of leaders. You need both ingredients in a socialist revolution: the highest level of consciousness possible and the highest level of self-organization and self-activity by the broadest possible segment of the population. All the problems of the relations between a vanguard organization and the masses stem from that basic contradiction.

If we look at the real world, the real development in bourgeois society for the last 150 years (more or less since the origin of the modern labor movement), we again see this striking contradiction. It helps us overcome one of the main disputes about the working class and the labor movement which has been going on a long time, and which is right in the middle of the political debate today. Is the working class an instrument for revolutionary

This article appeared in the *Mid-American Review of Sociology*, (Vol. 8, no. 2 (1983), pp. 3–21. An introductory note explained, "This is a substantively unaltered version of an address delivered at the Marx Centenary Conference—'Marxism: The Next Two Decades'—held at the University of Manitoba in Winnipeg, Manitoba, Canada, March 12–15, 1983."

social change? Is the working class integrated in bourgeois society? What has been its real role for the last 150 years? What does the historical balance sheet tell us about these questions?

The only conclusion you can draw from the real historical movement is that by and large, in day-to-day life, what Lenin called trade union consciousness dominates the working class. I would call it elementary class consciousness of the working class. This does not lead to permanent, day-to-day revolt against capitalism, but it is absolutely essential and necessary, as Marx pointed out many times, for an anticapitalist workers' revolt to occur sometime. If the workers do not fight for higher wages, if they do not fight for a shorter workday, if they do not fight for, let us say it in a provocative way, day-to-day *economic* issues, they become demoralized slaves. With demoralized slaves you are never going to make a socialist revolution or even acquire elementary class solidarity. So they *have* to fight for their immediate demands. But the fight for these immediate demands does not lead them automatically and spontaneously to challenge the existence of bourgeois society.

The other side of the story is also true. Periodically, the workers *do* revolt against bourgeois society, not by a hundred, five hundred, or a thousand, but by the millions. After all, the history of the 20th century *is* the history of social revolutions. Anybody who denies that should read the history books again, not to mention the newspapers. There has been hardly a single year since 1917, and in a certain sense since 1905, without a revolution somewhere in the world in which the workers participated in a rather important way. It is true that they did not always constitute the majority of the revolution's combatants. But that is going to change because the working class has become a majority in society in practically all the important countries of the world. So periodically, the workers *do* revolt against bourgeois society, as the statistics of the last 20 years in Europe attest. There was a real workers' challenge against the basic setup of capitalism in 1960–61 in Belgium, in 1968 in France, in 1968–69 in Italy, in 1974–75 in Portugal, and partially in Spain in 1975–76. And what was going on in Poland in 1980–81, if not a challenge against capitalism, was certainly a challenge for socialism. So this is a completely different picture from a permanently passive, integrated, bourgeoisified working class. More than 45 million workers have actively participated in these struggles.

The conclusion you can draw from these characteristics is that you have an *uneven development* of class activity and an *uneven development* of class consciousness in the working class. Workers do not strike every day, they cannot do that the way they function in the capitalist economy. The way they have to live by selling their labor power makes that impossible. They would starve if they would strike every day. And they certainly cannot make revolution every day, every year, or even every five years, for economic, social, cultural, political, and psychological reasons which I have no time to spell out. So you have a cyclical development of class militancy and class activity which is partially determined by an inner logic. If you fight for many years and the fight ends with grave defeats, then you will not start fighting at the same level or a higher level the year after the defeat. It will take you some time to recuperate; it might be 10 years, 15 years, or even 20 years. The opposite is also true. If you fight during some years with successes, even medium successes, you get momentum to fight on a broader and broader scale and on a higher and higher level. So we have this cyclical movement in the history of the international class struggle which we could describe in detail. Very closely combined with that uneven development of class militancy is an uneven development of class consciousness, not necessarily a mechanical function of the first. You can have high levels of class activity with a relatively low level of class consciousness. And the opposite is also true. You can have relatively high levels of class consciousness with a lower level of class militancy than one would have expected. I am talking, of course, about class consciousness of broad masses, of millions of people, not class consciousness of small vanguard layers.

Coming out of all these basic conceptual distinctions we can conclude the necessity of a vanguard formation nearly immediately. You need a vanguard organization in order to overcome the dangerous potential brought about by the uneven development of class militancy and class consciousness. If the workers would be at the highest point of militancy and consciousness all the time, you would not need a vanguard organization. But, unfortunately, they are not and cannot be there under capitalism. So you need a group of people who embody a permanently high level of militancy and activity and a permanently high level of class consciousness. After each wave of rising class struggle and rising class consciousness, when a turning point arrives and the actual activity of the masses declines, consciousness falls to a lower level and activity falls to nearly zero. The first function of a revolutionary vanguard organization is to maintain the continuity of the theoretical, programmatic, political, and organizational acquisitions of the previous phase of high class activity and of high working-class consciousness. It serves as the permanent memory of the class and of the labor movement—a memory which is codified, one way or another, in a program in which you can educate the new generation, which then does not need to start from scratch in its concrete intervention in the class struggle. This first function, then, is to assure a continuity of lessons drawn from the accumulated historical experience, because that is what a socialist program is: the sum total of the lessons drawn from all the experiences of real class struggles, real revolutions, and real counter-revolutions in the last 150 years. Very few people can cope with that, and nobody, absolutely nobody, can cope with that *alone*. You need an organization, and given the world nature of this experience, you need both a national *and* a worldwide organization to be able to constantly assess that sum total of historical and current experience of class struggle and revolution, to enrich it by new lessons coming out of new revolutions, to make it more and more adequate to the needs of class struggles and revolutions going on right at this time.

There is a second dimension. It is the organizational dimension, which is really not solely organizational but is, in reality, also political. Here we come to that famous question of centralization. Revolutionary Marxists stand for democratic centralism. But the word centralization is not to be taken in the first place as an organizational dimension, and in no way whatsoever is it essentially an administrative one. It is political. What does "centralization" mean? It means centralization of experience, centralization of knowledge, centralization of conclusions drawn out of actual militancy. Here again, we see a tremendous danger for the working class and the labor movement if there is no such centralization of experience: this is the danger of sectoralization and fragmentation, which does not enable anyone to draw adequate conclusions for action.

If we have women militants engaged only in feminist struggles, if we have young militants engaged only in youth struggles, if we have students engaged only in student struggles, if we have immigrant workers engaged only in immigrant worker struggles, if we have oppressed nationalities engaged only in oppressed nationalities' struggles, if we have unemployed engaged only in unemployed struggles, if we have trade unionists engaged only in trade union struggles, if we have unorganized, unionized, essentially unskilled workers engaged only in their own struggles, if we have political militants engaged only in election campaigns or in the publication of newspapers, and if each of them operates separately from each other, then they operate only on the basis of limited and fragmented experience and they *cannot* (for basic, I would say epistemological, reasons) draw correct conclusions from their own experience. They have fragmented struggles, fragmented experience, fragmented partial consciousness. They see only part of the whole picture. The conclusions which they come up with will be, you can say *a priori*, at least partially wrong. They cannot have an overall, total correct view of reality because they see only a fragmented part of that reality.

The same thing is true, of course, from an international point of view. If you concentrate only on Eastern Europe, you have a partial view of world reality. If you concentrate only on the underdeveloped, semi-colonial, dependent countries, you have a partial view of world reality. If you concentrate only on the imperialist countries, you have a partial view of world reality. Only if you bring together the experience of the concrete struggles conducted by the real masses in the three sectors of the world (which are also called the three sectors of world revolution),[1] then you have an overall, correct view of world reality. That is the big advantage of the Fourth International, because it is an international organization, which has comrades actually fighting, not only theoretically analyzing, in all these three sectors of the world, and it is concretely related to the struggles in all these three sectors of world revolution. This superiority is not due to the great intelligence of the leaders of the Fourth International. It is simply due to that elementary centralization of concrete experience of struggles on a global scale, added to a correct historical program.

That is what centralization is all about. It means that, I would not say the best because that is exaggerated, but at least *good* fighters in the unions, *good* fighters among unskilled workers and the unemployed, *good* fighters among oppressed nationalities, *good* fighters among women, youth, and students, *good* anti-imperialist fighters, *good* fighters in all these sectors of actually militant, oppressed, and exploited people in each state and on a world scale, come together to centralize their experiences in order to compare the lessons of their struggles on a statewide and worldwide scale, draw relevant conclusions, examine and reexamine in a critical way at each stage their program and their political line, in the light of lessons to be drawn out of all these experiences, in order to have an overall view of society, of the world, of its dynamics, and of our common socialist goal and how to get there. That is what we call, in our jargon, a correct program, a correct strategy, and correct tactics. Given the uneven development of class consciousness and the uneven and discontinuous level of class activity, this cannot be done by the masses in their totality. To believe otherwise is just a utopian and spontaneist daydream.

This can only be done by those people who claim for themselves the terribly "elitist" merit of being active in a more permanent way, in a more continuous way, than others. That is the only quality they claim for themselves, but it is a quality which is proven in life. And all those who do not have that quality also prove it in practice by ceasing political activity. All those who do have that quality, however, continue to fight even when the masses periodically stop fighting, do not stop developing class consciousness when the masses do (anybody who challenges this right challenges an elementary democratic and human right), continue to elaborate politics and theory, and constantly attempt to intervene in society in a permanent and continuous way. Out of that "merit," however modest and limited it is, grow a series of concrete and practical qualities which then constitute the basis for the justification of a vanguard organization.

As I said before, there is a real contradiction in the relationship between a vanguard organization and the broader masses. There is a real dialectical tension, if we can call it that, and we have to address ourselves to that tension. First of all, I used the words "vanguard organizations"; I did not use the words "vanguard parties." This is a conceptual difference I introduce on purpose. I do not believe in self-proclaimed parties. I do not believe in 50 people or 100 people standing in Market Square beating their breasts and saying, "We are the vanguard party." Perhaps they are, in their own consciousness, but if the rest of society does not give a damn about them, they will be shouting in that marketplace for a long time without this having any result in practical life, or worse, they will try to impose their convictions on an unreceptive mass through violence. A vanguard organization is something which is permanent. A vanguard party has to be constructed, has to be built through a long process. One of the characteristics of its existence is that it becomes recognized as such by at least a substantial minority of the class itself. You cannot have a vanguard party which has no following in the class.

A vanguard organization becomes a vanguard party when a significant minority of the real class, of the really existing workers, poor peasants, revolutionary youth, revolutionary women, revolutionary oppressed nationalities, recognizes it as their vanguard party, that is, follows it in action. Whether that must be 10 percent or 15 percent, that does not matter, but it must be a real sector of the class. If it does not exist, you have no real party, you have only the nucleus of a future party. What will happen to that nucleus will be shown by history. It remains an open question, not yet solved by history. You need a permanent struggle to transform that vanguard organization into a real revolutionary vanguard party rooted in the class, present in the working-class struggle, and accepted by at least a significant fraction of the real class as such.

Here we have to bring in another concept. I said before that the class is not permanently active and permanently on a high level of class consciousness. Now I have to introduce a distinction. The *mass* of the class is not, but the class is not homogeneous, not only because there are individuals who are members of different political groupings, at different levels of political awareness, influenced to different degrees by bourgeois ideology, but also because there is a differentiation going on within its own massive framework. There is a process of social and of political differentiation going on in the real working class all the time. There is a mass-vanguard distillation going on in the working class during certain periods. Lenin wrote a lot about it; Trotsky wrote a lot about it; Rosa Luxemburg, surprised as some of you may be, wrote a lot about it. People who have the ambition of being active in building revolutionary organizations, as I am, can give you the names, addresses, and telephone numbers of these vanguard workers in their own countries. It is not a mysterious question. It is a practical problem. Who are these vanguard workers in Belgium, France, Italy, Spain, Portugal, West Germany? They are those who are leading real strikes, who are organizing trade union militant oppositions, who are preparing mass demonstrations and mass struggles, who are differentiating themselves from the traditional bureaucratic apparatus.

It is both a social differentiation and a political differentiation, although one can discuss the exact weight of each element, which is not identical in each situation. But the layers as such are very real. The dimension of the layers is different in different periods. The "Revolutionary Obleute," as they are called in Germany, of the trade unions and the big factories of Berlin who were leading the November 1918 revolution and building the Independent Socialist Party, who afterwards moved to the Communist Party when the left wing of the Independent Socialist Party fused with the Communist Party at the Congress of Halle, were a very concrete layer in German society, not only in Berlin, but also in many of the industrial areas of the country. Everybody knew them, they were not an unknown quantity. They were tens and tens of thousands of people. If you look at the vanguard of the German working class 15 years later, say around 1932–33, this layer had strongly decreased in number, but it was still there.

If you study Russia, you see the same thing. In 1905, everybody knew these people. They were those who were leading the strikes, the real mass struggles at rank-and-file levels against the tsar. They were, in their majority, outside of social democracy before 1905, tended to come to social democracy during the 1905–06 revolution, and again partially left the party (Mensheviks as well as Bolsheviks) in the period of reaction. They reentered politics and grew on a massive scale in 1912 and especially with the beginning of the February 1917 revolution, and then the majority of them were absorbed by the Bolshevik Party after April 1917, after the Bolshevik Party took a straight and clear line for "All Power to the Soviets," that is to say, for the dictatorship of the proletariat.

One can discuss whether the Bolsheviks became a vanguard *party* in the true sense of the word in 1912–13, or only in 1917. I would tend to say that they became one in 1912–13; otherwise it would have been very difficult for them to grow as quickly as they did in the spring of 1917. But that is just a point of historical analysis. The real notion is that of the *fusion in real life* between this vanguard layer of the working class, the real leaders of real struggles of workers at factory and neighborhood levels, of women's struggles, of youth struggles, of national minority struggles, and the political vanguard organization. When that fusion has taken place, at least in part, you have a real vanguard party, recognized as such by a significant minority of the class. It will then become a majority probably only during the revolutionary crisis itself, on the condition of following a correct political line. If you do not have that fusion, you have only the nucleus of a future vanguard party, you have a vanguard organization, which is a precondition for that fusion at a later stage.

Then comes a third dimension: the self-organization of the class. Self-organization of the class goes through different forms at different stages of the class struggle. The most elementary self-organizations are trade unions. Then you have mass political parties at different levels of consciousness, bourgeois labor parties, independent labor parties, and revolutionary workers' parties. Only under conditions of revolutionary crises do you have the highest level of self-organization: this is the Soviet type of organization, which is to say, workers' councils, people's councils, call them what you want, popular committees.

Why do I say highest? Because they engulf the great majority of the workers, who generally, under nonrevolutionary conditions, you find neither in trade unions nor in political parties. Direct self-organization through a workers' council type of self-organization of the class is the highest form, not because I have a theoretical or ideological or moral or sentimental predilection for them—which of course I have—but for the simple, objective reason: they organize a much higher percentage of the workers and the exploited masses. Under normal conditions, unrestricted by bureaucratic apparatuses and leadership, they should organize up to 90 to 95 percent of the exploited masses, which you *never* find in trade unions or political parties. So they are the highest forms of self-organization.

Furthermore, there is absolutely no contradiction between the separate organizations of revolutionary vanguard militants and their participation in the mass organizations of the working class. On the contrary, history generally confirms that the more conscious and the better organized you are in vanguard groupings, the more constructively you operate in the mass organizations of the working class. This means that you have to avoid the theoretical foundations of sectarianism, that you have to respect workers' democracy, socialist democracy, soviet or workers' councils, or popular councils' democracy, in a very thorough way. But this being said, there is no contradiction whatsoever. Again, the only right you claim for yourself inside the unions, inside the mass parties, inside the soviets, is to be a more devoted, more energetic, more dedicated, more courageous, more lucid, more self-denying *builder* of the unions, *builder* of the mass parties, *builder* of the soviets, defender of the general interests of the working class, without attributing to yourself any special privilege toward your fellow workers, except the right to try to convince them.

Our stance for working-class democracy, for socialist democracy, for socialist pluralism, is based on a programmatic understanding that there are no contradictions between the interests of communists, vanguard militants, the working class, and the labor movement in its totality. There are no conditions in which we subordinate the interests of the class as a whole to the interests of any sect, any chapel, any separate organization. It is out of a theoretical understanding of that truth that we can fight enthusiastically, that we can fight with devotion and with deep understanding for the workers' united front, for a policy of unification of all different tendencies of the labor movement and the working class for common goals, because we believe that the victory of socialism is impossible without the victory of the fight for these common goals.

There is also a basic theoretical appreciation underlying this position. We do not believe that Marxism is a full, final doctrine, dogma, or *Weltanschauung*. We do not believe that the Marxist program, which embodies the continuity of the experience of the actual class struggle and real revolutions of the last 150 years, is a definitively closed book. If you would believe that, then the best revolutionary Marxist would be a parrot who would just recite from memory, or someone who looks for an answer after feeding all the lessons into a computer. For us, Marxism is always open because there are always new experiences, there are always new facts, including facts about the past, which have to be incorporated into the corpus of scientific social- ism. Marxism is always open, always critical, always self-critical.

It is not by accident that when Marx was called to answer the question in the drawing room game, "What is your main life *dictum*?" he gave as the answer, "De omnibus est dubitandum" ("You have to doubt everything"). This is really the opposite attitude of the one which is so often stupidly and foolishly attributed to Marx, that he was building a new religion without God. The spirit to doubt everything and to put into question everything that you yourself have said is the very opposite of religion and of dogma. Marxists believe that there are no eternal truths and no people who know everything. The second stanza of our common anthem, *The Internationale*, starts with the wonderful words, in French:

Il n'y a pas de sauveur suprême
Ni Dieu, ni César, ni tribun,
Producteur sauvons—nous nous mêmes
Decrétons le salut commun.

In German it is even clearer:

Es rettet uns Kein hoh'res Wesen,
Kein Gott, Kein Kaiser, Kein Tribun
Uns aus dem Elend zu erlosen,
Konnen wir nur selber tun.[2]

Only the whole mass of the producers can emancipate themselves. There is no God, no Caesar, no unfailing Central Committee, no unfailing Chairman, no unfailing General Secretary or First Secretary who can substitute for the collective efforts of the class. That is why we try simultaneously to build vanguard organizations and mass organizations.

You cannot trick the working class or "lead" the working class to do something which it does not want to do. You have to convince the working class. You have to help the working class understand collectively and massively the need for a socialist transformation of society, for the socialist revolution. That is the dialectical relationship between the vanguard party and the mass self-organization of the working class. And that is why, for us, socialist pluralism, the debate, even when it takes an unhealthy and unhappy form of factionalism and bickering which gets on the nerves of all serious militants (I completely sympathize with them, because it is largely a waste of time), is an unavoidable price to be paid for keeping up that self-critical process. If nobody is, in advance, in possession of the whole truth and nothing but the truth, if each situation has always to be reexamined in a critical way against new experiences of working-class struggle and of real revolutions, then of course you *need* criticism, you *need* the confrontation of different proposed solutions, you *need* variants. It is not a luxury just in order to be truthful to an abstract formula of workers' democracy. NO! It is an absolutely essential precondition for making a victorious revolution which will lead to a classless society.

Revolution is not a goal in itself. Revolution is an instrument, as a party is an instrument. The goal is building a socialist classless society. Everything we do, even today, even with shorter-term perspectives like leading the masses in their day-to-day struggles, can never be done in such a way that it conflicts basically with the longer-term goal, which is the goal of self-emancipation of the working class and self-emancipation of all the exploited, by building a classless society without exploitation, without oppression, without violence of men and women against each other. Socialist democracy is not a luxury but an absolute, essential necessity for overthrowing capitalism and building socialism. Let me give two examples.

We understand today the functional aspect of socialist democracy in postcapitalist society (the societies of Eastern Europe, the Soviet Union, China, Vietnam, and Cuba). Without socialist pluralistic democracy you cannot find correct solutions for the basic problems of socialist planning. No party can substitute for the mass of the people to determine what the mass of the people want as priorities in the form of consumption, the division between the consumption fund and the investment fund, between individual and collective consumption, between the productive and unproductive consumption fund, between the productive and unproductive investment fund, and so forth. Nobody can do that. Again, to believe otherwise is a utopian daydream.

And if the mass of the people do not accept your choice of priorities, no power on earth, even the biggest terror of Stalin, can force them to do the one key thing that you need to build socialism: have a constructive, creative, and convinced participation in the production process. There is one form of opposition that the bureaucracy has not succeeded in crushing. It is becoming bigger and bigger: the opposition which expresses itself by not caring about what is going on in production. You know the famous joke they tell in Eastern Germany. The journalist comes to a factory and asks the director, "Comrade manager, how many workers are working in your factory?" He answers, "Oh, at least half of them." This is reality in all the bureaucratized, so-called socialist countries. No terror can overcome that. Only socialist democracy can overcome that, only pluralism, only the possibility of the mass of the producers and the consumers to choose between different variants of the plan which conforms the most to their interests as they understand them.

Socialist democracy is not a luxury and its need is not limited to the most advanced industrial countries. It is true of China; it is true for Vietnam. It is the only way to rapidly correct the disastrous effects of grave policy mistakes. Without pluralism, without a broad public debate, without a legal opposition, it might take 15 years, it might take 25 years, it might take 30 years before you correct those mistakes. We have seen the historical record and it shows the terrible price the working class has to pay if you take such a long time before you correct your mistakes.

Mistakes in themselves are *unavoidable*. As Comrade Lenin said, the real key for a revolutionary is not that he avoids making mistakes (nobody avoids making mistakes) but how he goes about correcting them. Without internal party democracy, without the right to demonstrate, without the non-banning of factions or parties, without free public debate, you have great obstacles in correcting mistakes and you will pay a heavy price for this. So we are absolutely in favor of the right to different tendencies, full internal democracy, and the nonbanning of factions or parties.

I do not say the right to factions, because that is a false formulation. Factions are a sign of illness in a party. In an healthy party you have no factions—a healthy party from the point of view of both the political line and the internal party regime. But the right not to be thrown out of the party, if you create a faction, is a lesser evil than being thrown out and stifling the internal life of a party through excessive forbidding of internal debate.

It is not an easy question, especially in a proletarian party. The more revolutionary vanguard organizations are rooted in the working class, the less is their number of students and other nonproletarian members (I do not say that it is bad to have students or intellectuals; you need them, but they should not be the majority in a revolutionary organization). The more workers you have in your organization, the better you are implanted in the working class, the more likely you are to come up with the concrete problems of the class. Within that general framework is to be placed the functional nature of a vanguard organization for the class struggle, for the revolution, and for building socialism. You should never forget that there is a strict dialectical interrelation between the three. Otherwise we get off the track and we do not fulfill the historical role which we want to fulfill: to help the masses, the exploited and the oppressed of the world, build a classless society, a world socialist federation.

QUESTIONS AND ANSWERS

Question: I think that there was an important and perhaps not accidental omission. I agree that the importance of centralization flows out of the question of partial versus general experience, and something like a division of labor is necessary because everyone cannot have a personal participation and accurate summation of everything that is going on in the world. What is lacking in this formulation is that this summation must be made on the basis of the science of Marxism. Otherwise it leads to the pluralistic and agnostic mess which we see in many organizations. It is crucial to look at things through the prism of the collective experience of Marxism in its totality, including the experience of Stalin and Mao Tse Tung. If we do not use that prism to evaluate that experience, we will be back to empiricism.

Answer: I totally agree with the importance of science for building a revolutionary party. One of the biggest contributions of Marx to the labor movement was the building and developing of scientific socialism. I agree also with the formula that agnostic or empiricist alternatives to science are irrelevant. But you have to understand that science is always open. Science is based on what I would call optimistic skepticism or, as Marx said, optimistic doubt. And to cite Engels: the labor movement, the party, needs science and science cannot develop if it has not a *free* development. Tell that to Comrades Stalin and Mao Tse Tung.

Question: Where do the members of the vanguard get their class consciousness? How can those who are not of the class and, for the most part, do not share the conditions of lives of those in the class claim to have class consciousness? Not only that, but how can they claim to have one which is either more correct or higher than the workers themselves? How can we decide what is a higher level of consciousness?

Answer: On this question of higher consciousness, why do we claim higher consciousness? It is not a theoretical claim. We claim higher consciousness because of the confirmation in practice. The labor movement and the revolutionary movement are not a drawing room game. You are involving yourself with the destiny of millions of human beings. Who had a higher consciousness, those who supported the first imperialist war or those who were against the war from the beginning? *It is a practical question and you get a practical answer.* Can anybody give an agnostic answer? Would it have been correct to wait and see? Who had the higher consciousness, those who said Hitler is not so important because after Hitler it will be our turn, or those who said in 1930 and 1931 that it was vital to fight for the workers' united front from top to bottom of the labor movement and, by all means and with all sacrifices, to prevent this fascist criminal from coming to power, because he would kill tens of millions of human beings? Did he not? Again it was a practical question who had a higher consciousness, those who opposed or those who went along with Stalin? You can discuss every single one of the key political questions since 1848 or 1877 or 1917 or 1933. If a tendency of the world labor movement has been right on all of them, that is, has a correct program and a correct strategy, it can claim histori- cally higher consciousness. This does not mean that it has been right on everything, but it has been generally historically right, much more so than any other current or layer inside the working class. That is where the problem of higher consciousness can be decided. As to the question of how non-working-class members get class consciousness, one must give two answers.

In the first place, as the *Communist Manifesto* already pointed out, *indi- vidual* members of other social classes than the proletariat can assimi- late class consciousness through the acquisition of science—scientific socialism—and through a practical engagement on the side of working- class and revolutionary struggles. This is a political-moral way of acquiring such consciousness, different from the existential social way. It has to be constantly reaffirmed and reassessed through practical commitments. It leads to many political and individual crises, not only through the pressure of bourgeois and petty-bourgeois ideology, strengthened by non- proletarian living conditions, but also through its dialectical opposite, a feeling of guilt which makes such intellectuals easy prey for demagogy by bureaucrats ("If you do not accept the party leadership's *fiat*, it is because you are a petty-bourgeois intellectual."). But strict adherence to the princi- ples of scientific analysis and of revolutionary commitment (of the defense of all exploited and oppressed peoples everywhere) makes it possible to overcome such obstacles.

Still, it remains true that a revolutionary organization which is not deeply rooted in the working class, which has not a majority of wage-earners in its own ranks, which does not in practice have its finger on the pulse of the working class, cannot function as a real revolutionary *vanguard* organiza- tion, as a nucleus of a revolutionary vanguard *working-class* party. The danger that it will go astray on key questions of working-class strategy, not to say politics and tactics, will grow tremendously. So the real basis of higher working-class consciousness inside the revolutionary vanguard organization is *both* socialist science (the revolutionary Marxist program and principles) and the actual involvement in its ranks and leadership by real vanguard workers, who serve as transmission belts for what is really happening in the class, and who have higher class consciousness because they combine correct principles with the real experience of workers and mass struggles, in which they begin to play a leadership role.

Question: As an ex-member of the Revolutionary Workers League (R.W.L.) I would like to raise questions about actually existing Leninism rather than Leninism on the theoretical level. I lived that experience for many years, struggling for the integration of a gay liberation politics and a feminist politics into the life of the R.W.L. In that endeavor we were defeated. In fact, it was the gay question around which the majority of the organization was actually constructed in favor of an industrial turn by attacking us and our rights to raise our position in that debate, by denying the experiences we had learned in the autonomous mass movement, by denying our right to form caucuses of gays or other especially oppressed groups in the organization. If we are to overcome the crisis of actually existing Leninism we have to seriously look at how the oppressions of outside society are internalized, reproduced, and lived in those organizations.

Answer: The speaker makes a mistake in analysis. While I completely agree that you should not internalize the oppressions of bourgeois society inside a revolutionary party, you have to ask yourself, What is the *biggest* oppression in bourgeois society? It is not that of women in general and it is not that of gays in general. It is the working class which is the most oppressed layer of bourgeois society. Of course, women workers and gay workers are even more oppressed than other workers. I do not deny that. But I deny that a woman intellectual or a bourgeois woman is more oppressed in capitalist society than a male worker. I deny that strictly on material terms. Prove to me the opposite! Prove to me that the average worker is educated and developed in this society so he can freely speak in a meeting like this as you speak. I say NO! He is *more* oppressed, he is *more* exploited. And if you have a regime in a revolutionary organization where you do not allow the workers to discuss, where you do not allow the workers to decide, you are internalizing workers' oppression in your organization *more* than you are internalizing the oppression of women or the oppression of gays. So that is the real problem. If you see what the situation of the working class is in bourgeois society, you understand that there is a contradiction which is not something that can be solved by an easy decree or an administrative rule.

Question: The Workers Community Party (W.C.P.), as a vanguard organization, has experienced a profound crisis in the last few years. This led to a recognition that there have been serious errors in the political line, in the internal organization, and in the relations with individuals and forces outside of the W.C.P. There is also general agreement that there are a number of areas in particular that must be addressed. But in my opinion the central argument going on in the W.C.P., as in many left organizations, is the question of power. I am specifically talking about the disenfranchisement of women, oppressed nationalities, and working-class members in these parties and other working-class organizations through the seizure of power by certain elements within these organizations.

Answer: I will just concentrate on one key question, the question of power inside a revolutionary organization. This is an old question. I do not say that in a pejorative way. But it is as old as the socialist movement, the existence of socialism. The main objection raised against the first socialist thinkers in the 18th and the 19th centuries, the so-called utopian socialists, was in essence the same question.

People are the products of their conditions, of their circumstances. The circumstances in this society are bad. How can bad circumstances create good people who will change that society? This question is 200 years old. You can say that this leads to a power bias or a competition bias between individuals, which is true. Competition between individuals, and therefore the search for individual advantages, is the essential result of private property and commodity production. These are the very essence of bourgeois society. And how could anybody in this society be completely free of that influence? That is impossible. To develop perfect men ad women as products of an imperfect, bad, inhumane society is impossible.

But Karl Marx gave an answer to that dilemma in his *Theses on Feuerbach*. It is a double answer, which is the theoretical basis of my introduction. On the one hand, he said, this contradiction can only be solved through revolutionary activity. It is revolutionary activity which *transforms* human beings in the process of trying to revolutionize society. You will never have perfect human beings to build a perfect party which makes a perfect revolution. If you want that, you had better get out of politics. But you will have better and better revolutions, more and more conscious men and women, who will build a better and better revolutionary party, which will come out with a better and better transitional society, nearer and nearer to socialism. This is the self-critical nature of socialist revolutions, which Marx analyzed at great length in his preface to the *18th Brumaire of Louis Bonaparte*.

But there is also a second thesis on Feuerbach which I recommend, for example, to my comrades of Spartacist persuasion. This is the thesis in which Marx says: "Do not forget that the educators need to be educated."

You do not have people who are in possession of the full truth and who go to the masses in order to preach this full truth.

If you are unable to learn from reality, you do not understand that the Polish workers were *real* socialists, independently from their ideology, because they were trying to install a social order in which the workers themselves, with great sacrifice, would try to run the economy and the whole of society in the interests of the working class. That is essentially what socialism is all about, not whether you go to church or not. A Catholic worker who wants the workers to run the factories in my eyes has a thousand times higher class consciousness than a so-called communist worker who accepts that bosses run the factories.

So if we take these two things together, we try to transform ourselves by revolutionary praxis, by revolutionary activity, and if we remain modest, if we are not arrogant, if we understand that we have to learn from the masses as well as to teach them, then we can go very far. I do not say we shall have an ideal party but we can advance very far in the direction of such a party, but on two conditions. First, it has to have internal democracy, and there have to be substantial *institutional* safeguards against bureaucratization. Second, it has to be based on Marxism, that is, on a clear and correct program on the key issues of today's class struggle, of today's mass struggle in the world.

You cannot have people in the same party who would shoot each other, because that is what it amounts to under certain circumstances, in the literal sense of the word. If you have a wrong position on Central American revolution because of some weird theory you hold on the nature of the Soviet Union, at the border of Nicaragua you are confronted with a very concrete question: "On what side are you shooting?" The same thing is true for Poland. If you have a wrong position on the Polish workers' struggles, which are part and parcel of the world working-class struggle, you are in deep trouble. You cannot have in the same party those who want to put the strikers in jail or those who are willing to shoot strikers, and those who want the strikers to be free to strike and to organize, nor those who accept a ban on strikes and those who support the organizations the strikers set up independent from the state.

Such big divisions inside the same party are just not practical. They do not lead to common action, they lead to complete paralysis. I am not for *banning anybody in the labor movement.* I am for the right of the Stalinists to exist freely inside the labor movement. I was against the banning of the pro-government unions in Poland. It happened that the great majority of the Solidarity comrades were of the same opinion. We do not want to ban anybody inside the labor movement. Full freedom, but not in the same party. Those who do not agree on the basic program, let them build their own party. That is their right. So you need a programmatic discussion and programmatic clarification on the key questions of the class struggle in the world today before you can build a revolutionary party.

Notes

1. *Editor's note*—The "three sectors of the world revolution" referred to here are described earlier in the paragraph: the advanced industrialized (imperialist) countries, the less developed and underdeveloped nations of the "third world," and the bureaucratized workers' states (in Eastern Europe, the U.S.S.R., China, etc.).
2. *Editor's note*—The generally accepted English translation of these lines reads:

   We want no condescending saviors
   To rule us from their judgment hall.
   We workers ask not for their favors;
   Let us consult for all.

   A more faithful translation of the French original cited by Mandel would be:

   There is no supreme savior.
   Not god, not Caesar, not tribune.
   We producers must liberate ourselves,
   Proclaim our collective salvation.

6

The Leninist Theory of Organization: Its Relevance for Today

A serious discussion of the historical importance and current relevance of the Leninist theory of organization is possible only if one determines the exact position of this theory in the history of Marxism—or to be more precise, in the historical process of the unfolding and development of Marxism. This, like any process, must be reduced to its internal contradictions through the intimate interrelationship between the development of theory and the development of the actual proletarian class struggle.

Approached in this way, the Leninist theory of organization appears as a dialectical unity of three elements: a theory of the present relevance of revolution for the underdeveloped countries in the imperialist epoch (which was later expanded to apply to the entire world in the epoch of the general crisis of capitalism); a theory of the discontinuous and contradictory development of proletarian class consciousness and of its most important stages, which should be differentiated from one another; and a theory of the essence of Marxist theory and its specific relationship to science on the one hand and to proletarian class struggle on the other.

Looking more closely, one discovers that these three theories form, so to speak, the "social foundation" of the Leninist concept of organization, without which it would appear arbitrary, nonmaterialist and unscientific. The Leninist concept of the party is not the only possible one. It is, however, the only possible concept of the party which assigns to the vanguard party the historic role of leading a revolution which is considered,

This article appeared in what was at that time the theoretical magazine of the Socialist Workers Party in the United States, *International Socialist Review*, Vol. 31, no. 9 (December 1970), p. 26.

in an intermediate or long-range sense, to be inevitable. The Leninist concept of the party cannot be separated from a specific analysis of proletarian class consciousness, that is, from the understanding that *political* class consciousness—as opposed to mere "trade union" or "craft" consciousness— grows neither spontaneously nor automatically out of the objective developments of the proletarian class struggle.[1] And the Leninist concept of the party is based upon the premise of a *certain degree of autonomy of scientific analysis*, and especially of Marxist theory. This theory, though conditioned by the unfolding of the proletarian class struggle and the embryonic beginnings of the proletarian revolution, should not be seen as the mechanically inevitable product of the class struggle but as the result of a theoretical practice (or "theoretical production") that is able to link up and unite with the class struggle only through a prolonged struggle. The history of the worldwide socialist revolution in the 20th century is the history of this prolonged process.

These three propositions actually represent a deepening of Marxism, that is, either of themes that were only indicated but not elaborated upon by Marx and Engels or of elements of Marxist theory which were scarcely noticed due to the delayed and interrupted publication of Marx's writings in the years 1880–1905.[2] It therefore involves a further deepening of Marxist theory, brought about because of gaps (and in part contradictions) in Marx's analysis itself, or at least in the generally accepted interpretation of it in the first quarter century after Marx's death.

What is peculiar about this deepening of Marx's teaching is that, setting out from different places, it proceeds toward the same central point, namely, to a determination of the specific character of the proletarian or socialist revolution.

In contrast to all previous revolutions—not only the bourgeois revolutions, whose laws of motion have been studied in great detail (in the first place by Marx and Engels themselves), but also those revolutions which have hitherto been far less subjected to a systematic, generalized analysis (such as the peasant revolutions and those of the urban petty bourgeoisie against feudalism; the uprisings of slaves and the revolts of clan societies against slaveholding society; the peasant revolutions that occurred as the old Asiatic mode of production periodically disintegrated and so forth)—the proletarian revolution of the 20th century is distinguished by four particular features. These give it a specific character, but also, as Marx foresaw,[3] make it an especially difficult undertaking.

1. The proletarian revolution is the first successful revolution in the history of mankind to be carried out by the lowest social class. This class disposes of a potentially huge, but actually extremely limited, economic power and is largely excluded from any share in the social wealth (as

opposed to the mere possession of consumer goods which are continuously used up). Its situation is quite different from the bourgeoisie and the feudal nobility, who seized political power when they already held the economic power of society, as well as from the slaves, who were unable to carry through a successful revolution.

2. The proletarian revolution is the first revolution in history aimed at a consciously planned overthrow of society, that is, which does not seek to restore a previous state of affairs (as did the slave and peasant revolutions of the past) or simply legalize a transfer of power already achieved on the economic field, but rather to bring into being a completely new process, one which has never existed and which has been anticipated only as a "theory" or a "program."[4]

3. Just as every other social revolution, the proletarian revolution grows out of the internal class antagonisms and the class struggle they inevitably produce within society. But while revolutions in the past could by and large be satisfied with pushing this class struggle forward until a culminating point was reached—because for them it was not a question of creating completely new and consciously planned social relations—the proletarian revolution can become a reality only if the proletarian class struggle culminates in a gigantic process, stretching out over years and decades. This process is one of systematically and consciously overturning all human relations and of generalizing, first, the independent activity of the proletariat and, later (on the threshold of the classless society), that of all members of society. While the triumph of the bourgeois revolution makes the bourgeoisie into a conservative class (which is still able to achieve revolutionary transformations in the technical and industrial fields, and which plays an objectively progressive role in history for a rather long period of time, but which pulls back from an active transformation of social life, since in that sphere mounting collisions with the proletariat that it exploits make the bourgeoisie increasingly reactionary), the conquest of power by the proletariat is *not the end but the beginning* of the activity of the modern working class in revolutionizing society. This activity can end only when it liquidates itself as a class, along with all other classes.[5]

4. In contrast to all previous social revolutions, which have essentially taken place within a national or an even more limited regional framework, the proletarian revolution is by nature international and can reach its conclusion only in the worldwide construction of a classless society. Although it certainly can achieve victory at first within a national framework alone, this victory will constantly be endangered and provisional so long as the class struggle on an international scale has not inflicted a decisive defeat upon capital. The proletarian revolution, then, is a world revolutionary process, which is carried out neither in a linear fashion nor with uniformity. The

imperialist chain breaks first at its weakest links, and the discontinuous ebb and flow of the revolution occurs in conformity with the law of uneven and combined development. (This is true not only for the economy but also for the relationship of forces between classes; the two by no means automatically coincide.)

The Leninist theory of organization takes into account all these peculiarities of the proletarian revolution. It takes into consideration the peculiarities of this revolution in light of, among other things, the peculiarities and contradictions in the formation of proletarian class consciousness. Above all, it expresses openly what Marx only intimated, what his epigones scarcely understood at all, namely, that there can be neither an "automatic" overthrow of the capitalist social order nor a "spontaneous" or "organic" disintegration of this social order through the construction of a socialist one. Precisely because of the uniquely conscious character of the proletarian revolution, it requires not only a maturity of "objective" factors (a deep, ongoing social crisis which expresses the fact that the capitalist mode of production has fulfilled its historic mission) but also a maturity of so-called subjective factors (maturity of proletarian class consciousness and of its leadership). If these "subjective" factors are not present or are present to an insufficient extent, the proletarian revolution will not be victorious at that point, and *from its very defeat* will result the economic and social possibilities for a temporary consolidation of capitalism.[6]

The Leninist theory of organization represents, then, broadly speaking, the deepening of Marxism, applied to the basic problems of the social superstructure (the state, class consciousness, ideology, the party). Together with the parallel contributions of Rosa Luxemburg and Trotsky (and, in a more limited sense, of Lukacs and Gramsci) it constitutes the *Marxist science of the subjective factor.*

BOURGEOIS IDEOLOGY AND PROLETARIAN CLASS CONSCIOUSNESS

The Marxian proposition that "the dominant ideology of every society is the ideology of the dominant class" appears at first glance to conflict with the character of the proletarian revolution as the *conscious* overturning of society by the proletariat, as a product of the conscious, independent activity of the wage-earning masses. A superficial interpretation of this proposition might lead to the conclusion that it is utopian to expect the masses, who under capitalism are manipulated and exposed to the constant onslaught of bourgeois and petty-bourgeois ideas, to be capable of carrying out a revolutionary class struggle against this society, let alone a social revolution. Herbert Marcuse, who draws this conclusion, is (for the time being) simply the latest in a long series of theoreticians who, taking as their point of departure the Marxian definition of the ruling class, finish by calling into question the revolutionary potential of the working class.

The problem can be solved by replacing the formalistic and static point of view with a dialectical one. The Marxian proposition simply needs to be made more "dynamic." The dominant ideology of every society is the ideology of the dominant class, in the sense that the latter has control over the means of ideological production which society has at its disposal (the church, schools, mass media, etc.), and uses these means in its own class interests. As long as class rule is on the upswing, stable, and hence hardly questioned, the ideology of the dominant class will also dominate the consciousness of the oppressed class. Moreover, the exploited will tend to formulate the *first phases* of the class struggle in terms of the formulas, ideals, and ideologies of the exploiters.[7]

However, the more the stability of the existing society is brought into question, the more the class struggle intensifies, and the more the class rule of the exploiters itself begins to waver in practice, the more will at least sections of the oppressed class begin to free themselves from the control of the ideas of those in power. Prior to, and along with, the struggle for the social revolution, a struggle goes on between the ideology of the rulers and the new ideals of the revolutionary class. This struggle in turn intensifies and accelerates the concrete class struggle out of which it arose by lifting the revolutionary class to an awareness of its historical tasks and of the immediate goals of its struggle. Class consciousness by the revolutionary class can therefore develop out of the class struggle in spite of and in opposition to the ideology of the ruling class.[8]

But it is only in the revolution itself that the majority of the oppressed can liberate themselves from the ideology of the ruling class.[9] For this control is exerted not only, nor even primarily, through purely ideological *manipulation* and the mass assimilation of the ruling class's ideological production but, above all, through the day-to-day workings of the economy and society and their effect on the consciousness of the oppressed. (This is especially true in bourgeois society, although parallel phenomena can be seen in all class societies.)

In capitalist society this control is exerted through the internalization of commodity relations, which is closely tied to the reification of human relations and which results from the generalized extension of commodity production and the transformation of labor power into a commodity, and from the generalized extension of the social division of labor under conditions of commodity production. It is also accomplished through the fatigue and brutalization of the producers as a result of exploitation and the alienated nature of labor, as well as through a lack of leisure time, not only in a quantitative but also in a qualitative sense, and so forth. Only when the workings of this imprisonment are blown apart by a revolution, that is, by a sudden, intense increase in *mass activity outside of the confines of alienated labor*—only then can the mystifying influence of this very imprisonment upon mass consciousness rapidly recede.

The Leninist theory of organization therefore attempts to come to grips with the inner dialectic of this formation of political class consciousness, which can develop fully only *during* the revolution itself, yet only on the condition that it has already begun to develop *before* the revolution.[10] The theory does this by means of three operative categories: the category of the working class in itself (the mass of workers); the category of that part of the working class that is already engaging in more than sporadic struggles and has already reached a first level of organization (the proletarian vanguard in the broad sense of the word);[11] and the category of the revolutionary organization, which consists of workers and intellectuals who participate in revolutionary activities and are at least partially educated in Marxism.

The category of "the class in itself" is linked to the objective class concept in the sociology of Marx, where a social layer is determined by its objective position in the process of production *independent* of its state of consciousness. (It is well known that the young Marx—in the *Communist Manifesto* and in his political writings of 1850–52, for instance—put forward a subjective concept of the class according to which the working class becomes a class only through its struggle, that is, by reaching a minimum degree of class consciousness. Bukharin, in connection with a formula from *The Poverty of Philosophy*, calls this the concept of "the class for itself," as opposed to the concept of the "class in itself.")[12] This objective concept of the class remains fundamental for Lenin's ideas on organization, as it did for Engels and the German Social Democracy under the influence of Engels, Bebel, and Kautsky.[13]

It is only because there exists an objectively revolutionary class that can, and is periodically obliged to, conduct a revolutionary class struggle, and it is only in relation to such a class struggle, that the concept of a revolutionary vanguard party (including professional revolutionaries) has any scientific meaning at all, as Lenin himself explicitly observed.[14] All revolutionary activity not related to this class struggle leads at best to a party *nucleus*, but not a party, it runs the risk of degenerating into sectarian, subjective dilettantism. According to Lenin's concept of organization, there is no self-proclaimed vanguard. Rather, the vanguard must win recognition as a vanguard (that is, the historical right to act as a vanguard) through its attempts to establish revolutionary ties with the advanced part of the class and its struggle.

The category of "advanced workers" stems from the objectively inevitable stratification of the working class. It is a function of their distinct historical origin, as well as their distinct position in the social process of production and their distinct class consciousness.

The formation of the working class as an objective category is itself a historical process. Some sections of the working class are the sons, grandsons, and great grandsons of urban wage laborers; others are the sons and grandsons of agricultural laborers and landless peasants. Still others are only first- or second-generation descendants of a petty bourgeoisie that owned some means of production (peasants, artisans, etc.). Part of the working class works in large factories, where both the economic and the social relations give rise to at least an elementary class consciousness (consciousness that "social questions" can be solved through collective activity and organization). Another part works in small or medium-sized factories in industry or in the so-called service sector, where economic self-confidence as well as an understanding of the necessity for broad mass actions flow much less easily from the objective situation than in the large industrial plant. Some sections of the working class have been living in big cities for a long time. They have been literate for a long time and have several generations of trade union organization and political and cultural education behind them (through youth organizations, the workers' press, labor education, etc.). Still others live in small towns or even in the countryside. (This was true into the late 1930s, for instance, for a significant number of European miners.) These workers have little or no collective social life, scarcely any trade union experience, and have received no political or cultural education at all in the organized workers' movement. Some sectors of the working class are born from nations which were independent for a thousand years and whose ruling class oppressed other nations for long periods. Other workers are born from nations which fought for decades or centuries for their national freedom—or lived in slavery or serfdom no more than one hundred years ago.

If one adds to all these historical and structural differences the various personal abilities of each wage worker—not just differences in intelligence and ability to generalize from immediate experiences, but differences in the amount of energy, strength of character, combativity, and self-assurance too—one understands that the stratification of the working class into various layers, depending on the degree of class consciousness, is an inevitable phenomenon in the history of the working class itself. *It is this historical process of becoming a class which, at a given moment, is reflected in the various degrees of consciousness within the class.*

The category of the revolutionary party stems from the fact that Marxian socialism is a *science* which, in the final analysis, can be completely assimilated only in an individual and not in a collective manner. Marxism constitutes the culmination (and in part also the dissolution) of at least three classical social sciences: classical German philosophy, classical political economy, and classical French political science (French socialism and historiography). Its assimilation presupposes at least an understanding of the materialist dialectic, historical materialism, Marxian economic theory, and the critical history of modern revolutions and of the modern labor movement. Such an assimilation is necessary if it is to function, in its totality, as an instrument for analyzing social reality and as the compilation of the experiences of a century of proletarian class struggle. The notion that this colossal sum of knowledge and information could somehow "spontaneously" flow from working at a lathe or a calculating machine is absurd.[15]

The fact that as a science Marxism is an expression of the *highest degree* in the development of proletarian class consciousness means simply that it is only though an *individual* process of selection that the best, most experienced, most intelligent, and most combative members of the proletariat are able to directly and independently acquire this class consciousness in its most potent form. To the extent that this acquisition is an individual one, it also becomes accessible to other social classes and layers (above all, the revolutionary intelligentsia and the students).[16] Any other approach can lead only to an idealization of the working class—and ultimately of capitalism itself.

Of course, it must always be remembered that Marxism could not arise independently of the development of bourgeois society and of the class struggle that was inevitably unfolding within it. There is an inextricable tie between the collective, historical experience of the working class in struggle and its scientific working out of Marxism as collective, historical class consciousness in its most potent form. But to contend that scientific socialism is a historical product of the proletarian class struggle is not to say that all or even most members of the class can, with greater or lesser ease, reproduce this knowledge. Marxism is not an automatic product of the class struggle and class experience but a result of scientific, theoretical production. Such an assimilation is made possible only through participation in that process of production; and this process is by definition an *individual* one, even though it is only made possible through the development of the social forces of production and class contradictions under capitalism.

PROLETARIAN CLASS STRUGGLE AND PROLETARIAN CLASS CONSCIOUSNESS

The process whereby the proletarian mass, the proletarian vanguard, and the revolutionary party are united depends on the elementary proletarian class struggle growing over into *revolutionary* class struggle—the proletarian revolution. It also depends on the effects this has on the wage-earning masses. Class struggle has taken place for thousands of years without those who struggled being aware of what they were doing. Proletarian class struggle was conducted long before there was a socialist movement, let alone scientific socialism. Elementary class struggle—strikes, work stoppages around wage demands or for shorter working hours and other improvements in working conditions—leads to elementary forms of class organization (mutual aid funds, embryonic trade unions), even if these are short-lived. (It also gives rise to a general socialist ideal among *many* workers.) Elementary class struggle, elementary class organization, and elementary class consciousness are born, then, *directly out of action*, and only the experience arising out of that action is able to develop and accelerate consciousness. It is a general law of history that only through action are *broad masses* able to elevate their consciousness.

But even in its most elementary form, the spontaneous class struggle of the wage earners under capitalism leaves behind a residue in the form of a *consciousness crystallized in a process of continuous organization*. Most of the mass is active only during the struggle; after the struggle it will sooner or later retreat into private life ("into the struggle for existence"). What distinguishes the workers' vanguard from this mass is the fact that even during a lull in the struggle it does not abandon the front lines of the class struggle but continues the war, so to speak, "by other means." It attempts to solidify the resistance funds generated in the struggle into ongoing resistance funds—into unions.[17] By publishing workers' newspapers and organizing educational groups for workers, it attempts to crystalize and heighten the elementary class consciousness generated in the struggle. It thus helps give form to a factor of continuity, as opposed to the necessarily discontinuous action of the mass,[18] and to a factor of consciousness, as opposed to the spontaneity of the mass movement in and of itself.

However, advanced workers are driven to continuous organization and growing class consciousness less by theory, science, or an intellectual grasp of the social whole than by the practical knowledge acquired in struggle. Since the struggle shows[19] that the dissolving of the resistance funds after each strike damages the effectiveness of the strike and the working sums in hand, attempts are made to go over to the permanent strike fund. Since experience shows an occasional leaflet to have less effect than a regular newspaper, the workers' press is born. Consciousness arising directly out of the practical experience of struggle is *empirical and pragmatic consciousness*, which can enrich action to a certain extent, but which is far inferior to the effectiveness of a *scientifically global* consciousness, that is, of theoretical understanding.

Based on its general theoretical understanding, the revolutionary vanguard organization can consolidate and enrich this higher consciousness, provided it is able to establish ties to the class struggle, in other words, provided it does not shrink from the hard test of verifying theory in practice, of reuniting theory and practice. From the point of view of mature Marxism—as well as that of Marx himself and Lenin—a "true" theory divorced from practice is as much an absurdity as a "revolutionary practice" that is not founded on a scientific theory. This in no way diminishes the decisive importance and absolute necessity for theoretical production. It simply emphasizes the fact that wage-earning masses and revolutionary individuals, proceeding from different starting points and with a different dynamic, can bring about the unity of theory and practice.

This process can be summarized in the following diagram:

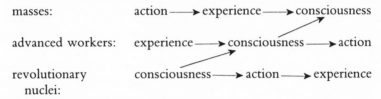

If we rearrange this diagram so that certain conclusions can be drawn from it, we get the following:

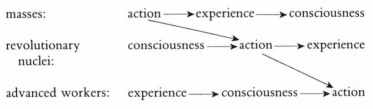

This formal diagram reveals a series of conclusions about the dynamics of class consciousness that were already anticipated in the analysis but only now obtain their full value. The collective action of the advanced workers (the "natural leaders" of the working class in the shops) is, relatively speaking, more difficult to attain because it can be aroused neither through pure conviction (as with the revolutionary nuclei) nor through purely spontaneous explosiveness (as with the broad masses). It is precisely the struggle *experience*—the important motivating factor in the actions of the advanced workers—that makes them much more careful and cautious before they undertake action on a broad scale. They have already digested the lessons of past actions and know that an explosion is not at all sufficient for them to be able to reach their goal. They have fewer illusions about the strength of the enemy (not to mention his "generosity") and about the durability of the mass movement. The greatest "temptation" of economism (that political organizing strategy focused purely on wages, working conditions, etc.) can be traced to this very point.

To summarize: the building of the revolutionary class party is the merging of the consciousness of the revolutionary nuclei with that of the advanced workers. The ripening of a prerevolutionary situation (of potentially revolutionary explosion) is the merging of action by the broad masses with that of the advanced workers. A revolutionary situation—the possibility of a revolutionary conquest of power— arises when a merging of *action* by the vanguard and the masses with the *consciousness* of the vanguard and revolutionary layers has been accomplished.[20] For the broad masses, the elementary class struggle arising from the contradictions of the capitalist mode of production is always kindled only by matters of immediate concern. The same is true for all mass actions, even political ones. Thus the problem of the broad mass struggle growing over into a revolutionary one depends not only on a quantitative factor but also on a qualitative one. This requires the existence of sufficiently advanced workers within the masses or the mass movement, who, on the basis of the stage of consciousness they have already reached, are capable of sweeping broader masses into action around objectives that challenge the continued existence of bourgeois society and the capitalist mode of production.

This also highlights the central importance of transitional demands,[21] the strategic position of advanced workers already trained in propagating these transitional demands, and the historical importance of the revolutionary organization, which alone is capable of working out a comprehensive program of transitional demands corresponding to the objective historical conditions, as well as to the subjective needs, of the broadest layers of the mass. *A successful proletarian revolution is only possible if all these factors are successfully combined.*

We have already stated that Lenin's theory of organization is above all a theory of revolution. To have misunderstood this is the great weakness of Rosa Luxemburg's polemic against Lenin in 1903–04. It is characteristic that the concept of centralization which is attacked in the essay "Organizational Question of Social Democracy" is—and this is clear if it is read attentively—a purely organizational one. (Yet, while it is attacked it is also confirmed. On this point modern "Luxemburgists" ought to read their "Rosa" more carefully and more thoroughly!) Lenin is accused of advocating an "ultracentralist" line, of dictating the composition of local party committees, and of wishing to stymie any initiative by lower party units.[22]

When we turn to the Leninist theory of organization as developed by Lenin himself, however, we see that the emphasis is by no means upon the formal, organizational side of centralization but upon its *political and social function*. At the heart of *What Is to Be Done?* is the concept of the transformation of proletarian class consciousness into political class consciousness *by means of a comprehensive political activity* that raises and, from a Marxist point of view, answers all questions of internal and external class relations: "In reality, it is possible to 'raise the activity of the working masses' *only* when this activity *is not restricted* to 'political agitation on an economic basis.' A basic condition for the necessary expansion of political agitation is the organization of *comprehensive* political exposure. *In no way* except by means of such exposures *can* the masses be trained in political consciousness and revolutionary activity."

And further:

> The consciousness of the working masses cannot be genuine class consciousness, unless the workers learn, from concrete, and above all from topical, political facts and events to observe *every* other social class in *all* the manifestations of its intellectual, ethical, and political life; unless they learn to apply in practice the materialist analysis and the materialist estimate of all aspects of the life and activity of *all* classes, strata, and groups of the population. Those who concentrate the attention, observation, and consciousness of the working class exclusively, or even mainly, upon itself alone are not Social Democrats; for the self-knowledge of the working class is indissolubly bound up, not solely with a fully clear theoretical understanding—it would be even truer to say, not so much with the theoretical, as with the practical, understanding—of the relationships between *all* the various classes of modern society, acquired through the experiences of political life.[23]

And it is for the same reason that Lenin emphasizes so strongly the absolute necessity for the revolutionary party to make *all* progressive demands and movements of *all* oppressed social layers and classes its own—even "purely democratic" ones. The central strategic plan advanced by Lenin in *What Is to Be Done?*[24] is therefore one of party agitation that unites all elementary, spontaneous, dispersed, and "merely" local or sectional protests, revolts, and movements of resistance. The emphasis of centralization clearly lies in the political and not in the formal, organizational sphere. The aim of formal organizational centralization is only to make possible the realization of this strategic plan.

Although she does not recognize this essence of Lenin's "centralism," Luxemburg is compelled in her polemic to indirectly counterpose to it another conception of the formation of political class consciousness and the preparation of revolutionary situations. Her doing so emphasizes even more poignantly how utterly wrong she was in this debate. Luxemburg's concept that "the proletarian army is recruited and becomes aware of its objectives in the course of the struggle itself"[25] has been completely refuted by history. In even the broadest, longest, and most vigorous of workers' struggles, the working masses have *not* gained a clear understanding of the tasks of the struggle, or did so only to an insufficient degree. (One need only recall the French general strikes of 1936 and 1968, the struggles of the

German workers from 1918 to 1923, the great struggles of the Italian workers in 1920, 1948, and 1969, as well as the prodigious class struggles in Spain from 1931 to 1937, to mention only four European countries.)

Experience in struggle is by no means sufficient for clarity on the tasks of a broad prerevolutionary, or even a revolutionary, mass struggle to be attained. These tasks are, of course, connected to the immediate motives that set off the struggle. But they can be grasped only with a comprehensive analysis of the overall social development, of the historical position achieved by the capitalist mode of production and its internal contradictions, and of the national and international relationship of forces between classes. Without protracted and consistent preparation, without the education of hundreds and thousands of advanced workers in the spirit of a revolutionary program, and without the practical experience accumulated over the years by these advanced workers through attempting to bring this program to the broad masses, it would be absolutely illusory to assume that suddenly, overnight so to speak, with the mere aid of mass *actions*, a consciousness equal to the demands of the historical situation could be created among these broad masses.

Actually, one could turn Luxemburg's proposition around and say that the proletarian army will *never* reach its historic objectives if the necessary education, schooling, and testing of a proletarian vanguard party in the working-out and agitational application of the revolutionary program in struggle has not taken place *before* the outbreak of the broadest mass struggles, which by themselves create only the *possibility* of the broad masses attaining revolutionary consciousness. That is the tragic lesson of the German revolution after the First World War, which was crushed precisely because of the lack of such a trained vanguard.

The objective of Lenin's strategic plan is to create such a party through an organic union of individual revolutionary nuclei with the vanguard of the proletariat. Such a fusion is impossible without a comprehensive *political* activity that takes the advanced workers beyond the confines of a horizon limited to the trade union or the factory. Empirical data available today confirm that Lenin's party, before and during the revolution of 1905 and after the mass movement began to pick up again in 1912, was such a party.[26]

To fully grasp the profoundly revolutionary nature of Lenin's strategic plan, it must be approached from yet another point of view. Any concept based on the probability, if not the inevitability, of a *revolution* occurring in the not too distant future must inevitably deal with the question of a direct collision with state power, that is, the question of the conquest of political power. As soon as this difficulty is built into the concept, however, the result is one more argument in favor of centralization. Lenin and Luxemburg agreed that capitalism itself and the bourgeois state exert a powerful centralizing influence on modern society,[27] and that it is in turn absolutely

illusory to think that this centralized state power can be gradually disman-
tled, as for instance a wall can be taken apart brick by brick.

In the final analysis, the ideological essence of the reformism and revisionism rejected by Luxemburg and Lenin, with equal passion,[28] was
rooted in the illusion that this could be done. Once the question of the
conquest of state power is no longer placed far off in the distance, however,
but is recognized to be an objective for the near or not-too-distant future,
the revolutionary is immediately confronted with the question of the means
necessary for achieving the revolutionary conquest of power. Here again,
Luxemburg misconstrued the *import* of Lenin's purely polemical use of the
notion of "Jacobins inseparably linked to the organization of the class-
conscious proletariat." What Lenin meant with this idea was certainly *not* a
brand of Blanquist conspirators but an *advanced group oriented, like the
Jacobins, toward an unremitting attempt to carry out the revolutionary tasks*; a
group that does not permit itself to be diverted from concentrating on *these*
tasks by the inevitable conjunctural ebb and flow of the mass movement.

Yet, to do justice to Luxemburg, it must be added that, in the first place,
she took up—in fact *had* to take up—this question from a different historical viewpoint, since by 1904 she was already influenced more by German
than by Russian or Polish reality; and second, that she completely drew the
necessary conclusions in the Leninist sense as soon as it became clear that in
Germany too the coming of the revolution was an immediate possibility.[29]

The young Trotsky likewise made a serious error in his polemic against
Lenin when he reproached him for this "substitutionism," that is, the
replacement of the initiative of the working class with that of the party
alone.[30] If we remove the core of this reproach from its polemical shell, we
find here too an idealistic, inadequate conception of the evolution of the
class consciousness of the proletariat: "Marxism teaches that the interests of
the proletariat are determined by its objective conditions of life. These
interests are so powerful and so unavoidable that they eventually [!] compel
the proletariat to bring them into the scope of its consciousness, i.e., to
make the realization of its *objective* interests into its *subjective* interests."[31]
Today it is easy to see what a naively fatalistic optimism was concealed in
this inadequate analysis. Immediate interests are here put on the same level
with historical interests, that is, with the unraveling of the most complex
questions of political tactics and strategy. The hope that the proletariat will
"eventually" recognize its historical interests seems rather shallow when
compared to the historical catastrophes that have arisen because, in the
absence of an adequate revolutionary leadership, the proletariat was not
even able to accomplish the revolutionary tasks of the here and now.

The same naive optimism is even more strikingly manifested in the
following passage from the same polemic:

The revolutionary social democrat is convinced not only of the inevitable [!] growth of the political party of the proletariat, but also of the inevitable [!] victory of the ideas of *revolutionary* socialism within this party. The first proof lies in the fact that the development of bourgeois society spontaneously leads the proletariat to politically demarcate itself; the second in the fact that the objective tendencies and the tactical problems of this demarcation find their best, fullest and deepest expression in revolutionary socialism, i.e., Marxism.[32]

This quotation makes clear that what the young Trotsky was championing in his polemic against Lenin was the "old, tested tactic" and the naive "belief in the inevitability of progress," à la Bebel and Kautsky, which prevailed in international Social Democracy from the time of Marx's death until the First World War. Lenin's concept of class consciousness was incomparably richer, more contradictory, and more dialectical precisely because it was based on a keen grasp of the relevance of the revolution for the present (not "finally some day" but in the coming years).

To round out the historical development it must be added that following the outbreak of the Russian revolution in 1917, Trotsky fully adopted Lenin's analysis of the formation of proletarian class consciousness and hence also Lenin's theory of organization, and until his death he stubbornly defended them against all skeptics and archpessimists (who claimed to detect in them the "embryo" of Stalinism). Thus he wrote in his last, unfinished manuscript:

A colossal factor in the maturity of the Russian proletariat in February or March 1917 was Lenin. He did not fall from the skies. He personified the revolutionary tradition of the working class. For Lenin's slogans to find their way to the masses, there had to exist cadres, even though numerically small at the beginning; there had to exist the confidence of the cadre in the leadership, a confidence based upon the entire experience of the past. To cancel these elements from one's calculations is simply to ignore the living revolution, to substitute for it an abstraction, the "relationship of forces," because the development of the revolution precisely consists of this, that the relationship of forces keeps incessantly and rapidly changing under the impact of the changes in the consciousness of the proletariat, the attraction of backward layers to the advanced, the growing assurance of the class in its own strength. The vital mainspring in this process is the party, just as the vital mainspring in the mechanism of the party is its leadership.[33]

THE REVOLUTIONARY VANGUARD AND SPONTANEOUS MASS ACTION

It would be a great injustice to Lenin to characterize his life work as a systematic "underestimation" of the importance of spontaneous mass actions as opposed to their "appreciation" by Luxemburg or Trotsky. Apart from polemical passages, which can only be understood when seen in context, Lenin welcomed huge, spontaneous outbreaks of mass strikes and demonstrations just as enthusiastically and just as explicitly as Rosa Luxemburg and Trotsky.[34] Only the Stalinist bureaucracy falsified Leninism with its increasing distrust of spontaneous mass movements—which after all is characteristic of any bureaucracy.

Luxemburg is completely correct to say that the outbreak of a proletarian revolution cannot be "predetermined" by the calendar, and nothing to the contrary will ever be found in Lenin. Lenin, like Luxemburg, was convinced that these elemental mass explosions, without which a revolution is unthinkable, can neither be "organized" according to rules nor "commanded" by a row of disciplined noncommissioned officers. Lenin, like Luxemburg, was convinced of the mighty arsenal of creative energy, resourcefulness, and initiative that a truly broad mass action unfurls and will always unfurl.

The difference between the Leninist theory of organization and the so-called theory of spontaneity—which can be attributed to Luxemburg only with important reservations—is thus to be found *not in an underestimation of mass initiative but in an understanding of its limitations*. Mass initiative is capable of many magnificent accomplishments. But by itself it is not able to draft, in the course of the struggle, a complete, comprehensive program for a socialist revolution touching upon all social questions (not to mention socialist reconstruction); nor is it alone capable of bringing about a sufficient centralization of forces to make possible the downfall of a centralized state power, with its repressive apparatus resting on a full utilization of the advantages of its "inside lines" of communication. In other words, the limitations of mass spontaneity begin with the understanding that a victorious socialist revolution *cannot be improvised*. And "pure" mass spontaneity always boils down to improvisation.

What is more, "pure" spontaneity exists only in books containing fairy tales about the workers' movement—but not in its real history. What is understood by "spontaneity of the masses" are movements that have not been planned out in detail ahead of time by some central authority. What is *not* to be understood by "spontaneity of the masses" are movements that take place without "political influence from the outside." Scratch off the blue coat of an ostensibly "spontaneous movement" and you will find the unmistakable residue of a bright red veneer. Here a member of a "vanguard" group who set off a "spontaneous" strike. There a former member of another "left-deviationist" affiliation, who has long since left it but who received sufficient mental equipment to be able, in an explosive situation, to react with lightning speed while the anonymous mass was still hesitating.

In one case, we will be able to detect in "spontaneous" action the fruits of years of "underground activity" by a trade union opposition or a rank-and-file group; in another case, the result of contacts that, for a rather long period of time, have patiently—and without apparent success—been nurtured by shop colleagues in a neighboring city (or a neighboring factory), where the "left wingers" are stronger. In the class struggle, too, there is no such thing as a goose falling "spontaneously" from heaven, already cooked.

Thus, what differentiates "spontaneous" actions from the "intervention of the vanguard" is not at all that in the former everyone in the struggle has reached the same level of consciousness, whereas in the latter "the vanguard" is distinct from "the mass." What differentiates the two forms of action is also not that in "spontaneous" actions no solutions have been carried into the proletariat from "outside," while an organized vanguard relates to the elementary demands of the mass "in an elitist fashion," "imposing" a program upon it. Never have there been spontaneous actions without some influence from vanguard elements. The difference between "spontaneous" actions and those in which "the revolutionary vanguard intervenes" is essentially that in "spontaneous" actions *the nature of the intervention of the vanguard elements is unorganized, improvised, intermittent, and unplanned* (occurring by chance in this plant, that district, or that city), while the existence of a revolutionary organization makes it possible to coordinate, plan, consciously synchronize, and continuously shape this intervention of the vanguard elements in the "spontaneous" mass struggle. Nearly all the requirements of Leninist "supercentralism" are based on this and this alone.

Only an incorrigible fatalist (a mechanical determinist) could be convinced that all mass explosions *had* to take place on a given day just because they broke out on that day and that, conversely, in all cases where mass explosions did not occur it was because they were not possible. Such a fatalistic attitude (common to the Kautsky-Bauer school of thought) is in reality a caricature of the Leninist theory of organization. In any case, it is characteristic that many opponents of Leninism, who in opposing Lenin have so much to say about "mass spontaneity," at the same time fall into this vulgar, mechanical determinism without realizing how much it contradicts their "high esteem" for "mass spontaneity."

If, on the other hand, one proceeds from the inevitability of periodic spontaneous mass explosions (which occur when socio-economic contradictions have ripened to the point where the capitalist mode of production in fact *has* to periodically produce such prerevolutionary crises), then one has to understand that it is impossible to determine the exact moment when this will happen, since thousands of minor incidents, partial conflicts, and accidental occurrences could play an important role in determining it. For this reason, a revolutionary vanguard which at decisive moments is able to concentrate its own forces on the "weakest link" is incomparably more effective than the diffuse performance of large numbers of advanced workers who lack this ability to concentrate their forces.[35]

The two greatest workers' struggles to take place in the West—the French May 1968 and the Italian fall 1969—entirely confirmed these views. Both began with "spontaneous" struggles prepared neither by the trade unions nor by the big social-democratic or "communist" parties. In both cases individual, radical workers and students or revolutionary nuclei played a decisive role in triggering, here or there, a first explosion and providing the working masses with an opportunity to learn from an "exemplary experience." In both cases millions upon millions came into the struggle—up to 10 million wage earners in France, up to 15 million in Italy. This is more than had ever before been seen—even during the greatest class struggles following the First World War.

In both cases the spontaneous tendency demonstrated by the workers went far beyond the "economism" of a purely economic strike. In France this was attested to by the factory occupations and numerous partial initiatives, in Italy not only by huge street demonstrations and the raising of political demands but also by the embryonic manifestation of a tendency toward self-organization at the point of production, that is, by the attempt to take the first step toward establishing dual power: the election of *delegati di reparto*. (In this sense the vanguard of the Italian working class was more advanced than the French, and it drew the first important historical lessons from the French May.)[36] But in neither case did these powerful, spontaneous mass actions succeed in overthrowing the bourgeois state apparatus and the capitalist mode of production, or even in advancing a mass understanding of the objectives that would have made such an overthrow possible within a short period of time.

To recall Trotsky's metaphor from *The History of the Russian Revolution*: the powerful steam simply evaporated for lack of a piston that it could drive at the decisive moment.[37] Certainly, in the final analysis, the driving force is the steam, the energy of mass mobilization and mass struggle, and not the piston itself. Without this steam the piston remains a hollow shell. Yet, without this piston even the most intense steam is wasted and accomplishes nothing. This is the quintessence of the Leninist theory of organization.

ORGANIZATION, BUREAUCRACY, AND REVOLUTIONARY ACTION

There is a difficulty in this connection, however, which Lenin, during the years of the most heated disputes with the Mensheviks, recognized either not at all (1903–05) or only to an insufficient degree (1908–14). Here the full value of the historic work of Trotsky and Rosa Luxemburg becomes clear in facilitating an understanding of the dialectical formula: "working class—advanced workers—workers' party."

A vanguard party and a certain *separation* between the party and the mass are made necessary precisely because of the inevitably inadequate level of class consciousness by the broad working masses. As Lenin repeatedly stressed, this is a complex dialectical relationship—a unity of separation and integration—which totally conforms to the historical peculiarities of the revolutionary struggle for a socialist revolution.

This separate party, however, originates within *bourgeois* society, which, with its inherent features of a universal division of labor and commodity production, tends to bring about a reification of *all* human relations.[38] This means that the building of a party apparatus separated from the working masses involves the danger of this apparatus becoming autonomous. When this danger develops beyond an embryonic stage, the tendency arises for the self-preservation of the apparatus to become an end in itself, rather than a means to an end (successful proletarian class struggle).

This is the root of the degeneration of both the Second and the Third Internationals, that is, the subordination of the mass social-democratic as well as the Communist parties of Western Europe to conservative, reformist bureaucracies, which, in their day-to-day practice, have become part of the status quo.[39]

Bureaucracy in workers' organizations is a product of the social division of labor, that is, of the inability of the working masses themselves, who are largely excluded from the cultural and theoretical process of production under capitalism, to regularly take care of all the tasks which must be dealt with within the framework of their organization. Attempts to overcome this anyway, which were often tried at the onset of the workers' movement, provide no solution because this division of labor completely corresponds to *material conditions* and is in no way invented by wicked careerists. If these conditions are overlooked, primitivism, ignorance, and the brawling it produces will place the same limitations on the movement as would otherwise be set by the bureaucracy. Having taken a different point of departure here—that of organizational *technique* instead of the level of consciousness—we have run up against the same problem which we had already cleared up earlier: namely, that it would be giving the capitalist mode of production too much credit to assume it to be a perfect school for preparing the proletariat for independent activity, or that it automatically creates the ability of the working masses to spontaneously recognize and achieve all the objectives and organizational forms of their own liberation.

Lenin, in his first debate with the Mensheviks, very much underestimated the danger of the apparatus becoming autonomous and the bureaucratization of the workers' parties. He proceeded from the assumption that the danger of opportunism in the modern labor movement was a threat coming mainly from petty-bourgeois academicians and petty-bourgeois "pure trade unionists." He made fun of the struggle of many of his comrades against the danger of "bureaucratism." Actually, history showed that the greatest source of opportunism in social democracy before the First World War came from neither the academicians nor the "pure trade unionists" but *from the social-democratic party bureaucracy itself,* from a practice of "legalism" limited on the one hand to electoral and parliamentary activity and on the other to a struggle for immediate reforms of an economic and trade union nature. (Merely to describe this practice is to confirm how much it resembles that of today's West European Communist parties!)

Trotsky and Luxemburg recognized this danger more accurately and earlier than Lenin. As early as 1904 Luxemburg expressed the thought that a "difference between the eager attack of the mass and the [overly] prudent position of the Social Democracy" was possible.[40] The thought is hardly expressed before it is discarded; the only possible validity it might have would be in the imaginary case of an "overcentralization" of the party along Leninist lines. Two years later Trotsky already expresses this with more precision:

> The European Socialist parties, particularly the largest of them, the German Social-Democratic Party, have developed their conservatism in proportion as the masses have embraced socialism and the more these masses have become organized and disciplined. As a consequence of this, Social Democracy as an organization embodying the political experience of the proletariat may at a certain moment become a direct obstacle to open conflict between the workers and bourgeois reaction. In other words, the propagandist-socialist conservatism of the proletarian parties may at a certain moment hold back the direct struggle of the proletariat for power.[41]

The prognosis has been tragically confirmed by history. Lenin did not see this until the eve of the First World War, whereas the German left had long before shed its illusions about the Social Democratic Party administration.[42]

ORGANIZATIONAL THEORY, REVOLUTIONARY PROGRAM, REVOLUTIONARY PRACTICE

After the traumatic shock suffered by Lenin on August 4, 1914, however, he too made a decisive step forward on this question. *From then on, the question of organization became one not only of function but also of content.* It is no longer simply a question of contrasting "the organization" in general to "spontaneity" in general, as Lenin frequently does in *What Is to Be Done?* and in

One Step Forward, Two Steps Backward. Now it is a question of carefully distinguishing between an objectively conservative organization and an objectively revolutionary one. This distinction is made according to *objective criteria* (revolutionary program, bringing this program to the masses, revolutionary practice, etc.), and the spontaneous combativity of the masses is consciously preferred to the actions or even the existence of conservative reformist mass organizations. "Naive" organizational fetishists might claim that after 1914 Lenin went over to the Luxemburgist view of "spontaneism," when, in conflicts between "unorganized masses" and the social-democratic organization, he systematically defended the former against the latter or accused the latter of betraying the former.[43] Lenin now even regarded the destruction of conservatized organizations as an inescapable prerequisite for the emancipation of the proletariat.[44]

Yet, the correction, or better yet completion, of his theory of organization, which Lenin undertook after 1914, was not a step backward to the worship of "pure" spontaneity but rather forward toward distinguishing between the *revolutionary* party and organization in general. Now, instead of saying that the purpose of the party is to develop the political class consciousness of the working class, the formula becomes much more precise: the function of the revolutionary vanguard consists in developing *revolutionary consciousness* in the vanguard of the working class. The building of the revolutionary class party is the process whereby the program of the socialist revolution is fused with the experience the majority of the advanced workers have acquired in struggle.[45]

This elaboration and expansion of the Leninist theory of organization, following the outbreak of the First World War, goes hand in hand with an expansion of the Leninist concept of the relevance of revolution to the present. Although before 1914 this was for Lenin limited by and large to Russia, after 1914 it was extended to all of Europe. (After the Russian revolution of 1905 Lenin had already recognized the immediate potential for revolution in the colonies and semi-colonies.)

Consequently, the validity of the Leninist "strategic plan" for the imperialist countries of Western Europe today is closely tied to the question of the nature of the historical epoch in which we live. From the standpoint of historical materialism, one is justified in deriving a conception of the party from the "present potential for revolution" only if one proceeds from the assumption—correct and provable, in our estimation—that, beginning with the First World War, and no later than the Russian October revolution, the worldwide capitalist system entered an epoch of historic structural crisis,[46] which *must* periodically lead to revolutionary situations. If, on the other hand, one assumes that we are still in an ascending stage of capitalism as a world system, such a conception would have to be rejected as being completely "voluntaristic." What is decisive in the Leninist strategic plan is certainly not revolutionary *propaganda*—which, of course, revolutionaries have to carry out even in nonrevolutionary periods—but its focus on revolutionary *actions* breaking out in the near or not distant future. Even in the ascending epoch of capitalism such actions were possible (note the Paris Commune), but only as unsuccessful exceptions. Under such conditions, building a party by concentrating efforts on preparing to effectively participate in such actions would hardly make sense.

The difference between a "workers' party" in general (referring to its membership or even its electoral supporters) and a revolutionary workers' party (or the nucleus of such a party) is to be found not only in program or objective social functions (which is to promote, not pacify, all objectively revolutionary mass actions, or all challenges and forms of action that attack and call into question the essence of the capitalist mode of production and the bourgeois state) but also in its ability to find a suitable pedagogical method enabling it to bring this program to ever-growing numbers of workers.

One can go further, however, and formulate the question more sharply: Is the danger of the apparatus becoming autonomous limited only to opportunist and reformist "workers'" organizations, or does it threaten *any* organization, including one with a revolutionary program and a revolutionary practice? Is not a developing bureaucracy the *unavoidable* consequence of *any* division of labor, including the one between "leadership" and "membership," and even in a revolutionary group? And is not, therefore, every revolutionary organization, once it has spread beyond a small milieu, condemned at a certain point in its development and in the development of mass struggles to become a brake on the struggle of the proletarian masses for emancipation?

If this line of argument were accepted as correct, it could lead to only one conclusion: that the socialist emancipation of the working class and of humanity is impossible—because the supposedly inevitable "autonomization" and degeneration of any organization must be seen *as one part of a dilemma*, the other part of which is represented by the tendency for all unorganized workers, all intellectuals only partially involved in action, and all persons caught up in universal commodity production to sink into a petty-bourgeois "false consciousness." Only a comprehensive, revolutionary practice aiming at total consciousness and enriching theory makes it possible to avoid the penetration of the "ideology of the ruling class" into even the ranks of individual revolutionaries. This can only be a collective and organized practice. If the above argument were correct, one would have to conclude that, with or without an organization, advanced workers would be condemned either not to reach political class consciousness or to rapidly lose it.

In reality this line of argument is false, since it equates the beginning of a process with its result. Thus, from the existence of a *danger* that even revolutionary organizations will become autonomous, it deduces, in a static and fatalistic fashion, that this autonomy is *inevitable*. This is neither empirically nor theoretically demonstrable. For the extent of the danger of bureaucratic degeneration of a revolutionary vanguard organization—and even more of a revolutionary party—depends not only on the *tendency* toward autonomy, which in fact afflicts all institutions in bourgeois society, but also upon existing *counter-tendencies*. Among these are the integration of the revolutionary organization into an international movement which is independent of "national" organizations and which constantly keeps a theoretical eye on them (not through an apparatus but through political criticism); a close involvement in the actual class struggle and actual revolutionary struggles that make possible a continuous selection of cadres in practice; a systematic attempt to do away with the division of labor by ensuring a continuous rotation of personnel between factory, university, and full-time party functionaries; and institutional guarantees (such as limitations on the income of full-timers and a defense of the organizational norms of internal democracy and the freedom to form tendencies and factions).

The outcome of these contradictory tendencies depends on *the struggle between them*, which, in turn, is ultimately determined by *two social factors*[47]: on the one hand the degree of *special social interests* set loose by the "autonomous organization" and on the other hand the extent of the *political activity* of the vanguard of the working class. Only when the latter decisively diminishes can the former decisively break out into the open. Thus, the entire argument amounts to a tedious tautology: during a period of *increasing passivity* the working class cannot be actively struggling for its liberation. It does not at all prove that, during a period of *increasing activity* on the part of advanced workers, revolutionary organizations are not an effective instrument for bringing about liberation, though their "arbitrariness" can and must be circumscribed by the independent activity of the class (or its advanced sections). The revolutionary organization is an instrument for making revolutions. Without the increasing political activity of broad masses of workers, proletarian revolutions are simply not possible.

ORGANIZATIONAL THEORY, DEMOCRATIC CENTRALISM, AND SOVIET DEMOCRACY

The objection was made to Lenin's theory of organization that through its exaggerated centralization it would prevent the development of internal party democracy. But this objection is a confused one, for inasmuch as the Leninist principles of organization restrict the organization to active members *operating under a collective control*, they actually expand rather than reduce the scope of party democracy.

Once a workers' organization surpasses a certain numerical size there are basically only two possible organizational models: the dues-paying electoral club (or territorial organization), which corresponds today to the organizational forms of the Social Democratic Party of Germany and of the French Communist Party; or a combat unit based on the selection of only active and conscious members. The first model, in theory, permits a certain latitude for grumblers and opponents to fool around in, but only in matters of secondary importance. *Otherwise, the great mass of the apolitical and passive membership provides the apparatus with a voting base that can always be mobilized* and that has nothing to do with class consciousness. (A not insignificant number of these members are even materially dependent on the apparatus— including the bulk of the municipal and administrative workers and employees and the employees of the workers' organization itself.)

In the combat organization, however, which is composed of members who have to exhibit a minimum of consciousness simply to become members, the possibility of finding independent thinking is actually much greater. Neither "pure apparatchiks" nor pure careerists can take over as easily as in an ordinary electoral club. So differences of opinion will be resolved less in terms of material dependency or abstract "loyalty" than according to substance. To be sure, the mere fact that the organization is composed in this fashion is no guarantee against bureaucratization, but at least it provides an essential condition for preventing it.[48]

The relationship between the revolutionary organization (a party nucleus or a party) and the mass of workers abruptly changes as soon as a revolutionary explosion occurs. At that point the seeds sown over the years by revolutionary and consciously socialist elements start sprouting. Broad masses are able to achieve revolutionary class consciousness at once. The revolutionary initiatives of broad masses can far outdistance those of many revolutionary groupings.

In his *History of the Russian Revolution* Trotsky emphasized in several instances that at certain conjunctures in the revolution the Russian working masses were even ahead of the Bolshevik Party.[49] Nevertheless, one should not generalize from this fact, and, above all, it must not be separated from the fact that, prior to Lenin's "April Theses," the Bolshevik Party's strategic conception of the nature and goal of the Russian revolution was insufficiently worked out.[50] The party ran the risk of having to pay for this until Lenin took decisive action with his "April Theses." He was able to do so with such ease, however, because the masses of educated worker-Bolsheviks were pushing him in that very direction and were themselves a reflection of the powerful radicalization of the Russian working class.

An objective, that is, comprehensive view of the role of the Bolshevik Party organization in the Russian revolution would no doubt have to be formulated somewhat differently. While the leading cadre of the party proved several times to be a conservative block preventing the party from going over to Trotsky's position on the struggle for the dictatorship of the proletariat (soviet power), at the same time it became evident that the crystallization of a revolutionary workers' cadre, schooled in two decades of revolutionary organization and revolutionary activity, was instrumental in making this decisive strategic turn a success. Should one wish to construct a correlation between the Stalinist bureaucracy and the "Leninist concept of the party," one would at least have to make allowances for this decisive element of intervention. *Stalin's victory was not the result of the Leninist "theory of organization" but the result of the disappearance of a decisive component of this concept: the presence of a broad layer of worker cadres, schooled in revolution and maintaining a high degree of activity, with a close relationship to the masses.* Moreover, Lenin himself would have in no way denied that in the absence of this factor the Leninist concept of the party could turn into its opposite.[51]

The Soviet system is the only universal answer discovered thus far by the working class to the question of how to organize its independent activity during and following the revolution.[52] It allows all of the forces within the class—and all the laboring and progressive layers of society in general—to be brought together in a simultaneous, open confrontation between the various tendencies existing within the class itself. Every true soviet system—one that is actually elected by the mass of the workers and has not been imposed upon them by one or another selective power apparatus— will for that reason only be able to reflect the social and ideological diversity of the proletarian layers emphasized above. A workers' council is in reality a united front of the most diverse political tendencies that are in agreement on one central point: the common defense of the revolution against the class enemy. (In the same way, a strike committee reflects the most widely differing tendencies among the workers, yet with one exception: it includes only those tendencies that are participating in the strike. Scabs have no place in a strike committee.)

There is no contradiction whatever between the existence of a revolutionary organization of the Leninist type and genuine soviet democracy, or soviet power. On the contrary, without the systematic organizational work of a revolutionary vanguard, a soviet system will either be quickly throttled by reformist and semi-reformist bureaucracies (see the German soviet system from 1918 to 1919) or will lose its political effectiveness from its inability to solve the central political tasks (see the Spanish revolutionary committees between July 1936 and spring 1937).

The hypothesis that a soviet system makes parties superfluous has one of two sources. Either it proceeds from the naive assumption that the introduction of soviets homogenizes the working class overnight, dissolves all differences of ideology and interest, and automatically and spontaneously suggests to the entire working class "the revolutionary solution" to *all* the strategic and tactical problems of the revolution. Or it is merely a pretext for giving to a small group of self-appointed "leaders" the opportunity to manipulate a rather broad, inarticulate mass, in that this mass is deprived of any possibility of systematically coming to grips with these strategic and tactical questions of the revolution, that is, *of freely discussing and politically differentiating itself.* (This is obviously the case, for example, with the Yugoslav system of so-called self-management.)

The revolutionary organization *can*, therefore, guarantee the working masses in the soviet system a greater degree of independent activity and self-awareness, and thereby of revolutionary class consciousness, than could an undifferentiated system of representation. But of course, to this end it must stimulate and not hold back the independent action of the working masses. It is precisely this independent initiative of the masses which reaches its fullest development in the soviet system. Again we reach a similar conclusion: the Leninist concept of organization, built upon a correct revolutionary strategy (on a correct assessment of the objective historical process), is simply the collective coordinator of the activity of the masses, the collective memory and digested experience of the masses, in place of a constantly repetitive and expanding discontinuity in time, space, and consciousness.

History has also shown in this connection that there is a substantial difference between a party *calling* itself a revolutionary party and actually *being* one. When a group of functionaries not only opposes the initiative and activity of the masses but seeks to frustrate them by any means, including military force (one thinks of Hungary in October–November 1956 or Czechoslovakia since August 1968), when this group not only finds no common language with a soviet system that springs spontaneously from mass struggles, but throttles and destroys this system behind a pretext of defending "the leading role of the party"[53]—then we are obviously no longer dealing with a revolutionary party of the proletariat but with an apparatus that represents the special interests of a privileged layer deeply hostile to the independent activity of the masses: the bureaucracy. The fact that a revolutionary party *can* degenerate into a party of bureaucracy, however, no more argues against the Leninist concept of organization than would the fact that doctors have killed, not cured, many patients argues against medical science. Any step away from this concept toward "pure" mass spontaneity would be comparable to reverting from medical science to quackery.

SOCIOLOGY OF ECONOMISM, BUREAUCRATISM, AND SPONTANEISM

When we emphasized that Lenin's concept of organization really represents a concept of the current potential for proletarian revolution, we touched upon the central factor in the Leninist theory of proletarian class consciousness: the problem of the definition of the revolutionary subject under capitalism.

For Marx and Lenin (as well as for Luxemburg and Trotsky, although they did not draw all the necessary conclusions from this fact until some time before 1914) the revolutionary subject is *the only potentially, only periodically revolutionary working class* as it works, thinks, and lives under capitalism, that is, in the totality of its social existence.[54] The Leninist theory of organization proceeds directly from this assessment of the position of the revolutionary subject, for it is self-evident that a subject, thus defined, can only be a *contradictory* one. On the one hand it is exposed to wage slavery, alienated labor, the reification of all human relations, and the influence of bourgeois and petty-bourgeois ideology. On the other hand, at periodic intervals it passes over into a radicalizing class struggle and even into open revolutionary battle against the capitalist mode of production and the bourgeois state apparatus. It is in this periodic fluctuation that the history of the *real* class struggle of the last 150 years is expressed. It is absolutely impossible to sum up the history of, say, the French or the German labor movements of the past 100 years with either the formula "increasing passivity" or "uninterrupted revolutionary activity." It is obviously a unity of *both* elements with an alternating emphasis on one or the other.

As ideological tendencies, opportunism and sectarianism have their deepest theoretical roots in an undialectical definition of the revolutionary subject. For the opportunists, this revolutionary subject is the *everyday worker.* Opportunists tend to imitate the attitude of this worker in everything and "to idolize his backward side," as Plekhanov put it so well. If the workers are concerned only with questions limited to the shops, then the opportunists are "pure trade unionists." If the workers are caught up in a wave of patriotic jingoism, they become social-patriots or social-imperialists. If the workers submit to cold war propaganda, they become cold-warriors: "The masses are always right." The latest and the most wretched expression of such opportunism consists of determining the program—let it be an electoral program—no longer through an objective scientific analysis of society but with the aid of . . . opinion polls.

But this opportunism leads to an insoluble contradiction. Fortunately, the moods of the masses do not stand still but can change dramatically in a rather short period of time. Today the workers are concerned only with internal shop questions, but tomorrow they will throng the streets in a political demonstration. Today they are "for" the defense of the imperialist fatherland against the "external enemy," but tomorrow they will be fed up with the war and again recognize their own ruling class as the main enemy. Today they passively accept collaboration with the bosses, but tomorrow they will move against them through a wildcat strike. The logic of opportunism leads—once the adaptation to bourgeois society has been excused through references to the attitude of the "masses"—to resistance *to these very masses* as soon as they begin, in a sudden reversal, to move into action against bourgeois society.

Sectarians simplify the revolutionary subject just as much as opportunists, but in the opposite sense. If only the everyday worker counts for the opportunists—that is, the worker who is assimilating and adapting to bourgeois relations—for the sectarians it is only the "ideal" proletarian who counts, one who acts like a revolutionary. If the worker does not behave in a revolutionary fashion, he has ceased to be a revolutionary subject: he is demoted to being "bourgeois." Extreme sectarians—such as certain ultraleft "spontaneists," certain Stalinists, and certain Maoists—will even go so far as to equate the working class with the capitalist *class* if it hesitates to completely accept the particular sectarian ideology in question.[55]

Extreme objectivism on the one hand ("everything the workers do is revolutionary") and extreme subjectivism on the other hand ("only those who accept our doctrine are revolutionary or proletarian") join hands in the final analysis when they deny the objectively revolutionary character of huge mass struggles led by masses with a contradictory consciousness. For the opportunist objectivists these struggles are not revolutionary, because "next month the majority will still go ahead and vote for the SPD [West German Social Democrats] or de Gaulle." For the sectarian subjectivists they have nothing to do with revolution, "because the [our] revolutionary group is still too weak."

The social nature of these two tendencies can be ascertained without difficulty. It corresponds to the petty-bourgeois intelligentsia: the opportunists for the most part represent the intelligentsia tied to the labor bureaucracy in mass organizations or in the bourgeois state apparatus, while the sectarians represent an intelligentsia that is either declassed or merely watches things from the sidelines, remaining outside of the real movement. In both cases there is a forced separation between the objective and subjective factors at work in the contradictory but undivided revolutionary subject, which corresponds to a divorce between practice and theory that leads only to an opportunist practice and to an idealizing "theory" embodying "false consciousness."

It is characteristic, however, for many opportunists (among others, trade union bureaucrats), as well as many sectarian literati, to accuse precisely the revolutionary Marxists of being petty-bourgeois intellectuals, who would like to "subjugate" the working class.[56] The question also plays a certain role in the discussions within the revolutionary student movement. Therefore, it is necessary to analyze more closely the problem of the sociology of the bureaucracy, of economism, and of spontaneism (or of the "handicraftsman's approach" to the question of organization).

The mediation between manual and mental labor, production and accumulation, occurs at several points in bourgeois society, though at different levels, for example, in the factory. What is meant by the general concept of "intelligentsia" or "intellectual petty bourgeoisie" or "technical intelligentsia" corresponds in reality to many diverse activities of such mediation, whose relation to the actual class struggle is quite distinct. One could essentially distinguish the following categories (we in no way claim that this constitutes a complete analysis):

1. The genuine intermediaries between capital and labor in the process of production, that is, the secondary officers of capital: foremen, timekeepers, and other cadre personnel in the factories, among whose tasks is the maintenance of labor discipline within the factory, in the interest of capital.

2. The intermediaries between science and technique, or between technique and production: laboratory assistants, scientific researchers, inventors, technologists, planners, project engineers, draftsmen. In contrast to category 1, these layers are not accomplices in the process of extracting surplus value from the producer. They take part in the material process of production itself and for that reason are not exploiters but producers of surplus value.

3. The intermediaries between production and realization of surplus value: advertising managers and offices, market research institutes, cadres and scientists occupied in the distribution sector, marketing specialists.

4. The intermediaries between buyers and sellers of the commodity labor power: above all, these are the trade union functionaries and, in a wider sense, all functionaries of the bureaucratized mass organizations of the labor movement.

5. The intermediaries between capital and labor in the sphere of the superstructure, the ideological producers (those who are occupied with producing ideology): a section of the bourgeois politicians ("public opinion makers"), the bourgeois professors of the so-called humanities, journalists, some artists.

6. The intermediaries between science and the working class, the theoretical producers, who have not been professionally incorporated into the ideological production of the ruling class and are relatively able, being free from material dependency on this production, to engage in criticism of bourgeois relations.

One could add a seventh group, which is partially included in the fifth, and partially in the sixth. In classical, stable bourgeois society, teaching as a profession falls into category 5, both because of the unlimited predominance of bourgeois ideology and because of the generally abstract and ideological character of all professional teaching. With the growing structural crisis in neocapitalist high schools and universities, however, a change in objective standards takes place. On the one hand the general crisis of capitalism precipitates a general crisis in neocapitalist ideology, which is increasingly called into question. On the other hand teaching serves less as abstract, ideological indoctrination and more as the direct technocratic preparation for the future intellectual workers (of categories 2 and 3) to be incorporated into the process of production. This makes it possible for the content of such teaching to be increasingly tied to a regained awareness of individual alienation, as well as to social criticism in related fields (and even to social criticism in general).

It now becomes clear which part of the intelligentsia will exert a negative influence upon the developing class consciousness of the proletariat: it is above all groups 3, 4, and 5. (We need say nothing about group 1 because in general it keeps its distance from the workers' organizations anyway.) What is most dangerous for the initiative and self-assurance of the working class is a symbiosis or fusion of groups 4 and 5, as has occurred on a broad scale since the First World War in the social-democratic and today already partially in the Moscow-oriented communist mass organizations in the West.

Groups 2 and 6, on the other hand, can only enhance the impact of the working-class and revolutionary organizations, *because they equip them with the knowledge that is indispensable for a relentless critique of bourgeois society and for the successful overthrow of this society, and even more for the successful taking over of the means of production by the associated producers.*

Those who rail against the growing union of workers' organizations with groups 2 and 6 of the intelligentsia objectively assist groups 3, 4, and 5 in exerting their negative influence on the working class. For never in history has there been a class struggle that has not been accompanied by an ideological struggle.[57] It boils down to a question of determining *which* ideology can sink roots in the working class; or, to phrase it better, whether bourgeois and petty-bourgeois ideology or Marxist scientific theory will develop among the workers. Whoever opposes "every outside intellectual influence" within the working class in struggle either forgets or pushes aside the fact that the influence which groups 1, 3, 4, and 5 exert on this working class is *permanently and unremittingly* at work upon the proletariat through the entire mechanism of bourgeois society and capitalist economy, and that the ultraleft "spontaneists" have no panacea at their disposal for putting an end to this process. To thunder against the influence of Marxist intellectuals within the working class means simply to allow the influence of the bourgeois intelligentsia to spread without opposition.[58]

Still worse: by resisting the formation of a revolutionary organization and the education of professional proletarian revolutionaries, Mensheviks and "spontaneists" are objectively forced to help perpetuate the division between manual and intellectual labor, that is, the spiritual subjugation of the workers to the intellectuals and the rather rapid bureaucratization of the workers' organizations. For, a worker who continuously remains within the capitalist process of production will most often not be in a position to globally assimilate theory, and will thereby remain dependent upon "petty-bourgeois specialists." For that reason, a decisive step can be taken within the revolutionary organization toward the intellectual emancipation of at least the most advanced workers and toward an initial victory over the division of labor within the workers' movement itself through the intermittent removal of workers from the factories.

This is not yet the final word on the sociology of spontaneism. We must ask ourselves: In which layers of the working class will the "antipathy" and "distrust" toward intellectuals have the most influence? Obviously, in those layers whose social and economic existence *most sharply subjects them to an actual conflict with intellectual labor.* By and large, these are the workers of the small and medium-sized factories threatened by technological progress; self-taught workers who, through personal effort, have differentiated themselves from the mass; workers who have scrambled to the top of bureaucratic organizations; workers who, because of their low education and cultural level, are the furthest removed from intellectual labor—and therefore also regard it with the greatest mistrust and hostility. In other words, the social basis of economism, spontaneism, the "handicraftsman's approach" to the question of organization and hostility toward science within the working class, is the craft layer of this class.

On the other hand, among the workers of the large factories and cities, of the extensive branches of industry in the forefront of technological progress, the thirst for knowledge, the greater familiarity with technical and scientific processes, and the greater audacity in projecting the conquest of power in both the factory and the state make it much easier to understand the objectively necessary role of revolutionary theoreticians and of the revolutionary organization.

The spontaneous tendencies in the labor movement often, though not always, correspond exactly to this social basis. This was especially true for anarcho-syndicalism in the Latin countries before the First World War. This was also true for Menshevism, which was thoroughly defeated by Bolshevism in the large metropolitan factories, but which found its most important proletarian base in the typically small-town mining and oil-field districts of southern Russia.[59] Attempts today, in the era of the third industrial revolution, to revive this craftsman-caste approach under the pretext of guaranteeing "workers autonomy" could only have the same result as in the past—namely, to dissipate the forces of the advanced and potentially revolutionary working class and to give a boost to the semi-craft, bureaucratized sections of the movement that are under the constant influence of bourgeois ideology.

SCIENTIFIC INTELLIGENTSIA, SOCIAL SCIENCE, AND PROLETARIAN CLASS CONSCIOUSNESS

The massive reintroduction of intellectual labor into the process of production brought about by the third industrial revolution, which was foreseen by Marx and whose foundations were already laid in the second industrial revolution,[60] has created the prerequisite for a much broader layer of the scientific intelligentsia to regain the awareness of alienation which it had lost through its removal from the process of direct production of surplus value and its transformation into a direct or indirect consumer of surplus value. For it, too, is overcome by alienation in bourgeois society. This is the material basis not only for the student revolt in the imperialist countries but also for the possibility of involving increasing numbers of scientists and technicians in the revolutionary movement.

The participation of the intelligentsia in the classical socialist movement before the First World War generally tended to decline. Though it was considerable at the start of the movement, it became smaller and smaller as the organized mass movement of the working class became stronger. In a little known polemic against Max Adler in 1910, Trotsky revealed the causes of this process to be on the whole materialistic: the intelligentsia's social dependency on the big bourgeoisie and the bourgeois state; an ideological identification with the class interests it thereby serves; and the inability of the workers' movement, organized as a "counter-society," to compete with its counterpart. Trotsky predicted that this would probably change very quickly, in a revolutionary epoch, on the eve of the proletarian revolution.[61]

From these correct premises, however, he drew what were already incorrect tactical conclusions, when, for instance, he failed to see the great importance which, in 1908–09, Lenin accorded the student movement (which was re-emerging in the middle of the victorious counter-revolution). Trotsky considered it an albatross for the subsequent, new rise in the revolutionary mass movement (that was to begin in 1912).

He even went so far as to maintain that it was the "fault" of the leading revolutionary intelligentsia in the Russian Social Democracy if the student movement was able to spread "its overall social characteristics: a spirit of sectarianism, an individualism typical of intellectuals, and ideological fetishism."[62] As Trotsky later admitted, at that time he underestimated the *political and social significance* of the faction fight between the Bolsheviks and the Liquidators, which was only an extension of the earlier struggle between Bolsheviks and Mensheviks. History was to show that this struggle had nothing to do with a product of "intellectual sectarianism" but with the separation of socialist, revolutionary consciousness from petty-bourgeois, reformist consciousness.[63]

It is correct, however, that the participation of the Russian revolutionary intelligentsia in the building of the revolutionary class party of the Russian proletariat was still a pure product of individual selection without any social roots. Since the October revolution, this has inevitably turned against the *proletarian* revolution, for the masses of the technical intelligentsia were not *able* to go over to the camp of the revolution. At first they sabotaged economic production and the methods of social organization on the broadest scale; then their cooperation had to be "bought" through high salaries; and finally they were transformed into the driving force behind the bureaucratization and degeneration of this revolution.

Inasmuch as the position of the technical intelligentsia (especially category 2 above) in the material process of production has today decisively changed, and since this technical intelligentsia is gradually being transformed into a section of the wage-earning class, the possibility of its massive participation in the revolutionary process and in the reorganization of society stands on much firmer ground than in the past. Frederick Engels had already pointed to the historically decisive role this intelligentsia could play in the construction of the socialist society.

> In order to take over and put into operation the means of production, we need people, and in large numbers, who are technically trained. We do not have them. . . . I foresee us in the next eight to ten years recruiting enough young technicians, doctors, lawyers and teachers to be in a position to let party comrades administer the factories and essential goods for the nation. Then our accession to power will be quite natural and will work itself out relatively smoothly. If, on the other hand, we prematurely come to power through a war, the technicians will be our main opponents, and will deceive and betray us whenever possible. We will have to use terror against them and still they will shit all over us.[64]

Of course, it must be added that in the course of this third industrial revolution the working class itself, which is much better qualified than in 1890, exhibits a far greater ability to directly manage the factories than in Engels's time. But in the final analysis it is technical abilities that are required for the broad masses to be able to exert political and social control over the "specialists" (a matter about which Lenin had so many illusions in 1918). A growing union between the technical intelligentsia and the industrial proletariat, and the growing participation of revolutionary intellectuals in the revolutionary party, can only facilitate that control.

As the contradiction between the objective socialization of production and labor on the one hand and private appropriation on the other intensifies (as the crisis of the capitalist relations of production sharpens—and today we are experiencing a new and sharper form of this contradiction, which underlay the May 1968 events in France and the mass struggles in Italy in 1969), and as neocapitalism seeks to win a new lease on life by raising the working class's level of consumption, science will increasingly become for the masses a revolutionary, productive force in two regards: with automation and the growing mountain of commodities it produces not only a growing crisis in the production and distribution process of capital, which is based upon generalized commodity production; it also produces revolutionary consciousness in growing masses of people by allowing the myths and masks of the capitalist routine to be torn away, and by making it possible for the worker, reconquering the consciousness of being alienated, to put an end to that alienation. As the decisive barrier which today holds back the working class from acquiring political class consciousness is found to reside less in the misery of the masses or the extreme narrowness of their surroundings than in the constant influence of petty-bourgeois and bourgeois ideological consumption and mystification, it is precisely then that the eye-opening function of critical social science can play a truly revolutionary role in the new awakening of the class consciousness among the masses.

Of course, this makes necessary the existence of concrete ties with the working masses—a requirement that can only be met by the advanced workers on the one hand and the revolutionary organization on the other. And this also requires the revolutionary, scientific intelligentsia not to "go to the people" with the modest populist masochism that restricts it to humbly supporting struggles for higher wages, but to bring the awakened and critical layers of the working class what they are unable to achieve by themselves, owing to their fragmented state of consciousness: the scientific knowledge and awareness that will make it possible for them to recognize the scandal of concealed exploitation and disguised oppression for what it is.

HISTORICAL PEDAGOGY AND COMMUNICATION OF CLASS CONSCIOUSNESS

Once it is understood that the Leninist theory of organization tries to answer the problems of the current potential for revolution and of the revolutionary subject, this theory leads directly to the question of historical pedagogy, that is, the problem of *transforming* potential class consciousness into actual class consciousness, and trade-unionist consciousness into political, revolutionary consciousness. This problem can only be resolved in the light of the classification of the working class delineated above—into the mass of the workers, advanced workers, and organized revolutionary cadre. To assimilate its growing class consciousness, each layer requires its own methods of instruction, goes through its own learning process, and needs to have a special form of communication with the class as a whole and with the realm of theoretical production. The historical role of the revolutionary vanguard party Lenin had in mind can be summed up as that of jointly expressing these three forms of pedagogy.

The broad masses learn only through action. To hope to "impart" revolutionary consciousness to them through propaganda is an endeavor worthy of Sisyphus—and just as fruitless. Yet, although the masses learn only through action, all actions do not necessarily lead to a mass acquisition of *revolutionary* class consciousness. Actions around immediately realizable economic and political goals that can be completely achieved within the framework of the capitalist social order do not produce revolutionary class consciousness. This was one of the great illusions of the "optimistic" Social Democrats at the end of the 19th century and the beginning of the 20th (including Engels), who believed that there was a straight line leading from partial successes in electoral struggles and strikes to revolutionary consciousness and to an increase in the proletariat's revolutionary combativity.[65]

This has proven to be historically incorrect. These partial successes certainly played a significant and positive role in strengthening the self-confidence and combativity of the proletarian masses in general. (The anarchists were wrong to reject these partial struggles out of hand.) Yet they did not prepare the working masses for revolutionary struggle. The German working class's lack of experience in revolutionary struggles on the one hand and the existence on the other hand of such experience in the Russian working class was the most important difference in consciousness between the two classes on the eve of the First World War. It decisively contributed to the dissimilar outcome of the revolutions of 1917–19 in Germany and in Russia.

Since the goal of mass actions is generally the satisfaction of immediate needs, it becomes an important aspect of revolutionary strategy to link these needs to demands that objectively cannot be achieved or coopted within the framework of the capitalist social order, and which produce an objectively revolutionary dynamic that has to lead to a test of strength between the two decisive social classes over the question of power. This is the strategy of transitional demands, which, through the efforts of Lenin, was incorporated into the program of the Communist International at its fourth congress, and which was later elaborated by Trotsky in the main body of the program of the Fourth International.[66]

The development of revolutionary class consciousness among the broad masses is possible only if they accumulate experiences of *struggles* that are not only limited to the winning of partial demands within the framework of capitalism. The gradual injection of these demands into mass struggles can come about only through the efforts of a broad layer of advanced workers who are closely linked to the masses and who disseminate and publicize these demands (which normally do *not* spontaneously grow out of the day-to-day experiences of the class) in the factories, experimenting with them in various skirmishes and spreading them through agitation, until a point is reached where favorable objective and subjective conditions converge, making the realization of these demands the actual objective of great strikes, demonstrations, agitational campaigns, and so on.

Although revolutionary class consciousness among the broad masses develops only out of the experience of *objectively revolutionary struggle*, among advanced workers it flows from the experience of life, work, and struggle in general. These experiences do not necessarily *need* to be revolutionary at all. From the daily experiences of class conflict, these advanced workers draw the elementary conclusions about the need for class solidarity, class action, and class organization. The programmatic and organizational forms through which this action and organization are to be led will differ greatly depending upon objective conditions and concrete experiences. But the advanced workers' experience of life, work, and struggle leads them to the threshold of understanding the inadequacy of activity which seeks merely to reform the existing society rather than abolish it.

The activity of the revolutionary vanguard can make it possible for the class consciousness of the advanced workers to cross over this threshold. It can, however, fulfill this role of catalyst neither automatically nor without regard for objective conditions. It can only fulfill it when it is itself equal to the task, that is, if the content of its theoretical, propagandistic, and literary activity corresponds to the needs of the advanced workers, and if the form of this activity does not trample underfoot the laws of pedagogy (avoiding ultimatistic formulations). At the same time, this kind of activity must be linked to *activity of a practical nature* and to a *political perspective*, thus enhancing the credibility of both the revolutionary strategy and the organization putting it forward.

In periods of abating class struggles, of a temporary decline in the self-confidence of the working class, during which the stability of the class enemy appears temporarily assured, the revolutionary vanguard will not be able to achieve its objectives even if its activity is completely equal to the task of catalyzing revolutionary class consciousness among the broadest layer of advanced workers. This belief that a mere defense of "the correct tactic" or "the correct line" is sufficient to miraculously generate a growing revolutionary force, even in periods of declining class struggle, is an illusion stemming from bourgeois rationalism, not from the materialist dialectic. This illusion, incidentally, is the cause of most splits within the revolutionary movement, because the organizational sectarianism of the splitters is based on the naive view that the "application of the correct tactic" can win over more people in the as yet untouched periphery than it can among revolutionaries who are already organized. As long as the objective conditions remain unfavorable, such splits, therefore, usually result in grouplets that are even weaker than those whose "false tactics" made them seem so worthy of condemnation in the first place.

This does not mean, however, that the work of the revolutionary vanguard among the advanced workers remains useless or ineffectual during unfavorable objective circumstances. It produces no great *immediate* successes, yet it is a tremendously important, and even decisive, *preparation* for that turning point when class struggles once again begin to mount!

For, just as broad masses with no experience of revolutionary struggle cannot develop revolutionary class consciousness, advanced workers who have never heard of transitional demands cannot introduce them into the next wave of class struggle. The patient, persistent preparation carried out, with constant attention to detail, by the revolutionary vanguard organization, sometimes over a period of years, pays off in rich dividends the day the "natural leaders of the class," still hesitating and not yet completely free from hostile influences, suddenly, during a big strike or demonstration, take up the demand for workers' control and thrust it to the forefront of the struggle.[67]

To be in a position, however, to convince a country's advanced workers and radical intelligentsia of the need to extend broad mass struggles beyond the level of immediate demands to that of transitional demands, it is not enough for the revolutionary vanguard organization to learn by heart a list of such demands culled from Lenin and Trotsky. It must acquire a twofold knowledge and a two-sided method of learning. On the one hand it must assimilate the body of the experiences of the international proletariat over more than a century of revolutionary class struggle. On the other hand it must carry on a continuous, serious analysis of the present overall social reality, national as well as international. This alone makes it possible to apply the lessons of history to the reality at hand. It is clear that on the basis of the Marxist theory of knowledge, only practice can ultimately provide the criterion for measuring the actual theoretical assimilation of present-day reality. For that reason, international practice is an absolute prerequisite for a Marxist international analysis, and an international organization is an absolute prerequisite for such a practice.

Without a serious assimilation of the entire historical experience of the international workers' movement from the revolution of 1848 to the present, it is impossible to determine with scientific precision either the contradictions of present neocapitalist society—on a world scale as well as in individual countries—or the concrete contradiction accompanying the formation of proletarian class consciousness, or the kind of struggles that could lead to a prerevolutionary situation. History is the only laboratory for the social sciences. Without assimilating the lessons of history, a pseudo-revolutionary Marxist today would be no better than a medical student who refused to set foot inside the dissecting laboratory.

It should be pointed out in this connection that all attempts to keep the newly emerging revolutionary movement "aloof from the splits of the past" demonstrate a complete failure to understand the socio-political nature of this differentiation within the international workers' movement. If one puts aside the inevitable personal and incidental factors involved in these differentiations, one has to conclude that the great disputes in the international workers' movement since the foundation of the First International (the disputes between Marxism and anarchism; between Marxism and revisionism; between Bolshevism and Menshevism; between internationalism and social-patriotism; between defenders of the dictatorship of the proletariat and defenders of bourgeois democracy; between Trotskyism and Stalinism; between Maoism and Khrushchevism) touch upon fundamental questions relating to the proletarian revolution and to the strategy and tactics of revolutionary class struggle. *These basic questions are products of the very nature of capitalism, the proletariat, and revolutionary struggle.* They will therefore remain pressing questions as long as the problem of creating a classless society on a world scale has not been solved in practical terms. No "tactfulness," no matter how artful, and no "conciliationism," no matter how magnanimous, can in the long run prevent these questions from rising out of practice itself to confront each new generation of revolutionaries. All that is accomplished by attempting to avoid a discussion of these problems is that instead of raising, analyzing, and solving them in a methodical and scientific fashion, this is done unsystematically, at random, without plan, and without sufficient training and knowledge.

However, while the assimilation of the historical substance of Marxist theory is necessary, it is nevertheless in and of itself an insufficient prerequisite for conveying revolutionary class consciousness to the advanced workers and the radical intelligentsia. In addition, a systematic analysis of the present is required, without which theory cannot furnish the means for disclosing either the immediate capacity of the working class for struggle or the "weak links" in the neocapitalist mode of production and bourgeois society; nor can it furnish the means for formulating the appropriate transitional demands (as well as the proper pedagogical approach to raising them). Only the combination of a serious, complete social and critical analysis of the present and the assimilation of the lessons of the history of the workers' movement can create an effective instrument for the theoretical accomplishment of the task of a revolutionary vanguard.[68]

Without the experience of revolutionary struggle by broad masses, there can be no revolutionary class consciousness among these masses. Without the conscious intervention of advanced workers, who inject transitional demands into workers' struggles, there can hardly be experiences of revolutionary struggle on the part of the broad masses. Without the spreading of transitional demands by a revolutionary vanguard, there can be no possibility of advanced workers influencing mass struggles in a truly anticapitalist sense. Without a revolutionary program, without a thorough study of the history of the revolutionary workers' movement, without an application of this study to the present, and without practical proof of the ability of the revolutionary vanguard to actually play a leading role in at least a few sectors and situations, there can be no possibility of convincing the advanced workers of the need for the revolutionary organization, and therefore no possibility (or only an unlikely one) that the appropriate transitional demands for the objective situation can be worked out by the advanced workers. In this way the various factors in the formation of class consciousness intertwine and underpin the timeliness of the Leninist conception of organization.

The process of building a revolutionary party acquires its unified character through jointly expressing the learning of the masses in action, the learning of the advanced workers in practical experience, and the learning of the revolutionary cadre in the transmission of revolutionary theory and practice. There is a constant interrelationship between learning and teaching, even among the revolutionary cadre, who have to achieve the ability to shed any arrogance resulting from their theoretical knowledge. *This ability proceeds from the understanding that theory proves its right to exist only through its connection to the real class struggle and by its capacity to transform potentially revolutionary class consciousness into the actual revolutionary class consciousness of broad layers of workers.* The famous observation by Marx that the educators must themselves be educated[69] means exactly what it says. It does not mean that a consciously revolutionary transformation of society is possible without a revolutionary pedagogy. And it is given a more complete expression in the Marxist proposition that "In revolutionary activity the changing of oneself coincides with the changing of circumstances."[70]

Notes

1. This concept was by no means invented by Lenin but corresponds to a tradition leading from Engels, through Kautsky, to the classical doctrines of international social democracy between 1880 and 1905. The Hainfeld Program of the Austrian Social Democracy, drafted in 1888–89, explicitly states: "Socialist consciousness is something that is brought into the proletarian class struggle from outside, not something that organically develops out of the class struggle." In 1901 Kautsky published his article "Akademiker und Proletarier" in *Neue Zeit* (19th year, Vol. 2, April 17, 1901), in which he expressed the same thought (p. 89) in a form that directly inspired Lenin's *What Is to Be Done?*

   It is well known that Marx developed no uniform concept of the party. But while he sometimes totally rejected the idea of a vanguard organization, he also formulated a conception which very closely approaches that of "introducing revolutionary-socialist consciousness" into the working class. Note the following passage from a letter, written by him on January 1, 1870, from the executive board of the First International to the federal committee of Romanic Switzerland: "The English possess all the necessary *material prerequisites* for a social revolution. What they lack is a *spirit of generalization and revolutionary passion.* That the executive board alone can remedy, and in doing so, hasten the development of a truly revolutionary movement in this country, and hence *everywhere.* The great successes that we have already achieved in this regard are being attested to by the wisest and most distinguished newspapers of the ruling class . . . not to mention the so-called radical members of the House of Commons and the House of Lords, who only a short time ago had quite a bit of influence on the leaders of the English workers. They are publicly accusing us of having poisoned and almost suffocated the *English spirit* of the working class, and of having driven it to revolutionary socialism." (Marx-Engels, *Werke,* Vol. 16 [Berlin: Dietz-Verlag, 1964], pp. 386–387.)

   The concept of the "current potential for revolution" in Lenin was first formulated by Georg Lukacs, as is well known, in *Geschichte und Klassenbewusstsein* (Berlin: Malik Verlag, 1923) and particularly in his *Lenin* (Cambridge, MA: MIT Press, 1971).

2. This is especially true for the crucial Marxian category of *revolutionary practice,* which was developed in the then unknown *German Ideology.*

3. It is in this sense that, among others, the famous statement by Marx at the beginning of *The Eighteenth Brumaire of Louis Bonaparte* must be understood, in which he stresses the constant self-critical nature of the proletarian revolution and its tendency to come back to things that appeared to have already been accomplished. In this connection, Marx speaks also of the proletariat as being hypnotized by the "undefined magnitude of its own objectives."

4. In the *Communist Manifesto* Marx and Engels state that communists "do not set up any special principles of their own, by which to shape and mold the proletarian movement." In the English edition of 1888, Engels substituted the word "sectarian" for the word "special." In doing so, he expresses the fact that scientific socialism certainly does try to advance "special" principles in the labor movement, but only those objectively resulting from the general course of the proletarian class struggle, i.e., from contemporary history, and not those peculiar only to the creed of a particular sect, i.e., to a purely incidental aspect of the proletarian class struggle.

5. This thought is poignantly expressed by Trotsky in the introduction to the first

Russian edition of his book, *The Permanent Revolution* (New York: Merit Publishers, 1969). Mao Tse Tung too has more than once called attention to this thought. In sharp contrast to it is the notion of a "socialist mode of production" or even of a "developed social system of socialism" in which the first stage of communism is regarded as something fixed and not as simply a transitional phase in the permanent revolutionary development from capitalism to communism.

6. Note Lenin's well-known statement that there are no "inextricable economic situations" for the imperialist bourgeoisie.

7. Thus the rising bourgeois class consciousness and even the rising plebeian or semiproletarian class consciousness in the 16th and 17th centuries were expressed within a completely religious framework, finding the way to overt materialism only with the full-blown decadence of the feudal absolutist order in the second half of the 18th century.

8. Gramsci's "concept of political and ethical hegemony," which an oppressed social class must establish within society before it can take political power, expresses this possibility especially well. See *Il Materialismo Storico e la Filosofia di Benedetto Croce* (Milan: Einaudi, 1964), p. 236; and also *Note sul Machiavelli* (Milan: Einaudi, 1964), pp. 29–37, 41–50 ff. This hegemony concept has been criticized or modified by numerous Marxist theoreticians. See, for example, Nicos Poulantzas, *Pouvoir politique et classes sociales* (Paris: Maspero, 1968), pp. 210–222. Concerning the significance of overall social *consensus* with the material and moral foundations of bourgeois class rule, see Jose Ramon Recalde, *Integracion y lucha de clases en el neo-capitalismo* (Madrid: Editorial Ciencia Nueva, 1968), pp. 152–157.

9. This is expressed by Marx and Engels in the proposition in *The German Ideology* that, "this revolution is necessary therefore, not only because the ruling class cannot be overthrown in any other way, but also because the class *overthrowing* it can only in a revolution succeed in ridding itself of all the muck of ages and become fitted to found society anew." Karl Marx and Frederick Engels, *The German Ideology* (Moscow: Progress Publishers, 1968), p. 87. See also the following observation by Marx in 1850 against the Schapper minority in the Communist League: "The minority substitutes a dogmatic approach for a critical one, and idealism for materialism. For it, the driving force of the revolution is mere will power, not actual conditions. We, on the other hand, tell the workers: 'You will have to go through 15, 20, 50 years of civil wars and people's struggles not only to change the conditions, *but in order to change yourselves* so you will be capable of exercising political rule.' You, on the contrary, say: 'If we can't take power right away we might as well go to bed.'" Karl Marx, *Enthullungen Ueber den Kommunistenprozess zu Koln* (Berlin: Buchandlung Vorwartz, 1914), pp. 52–53.

10. Note Lenin: "Our wiseacre fails to see that it is precisely during the revolution that we shall stand in need of the results of our [prerevolutionary—E.M.] theoretical battles with the Critics in order to be able resolutely to combat their *practical* positions!" *What Is to Be Done?* (Moscow: Progress Publishers, 1964, p. 163. How tragically this came true 17 years later in the German revolution.

11. In this connection in *What Is to Be Done?* Lenin speaks of the "social-democratic" and "revolutionary" workers in contrast to the "backward" workers.

12. N. Bukharin, *Theorie des Historischen Materialismus* (published by the Communist International, 1922), pp. 343–345.

"Economic conditions had first transformed the mass of the people of the country into workers. The combination of capital has created for this mass a common situation, common interests. This mass is thus already a class as against capital, but not yet for itself. In the struggle, of which we have noted only a few phases, this mass becomes united, and constitutes itself as a class for itself." Karl Marx, *The Poverty of Philosophy* (New York: International Publishers, 1963), p. 173.

13. See the section of the S.P.D.'s "Erfurt Program" that was not criticized by Engels, which describes the proletarians as simply the class of wage workers separated from the means of production and condemned to sell their labor power, and which describes the class struggle as the objective struggle between exploiters and exploited in modern society (i.e., without relation to the degree of organization or consciousness of the wage earners). Following this objective fact, which is established in the first four sections, comes the following addition to the conclusion of the general body of the program: "The task of the social-democratic party is to mold this struggle of the working class into a conscious and homogeneous one and to point out what is by nature its essential goal." This once again explicitly confirms that there can be classes and class struggle in capitalist society without the struggling working class being conscious of its class interests. Further on, in the eighth section, the program speaks of the "class-conscious workers of all countries," and Engels proposes a change which again underlines the fact that he made a definitive distinction between the "objective" and the "subjective" concept of class: "Instead of 'class conscious,' which for us is an easily understandable abbreviation, I would say (in the interests of general understanding and translation into foreign languages) 'workers permeated with the consciousness of their class situation,' or something like that." Engels, "Zur Kritik des sozialdemokratischen Programmentwurfs 1891," in Marx-Engels, *Werke*, Vol. 22 (Berlin: Dietz-Verlag, 1963), p. 232.

14. Lenin: "The basic prerequisite for this success [in consolidating the party— E.M.] was, of course, the fact that the working class, whose elite has built the Social Democracy, differs for objective economic reasons, from all other classes in capitalist society in its capacity for organization. Without this prerequisite, the organization of professional revolutionaries would only be a game, an adventure. . . ." Lenin, *Oeuvres Completes*, Vol. 12 (Paris: Editions Sociales, 1969), p. 74.

15. To counter this view, many critics of the Leninist concept of organization (beginning with Plekhanov's article, "Centralism or Bonapartism" in *Iskra*, 70 [Summer, 1904], refer to a passage in *The Holy Family*. The passage states: "When socialist writers ascribe this historic role to the proletariat, it is not, as Critical Criticism pretends to think, because they consider the proletarians as *gods*. Rather the contrary. Since the abstraction of all humanity, even of the *semblance* of humanity, is practically complete in the full-grown proletariat: since the conditions of life of the proletariat sum up all the conditions of life of society today in all their inhuman acuity; since man has lost himself in the proletariat, yet at the same time has not only gained theoretical consciousness of that loss, but through urgent, no longer disguisable, absolutely imperative *need*—that practical expression of *necessity*—is driven to revolt against that inhumanity; it follows that the proletariat can and must free itself. But it cannot free itself without abolishing the conditions of its own life. It cannot abolish the conditions of its own life without abolishing *all* the inhuman conditions of life of society today which are summed up in its own situation. Not in vain does it go

through the stern but steeling school of *labor*. The question is not what this or that proletarian, or even the whole of the proletariat, at the moment *considers* as its aim. The question is *what the proletariat is*, and what, consequent on that *being*, it will be compelled to do. Its aim and historical action is irrevocably and obviously demonstrated in its own life situation as well as in the whole organization of bourgeois society today. There is no need to dwell here upon the fact that a large part of the English and French proletariat is already *conscious* of its historic task and is constantly working to develop that consciousness into complete clarity." Karl Marx and Frederick Engels, *The Holy Family* (Moscow: Foreign Languages Publishing House, 1956), pp. 52–53.

Aside from the fact that Marx and Engels were hardly in a position in 1844–45 to produce a mature theory of proletarian class consciousness and proletarian organization (to become aware of this, one need only compare the last sentence of the above quotation with what Engels wrote 40 years later about the English working class), these lines say the very opposite of what Plekhanov reads into them. They say only that the social *situation* of the proletariat prepares it for radical, revolutionary *action*, and that the determination of the general socialist objective (the abolition of private property) is "prescribed" by its conditions of life. In no way do they indicate, however, that the proletariat's "inhuman conditions of life" will somehow mysteriously enable it to "spontaneously" assimilate all the social sciences. Quite the opposite! (Concerning Plekhanov's article, see Samuel H. Baron's *Plekhanov* [Stanford: Stanford University Press, 1963], pp. 248–253.)

16. Today it is almost forgotten that the Russian socialist movement too was founded largely by students and intellectuals, and that around three-fourths of a century ago they were faced with problems much like those we face today. Similar, but of course not identical: today there is an additional obstacle (the reformist, revisionist mass organizations of the working class), as well as an additional strength (historical experience, including the experience of great victory which the revolutionary movement has accumulated since then).

   In *What Is to Be Done?* Lenin speaks explicitly of the capacity of intellectuals to assimilate "political knowledge," i.e., scientific Marxism.

17. See Karl Marx, *The Poverty of Philosophy*. An absorbing description of the various early forms of trade unions and of workers' resistance funds can be found in E. P. Thompson's *The Making of the English Working Class* (Baltimore: Penguin Books, 1968).

18. The necessarily discontinuous nature of mass action is explained by the class condition of the proletariat itself. As long as a mass action does not succeed in toppling the capitalist mode of production, its duration will be limited by the financial, physical, and mental ability of the workers to withstand the loss of wages. It is obvious that this ability is not unlimited. To deny this would be to deny the material conditions of the proletariat's existence, which compel it, as a class, to sell its labor power.

19. See a few examples from the first years of the metal workers union of Germany: *Funfundsiebzig Jahre Industriegewerkshaft Metall* (Frankfurt: Europäische Verlagsantalt, 1968), pp. 72–78.

20. We cannot describe in detail here the differences between a prerevolutionary and a revolutionary situation. Simplifying the matter, we would differentiate a revolutionary from a prerevolutionary situation in this way: while a prerevolutionary situation is characterized by such extensive mass struggles that the

continued existence of the social order is *objectively* threatened, in a revolutionary situation this threat takes the form, organizationally, of the proletariat establishing organs of dual power (i.e., potential organs for the exercising of power by the working class), and *subjectively* of the masses raising directly *revolutionary* demands that the ruling class is unable to either repulse or co-opt.

21. See below, the Leninist origins of this strategy.

22. Rosa Luxemburg, "Organizational Question of Social Democracy," in Mary-Alice Waters, ed., *Rosa Luxemburg Speaks* (New York: Pathfinder Press, 1970), pp. 112–130.

23. Lenin, *What Is to Be Done?*, p. 66.

24. For a relating of this plan directly to revolution, see *What Is to Be Done?*, pp. 165–166. It is true that there are no *organizational* rules for centralization in *What Is to Be Done?*, but they are determined exclusively *by the conditions* imposed by illegality. Lenin recommends the broadest "democratism" for "legal" revolutionary parties: "The general control (in the literal sense of the term) exercised over every act of a party man in the political field brings into existence an automatically operating mechanism which produces what in biology is called the 'survival of the fittest.' 'Natural selection' by full publicity, election and general control provides the assurance that, in the last analysis, every political figure will be 'in his proper place,' do the work for which he is best fitted by his powers and abilities, feel the effects of his mistakes on himself, and prove before all the world his ability to recognize mistakes and to avoid them." Ibid., p. 130.

    Within her Polish party, which was also defined by highly conspiratorial restrictions, Luxemburg, for her part, practiced (or accepted) a centralism that was no less stringent than that of the Bolsheviks (compare the conflict with the Radek faction in Warsaw and the serious charges made against it).

25. *Rosa Luxemburg Speaks*, p. 118.

26. For this see David Lane, *The Roots of Russian Communism* (Assen: Van Gorcum and Co., 1969). Lane has attempted to analyze the social composition of the membership of the Russian Social Democracy and of the Bolshevik and Menshevik factions between 1897 and 1907 on the basis of empirical data. He comes to the conclusion that the Bolsheviks had more worker members and activists than the Mensheviks (pp. 50–51).

27. "Generally speaking it is undeniable that a strong tendency toward centralization is inherent in the social-democratic movement. This tendency springs from the economic makeup of capitalism, which is essentially a centralizing factor. The social-democratic movement carries on its activity inside the large bourgeois city. Its mission is to represent, within the boundaries of the national state, the class interests of the proletariat and to oppose those common interests to all local and group interests.

    "Therefore, the social democracy is, as a rule, hostile to any manifestations of localism or federalism. It strives to unite all workers and all worker organizations in a single party, no matter what national, religious, or occupational differences may exist among them." *Rosa Luxemburg Speaks*, p. 116.

28. Compare the thesis put forward by Andre Gorz, according to which a new party can be created only "from the bottom up" once the network of factory and rank-and-file groups "stretches out, over the entire national territory" ("Ni-Trade-Unionists, ni Bolcheviks," *Les Temps Modernes*, [October 1969]). Gorz has not understood that the crisis of the bourgeois state and the capitalist mode of production does not develop gradually "from the periphery toward the

center," but that it is a discontinuous process which tends toward a decisive test of strength once it reaches a definite turning point. If the centralization of revolutionary groups and combatants does not take place in time, attempts by the reformist bureaucracy to steer the movement back into acceptable channels will only be facilitated—as quickly happened in Italy, in fact, while Gorz was writing his article. This in turn quickly led to a setback for the "rank-and-file" groups. It did not at all lead to their spread throughout the whole country.

29. See Rosa Luxemburg's article on the founding of the Communist Party of Germany entitled "The First Convention": "The revolutionary shock troops of the German proletariat have joined together into an independent political party" (*The Founding Convention of the Communist Party of Germany* [Frankfort: Europäische Verlagsanstalt, 1969], p. 301). "From now on it is a question of everywhere replacing revolutionary moods with unflinching revolutionary convictions, the spontaneous with the systematic" (p. 303). See also (on p. 301) the passage from the pamphlet written by Luxemburg, *What Does the Spartacus League Want?*: "The Spartacus League is not a party that seeks to come to power over or with the help of the working masses. *The Spartacus League is only that part of the proletariat that is conscious of its goal*. It is that part which, at each step, points the working-class masses as a whole toward their historic task, which, at each separate stage of the revolution, represents the ultimate socialist objective and, in all national questions, the interests of the proletarian world revolution" (emphasis added). In 1904 Luxemburg had not yet understood the essence of Bolshevism—that "that part of the proletariat that is conscious of its goal" must be organized *separately* from the "broad mass."

It is a complete confirmation of our thesis that as soon as Luxemburg adopted the concept of the vanguard party, she too was accused by Social Democrats ("left" Social Democrats at that) of wanting "the dictatorship over the proletariat" (Max Adler, "Karl Liebknecht und Rosa Luxemburg," *Der Kampf*, XII, no. 2 [February 1919], p. 75).

30. Leon Trotsky, *Nos taches politiques* (Paris: Editions Pierre Belfond, 1970), pp. 123–129.
31. Ibid., p. 125.
32. Ibid., p. 186.
33. Leon Trotsky, "The Class, the Party and the Leadership," *Fourth International*, 1, no. 7 (December 1940), p. 193.
34. Numerous examples of this could be mentioned. See, among others, Lenin, *Collected Works*, Vol. 18 (Moscow: Foreign Languages Publishing House, 1963), pp. 471–477; Vol. 23, pp. 236–253; Vol. 10, pp. 277–278.
35. The impossibility of "spontaneous" concentration of the revolutionary vanguard elements on a national scale was demonstrated with particular clarity in the French general strike of May 1968.
36. Yet here too these initial forms of independent organization were unable, in the absence of an organized revolutionary vanguard, which would have carried out the necessary preparatory work, to neutralize for long, let alone to smash, the conservative centralization of the trade union and state apparatuses and of the entrepreneurs.
37. Leon Trotsky, *The History of the Russian Revolution* (Ann Arbor: University of Michigan Press, 1957), p. xix.
38. See, among others, Georg Lukacs, *Geschichte und Klassenbewusstsein* (Berlin: Malik Verlag, 1923), pp. 180–189 ff.

39. The defense of the political and material special interests of these bureaucracies is nevertheless the social substructure upon which the superstructure of this autonomy and its ideological sediment are able to arise.
40. *Rosa Luxemburg Speaks*, p. 121.
41. Leon Trotsky, "Results and Prospects," in *The Permanent Revolution*, p. 114.
42. Compare, for instance, Clara Zetkin's biting scorn for the S.P.D. executive committee (as well as Kautsky's lack of character), which she expressed in her correspondence concerning the party leadership's censorship in 1909 of the publication of Kautsky's *The Road to Power*. K. Kautsky, *Le Chemin de Pouvoir* (Paris: Editions Anthropos, 1969), pp. 177–212. Contrast this with the respect shown by Lenin for Kautsky in the same year.
43. Lenin, "Der Zusammenbruch der II Internationale," in Lenin and Zinoviev, *Gegen den Strom* (published by the Communist International, 1921), p. 164.
44. Ibid., p. 165.
45. Lenin, "'Left Wing' Communism, an Infantile Disorder," in *Collected Works*, Vol. 31 (Moscow: Foreign Languages Publishing House, 1966), pp. 17–118.

    See also the above mentioned passage from the pamphlet *What Does the Spartacus League Want?*, by Rosa Luxemburg.

    This conclusion was superior to that of Trotsky in 1906 or Luxemburg in 1904. In the face of a growing conservatism on the part of the social-democratic apparatus, they had illusions about the ability of the masses to solve the problem of the seizure of power with the aid of their revolutionary ardor alone. In "The Mass Strike, the Political Party and the Trade Unions" (in *Rosa Luxemburg Speaks*, pp. 153–219) Luxemburg even shifts the problem temporarily onto the "unorganized," i.e., the poorest, section of the proletariat, which for the first time attains consciousness during a mass strike. In his writings after 1914, Lenin too, explicitly contrasts these masses to the "labor aristocracy,' in a somewhat oversimplified manner, in my opinion. At that time the workers in the large steel and metal-processing plants, among others, belonged to the unorganized sectors of the German proletariat, and while they turned to the left *en masse* after 1918, they did not at all belong to the "poorest" layers.
46. This so-called general crisis of capitalism, i.e., the onset of the historical epoch of the decline of capitalism, should not be confused with conjunctural crises, i.e., periodic economic crises. These have occurred during the period of rising, as well as declining, capitalism. For Lenin, the epoch beginning with the First World War is the "era of beginning social revolution." See, among others, Lenin and Zinoviev, *Gegen den Strom*, p. 393.
47. Herein undoubtedly lies the greatest weakness of this fatalistic theory. Out of the tendency toward growing autonomy it automatically deduces a *social danger*, without including in its analysis the transmission of potential social power and specific social interests. The tendency for doormen and cashiers to develop their own interests does not give them power over banks and large firms—except for the "power" of robbery, which is effective only under very specific conditions. If the analysis of this tendency toward autonomy is to have any social content, therefore, it must be accompanied by a definition of these conditions.
48. The formal rules of democratic centralism are, of course, part of these prerequisites. These rules include the right of all members to be completely informed about differences of opinion in the leadership; the right to form tendencies and to present contradictory points of view to the membership before leadership elections and conventions; the regular convening of conventions; the right to

periodically revise majority decisions in the light of subsequent experiences, i.e., the right of minorities to periodically attempt to reverse decisions made by the majority; the right of political initiative by minorities and members at conventions; and so on.

These Leninist norms of democratic centralism were rather strikingly formulated in the new party statutes drawn up before August 1968 in preparation for the 14th convention of the Czechoslovakian C.P. The Moscow defenders of bureaucratic centralism reacted with the invasion. In fact, this proposed return to Leninist norms of democratic centralism was one of the most important "thorns" in the side of the Soviet bureaucracy as far as the developments in Czechoslovakia were concerned.

49. Leon Trotsky, *The History of the Russian Revolution.*
50. Between 1905 and 1917 the Bolshevik Party was educated in the spirit of achieving the "democratic dictatorship of the workers and peasants," i.e., in the spirit of a formula with its eye on the possibility of a coalition between a workers' party and a peasant party within the framework of capitalism— foreseeing, in other words, a *capitalist* development of Russian agriculture and industry. Lenin clung to this possibility until late 1916. Only in 1917 did he realize that Trotsky had been correct back in 1905, when he predicted that the agrarian question could only be solved by the dictatorship of the proletariat and the socialization of the Russian economy.

Hartmut Mehringer ("Introduction historique," in Trotsky, *Nos taches politiques,* pp. 17–18, 34 ff.) is completely wrong to link Lenin's theory of organization with his specific strategy in the Russian revolution, to explain it in terms of the "subordinate" role (?) of the working class in this strugge, and to trace Trotsky's theory of the gradual extension of class consciousness to the entire working class to the theory of the permanent revolution. Aside from the fact that Mehringer gives an inadequate and inaccurate outline of Lenin's revolutionary strategy (Lenin was for the *absolute independence* of the Russian working class in opposing the Russian bourgeoisie, and was completely in favor of this class playing a leading role in the revolution); and aside from the fact that, like Lenin, Luxemburg rejected as premature any attempt to establish the proletarian dictatorship in Russia and assigned the revolutionary struggle of the Russian proletariat the mere goal of carrying out the historical tasks of the bourgeois revolution (while at the same time she fought against Lenin's theory of organization), it appears obvious to us that the very theory of permanent revolution, (the task of establishing the proletarian dictatorship in an underdeveloped country) can be grasped with a minimum of realism only through the utmost concentration on the revolutionary tasks in general. Thus it leads not away from Lenin's theory of organization but straight to it. See in this regard also the excellent pamphlet by Denise Avenas, *Economie et politique dans la pensée de Trotsky* (Paris: Maspero, "Cahiers Rouges," 1970).
51. Lenin, *Oeuvres Completes,* Vol. 12 (Paris: Editions Sociales, 1969), p. 74. "The pamphlet *What Is to Be Done?* repeatedly emphasizes that the organization of professional revolutionaries which it proposes makes sense only insofar as it is connected to the 'truly revolutionary class irresistibly rising up in struggle.'" Lenin underlines the fact that the sickness of small group existence can only be overcome through "the ability of the party, through its open mass work, to reach our to proletarian elements" (ibid., p. 75).
52. Maspero in Paris will soon publish an anthology by us entitled "Workers"

Control, Workers' Councils and Workers' Self-Management," which attempts to prove this thesis. Europäischer Verlagsanstalt has announced plans to publish a German edition in 1971.

53. For Lenin the "leading role of the party" in the soviet system is a political one, not one of substitution. It is a question not of substituting itself for the majority in the soviet, but of convincing them of the correctness of the communist policy. The "leading role of the party" is not even mentioned in his basic work on soviets, *State and Revolution*. And if, in times of the greatest confusion and civil war, he sometimes made sharp sallies on tactical questions, arguments can be found in his writings against "soviets without communists," but no arguments in favor of "communists without soviets."

54. Georg Lukacs (*Geschichte und Klassenbewusstsein*, p. 306 ff.) is wrong to think that he discovers one of the roots of Luxemburg's "theory of spontaneity" in the illusion of a "purely proletarian revolution." Even in countries where the numerical and social importance of the proletariat is so overwhelming that the question of "allies" becomes insignificant, the separate organization of the vanguard remains absolutely necessary in a "purely proletarian revolution" because of the internal stratification of the proletariat.

55. A striking example of this is the Chinese Maoists, for whom one wing of their own party (including the majority of the central committee that led the Chinese revolution to victory) is said to be made up of "defenders of the capitalist line"—and even "capitalists" pure and simple.

   For the Italian Bordigists, the general strike of July 14, 1948, had nothing to do with proletarian class struggle, because the workers were striking in defense of the "revisionist" leader of the C.P., Togliatti.

   See also the lovely formulation of the French spontaneist Denis Anthler: "When the proletariat is not revolutionary, it does not exist, and revolutionaries cannot do anything with it. It is not they who, by assuming the role of educators of the people, will be able to create the historical situation in which the proletariat will become what it is; this can only be done by the development of modern society itself." (Preface to Leon Trotsky, "Rapport de la delegation siberlenne" [Paris: *Spartacus*, 1970], p. 12.) This quote also shows how clearly extreme subjectivism and extreme objectivism are related. And how is it explained that despite huge struggles the proletariat does not achieve victory? "Circumstances are to blame, the objective conditions were not ripe." Behind the ultraleft mask one can see those well-known "spontaneists" Karl Kautsky and Otto Bauer eagerly nodding their wise heads. The ridiculous conclusions to which this extreme fatalism and mechanical determinism lead become clear as soon as the "development of modern society itself" is expected to explain to us in concrete terms just why at a given moment the majority of factory A and city B (but not factory C or city D) come out in favor of the dictatorship of the proletariat and against reformism. Yet for better or for worse, the outcome of the revolution depends upon the answer to this question. As long as the "development of modern society itself" does not drop *all* factories and *all* cities like ripe fruit into the lap of the revolution, the "educators of the people," according to Anthler, should presumably refrain from doing violence to "objective conditions," by seeking to win the workers of C and D.

56. This reproach against Lenin and the Leninists was made by the Russian "Economists," and now today's spontaneists have rediscovered it.

57. On this subject see Nicos Poulantzas, *Pouvoir politique et classes sociales*, pp. 210–222.
58. It is interesting to confirm that after the split in the Russian Social Democracy there were many more intellectuals, including professional revolutionary intellectuals, with the Mensheviks than with the Bolsheviks. See in this connection David Lane, *The Roots of Russian Communism*, pp. 47, 50.
59. David Lane too, emphasizes the preponderance of the Bolsheviks in the cities with large factories and an old, stabilized working class. (Ibid., pp. 212–213.)
60. In his last work ("Zum allgemeinen Verhaltnis von wissenschafilicher Intelligenz und proletarischen Klassenbewusstsein," *SDS-Info*, 26–27 [Dec. 22, 1969]), Hans-Jurgen Krahl brought out "the" Marx quotation on this question which we are reprinting here. (It comes from the unincorporated section "Sechstes Kapitel, Resultate des unmittelbaren Produktionsprozesses" in the draft of Chapter Six of Book One of the first volume of *Capital*, which was published for the first time in the "Marx-Engels Archives" in 1933.) We should like to dedicate this article, which was intended to promote discussion and understanding with him, to this young friend who so tragically passed away.

"With the development of a real subsuming of labor under capital (or in the specifically capitalist mode of production), the real functionary in the overall labor process is not the individual worker, but increasingly a combined social capacity for work, and the various capacities for work, which are in competition with one another and constitute the entire productive machine, participate in very different ways in the direct process of creating commodities—or, more accurately in this sense, products—(one works more with his hands, another more with his head, one as a manager, an engineer, a technician, etc., another as a supervisor, and a third as a simple manual laborer, or even a helper). As a result of this, the functions of labor capacity will increasingly tend to be classified by the direct concept of productive labor, while those who possess that capacity will be classified under the concept of productive workers, directly exploited by capital and subordinated to its process of consumption and production." (Karl Marx, *Resultate* [Frankfurt: Neue Kritik, 1969], p. 66.)
61. Leon Trotsky, *The Intelligentsia and Socialism* (London: New Park Publishers, 1966).
62. Leon Trotsky, "Die Entwicklungstendenzen der russischen Sozioldemkratie," in *Die Neue Zeit*, XXVIII, no. 2 (1910), p. 862.
63. Already in his first polemical book against Lenin (*Nos taches politiques*, pp. 68–71, for example), Trotsky had undertaken to represent the entire Leninist polemic against "Economism" and the "handicraftsman's approach to organization" in *What Is to Be Done?* as a pure discussion between intellectuals, or at best an attempt to win over the best forces of the petty-bourgeois intelligentsia to the revolutionary Social Democracy. He did not understand that it was a question of repelling the petty-bourgeois, revisionist influence *upon the working class*. His polemic against Lenin from 1903 to 1914 was characterized by an underappreciation of the catastrophic consequences of opportunism for the working class and the labor movement. Only in 1917 did he overcome this underappreciation once and for all.
64. August Bebel, *Briefwechsel mit Friedrich Engels* (The Hague: Mouton and Co., 1965), p. 465.
65. The sole difficulty for the revolution seemed to them to lie in a necessary

reaction to any possible repeal of universal suffrage, as might happen in case of war. In contrast, Luxemburg, in dealing with the question of the mass strike, had undertaken a conscious attempt to develop the proletariat's forms of struggle by going beyond electoral and wage struggles and closely following the example of the Russian revolution of 1905.

Even today, Lelio Basso, in an interesting analysis of *Rosa Luxemburg's Dialektik der Revolution* (Frankfurt: Europäische Verlagsanstalt, 1969), pp. 82–83, attempts to present as the quintessence of Luxemburg's strategy a centrist reconciliation between day-to-day struggles and ultimate objectives which is limited to "sharpening the contradictions" of objective development. The fact that the deeper meaning of the mass strike strategy escapes him as a result of this error does not need to be dwelt on here.

66. See the discussion of the program at the fourth congress of the Communist International (*Protokoll des Vierten Kongresses der Kommunistischen Internationale* [published by the Communist International, 1923], pp. 404–448. It provisionally concluded with the following declaration of the Russian delegation, signed by Lenin, Trotsky, Zinoviev, Radek, and Bukharin: "The dispute over how the transitional demands should be formulated and in which section of the program they should be included has awakened a completely erroneous impression that there exists a principled difference. In light of this, the Russian delegation unanimously confirms that the drawing up of transitional slogans in the programs of the national sections and their general formulation and theoretical motivation in the general section of the program cannot be interpreted as opportunism" (p. 542). Trotsky seemed to foresee such a strategy already in 1904 when he wrote: "The party stands on the proletariat's *given lack of consciousness* . . . and attempts to implant itself in the proletariat by *raising* this level. . . ." (*Nos taches politiques*, p. 126.)

67. Georg Lukacs (*Lenine* [Paris: E.D.I., 1965], p. 57) is completely correct when he concludes from similar considerations that the Leninist revolutionary party cannot "make" a revolution, but can accelerate the tendencies that will lead to one. Such a party is *both* producer and product of the revolution—which amounts to a resolution of the antithetical positions of Kautsky ("The new party must prepare the way for the revolution") and Luxemburg ("The new party will be created by the revolutionary action of the masses").

68. Hans-Jurgen Krahl ("Zum allgemeinen Verhaltnis," p. 13 ff.) is quite correct when he reproaches Lukacs for his "idealizing" concept of the totality of proletarian class consciousness, and when he accuses him of an inability to combine empirical knowledge and abstract theory—itself based on an inability to transmit revolutionary theory to the working masses. He should have been able to conclude from our essay, however, that such a transmission can be completely achieved on the basis of the Leninist concept of organization—that it, in fact, lies at the very heart of this concept. Since he makes a sharp distinction between "alienated lot in life" and alienated process of production, however, he is predisposed by the Marcusian tendency to see the "alienation of the consumer" as the central problem, and as a result to regard the "civilized satisfaction of needs," which the neocapitalist system ostensibly makes possible for the working class, as an obstacle on its way toward acquiring proletarian class consciousness. Yet, the Achilles heel of the capitalist mode of production must more than ever be sought in the sphere of alienation in the production process; there alone can a truly revolutionary rebellion begin, as the events in

France and Italy have demonstrated. With that we are brought back to the process, which we described, of formulating and conveying class consciousness. In describing it, we, like Krahl (and, we are convinced, like Lenin and Trotsky), in no way substitute the naive concept of the "omniscient party" for that of the evolution of revolutionary theory *as a specific and permanent ongoing process of production*.

69. Karl Marx, "Theses on Feuerbach," third thesis: "The materialist doctrine concerning the changing of circumstances and upbringing forgets that circumstances are changed by men and that it is essential to educate the educators themselves." (Marx-Engels, *The German Ideology*, p. 660.)

70. Ibid., p. 234.

PART III
Marxist Program
and Theory

7

What Is the Theory of Permanent Revolution?

For 80 years the theory of permanent revolution has been the object of a permanent debate inside the international labor and revolutionary movement. A great number of articles and books have been devoted to the discussion. A significant number of revolutions and counter-revolutions have occurred in the less developed countries of the world in which this theory could be tested in the light of real historical development. But, as has happened so many times in the history of Marxist theory and politics, the initially clear terms of the theory became increasingly obscured by side issues, if not outright deformations, produced by the political needs, confusions, of prejudices of polemicists. (One historical precedent which immediately leaps to mind is Marx and Engels's theory of the state.)

Given the new debate[1] unfolding around the theory of permanent revolution, in which the theory is accused of having legitimized essentially ultraleft strategies and tactics, it therefore appears useful to restate in as clear and concise a manner as possible the basic themes of the theory as progressively developed by Leon Trotsky in his main writings on the subject, to wit: *Results and Prospects* (1906); *The Proletariat and the Russian Revolution* (1907); *1905* (1909); *From the October Revolution to the Peace of Brest Litovsk* (1918); Preface to *Results and Prospects* (1919); Preface to *1905* (1922); *Problems of (Everyday) Life* (1923); *The Third International after Lenin* (1928); *Permanent Revolution* (1930); *The History of the Russian Revolution* (1931–32); Introduction to Harold Isaacs, *The Tragedy of the Chinese Revolution* (1938); *The Transitional Programme* (1938); and *Three Concepts of the Russian Revolution* (1940).

We extend these theses to some new historical problems which have arisen since Trotsky's death, above all the question of nuclear weapons. We

This article appeared in a theoretical journal published by the United Secretariat of the Fourth International, *International Marxist Review*, Vol. 2, no. 1 (London, Summer 1986), p. 7.

do not quote from the successive writings of Trotsky, whose positions on permanent revolution obviously evolved through time, even if his main thesis was essentially already stated as early as 1906. We take the theory in its totality as it emerged in its final shape in the 1933–40 period.

1. *In the imperialist epoch, a full realization of the historic tasks of the national-democratic revolution in the less developed countries is impossible without the conquest of political power by the working class supported by the poor peasantry, that is, without the destruction of the bourgeois state (or the old state of the ruling class) and the establishment of the dictatorship of the proletariat.*

This thesis is based on the following propositions:

1.1. In the less developed countries the unfulfilled tasks of the national-democratic revolution are not only political: the overthrow of absolutist, semi-feudal, or other dictatorships; the full conquest of political democracy; national independence from imperialism; national liberation of oppressed nationalities; constitution of the united nation; and national appropriation of natural resources and big firms owned by foreign capital; and so on. They are also social and economic: agrarian revolution, creation of a united national market, and elimination of all major obstacles to the industrialization and overall modernization of the country. In that sense, in no way can one say that the February 1917 revolution realized, through the overthrow of tsarism, the main unfulfilled tasks of the national-democratic revolution in Russia. These were only realized through the October revolution.

1.2. Bourgeois state power is an obstacle to the full realization of the unfulfilled tasks of the national-democratic revolution in less developed countries, not only for functional reasons, such as the inability or fear of the bourgeoisie to sufficiently mobilize the masses, for example, but for reasons of social and economic *antagonism of interests* with those of the great mass of the people. It results in the final analysis from the operation of the *law of uneven and combined development*, that is, from the objective social-economic structure of these countries which increasingly *combines*, albeit in a "conflictual" way, landed property, industrial property and banking property, "nationalist" capitalist property, and foreign imperialist property.

1.3. In less developed countries there can exist no "intermediate" or "combined" state power between that of the bourgeoisie (or of the old ruling classes) on the one hand and proletarian state power supported by the poor peasantry on the other. More precisely, the peasantry cannot play an independent role in the field of government and state power on a national scale, although it can certainly represent the majority of participants in the revolutionary process in a number of less developed countries. It is historically condemned either to follow the bourgeoisie or to follow the proletariat. In all less developed countries, the establishment of the worker-peasant alliance is an indispensable precondition for the victory of the revolution. But this alliance can only lead to victory if the hegemony of the proletariat over the peasantry is firmly established, that is, if the revolution leads to the establishment of the dictatorship of the proletariat.

1.4. The theory of permanent revolution represents both an explanation of what actually occurs during revolutions in less developed countries and what is necessary for the triumph of these revolutions. In essence, therefore, the theory of permanent revolution *corresponds both to a real historical process of revolution* and to a *strategy necessary for bringing that process to a successful conclusion.* While the revolution generally starts with a struggle for national and democratic tasks (although it can also start with the issue of peace), as the main (but not necessarily the only) demands of the exploited and the oppressed, it can only triumph through the destruction of bourgeois state power and the establishment of the dictatorship of the proletariat.

1.5. The fact that a full and complete realization of the unfulfilled tasks of the national-democratic revolution in less developed countries is impossible without the dictatorship of the proletariat does not mean *either* that a partial realization of some of these tasks (formal independence or partial agrarian reform, for example) is impossible *or* that in *all* countries the dictatorship of the proletariat is possible. In some less developed countries where the proletariat is too weak or hardly exists there can obviously be no question of establishing its "dictatorship." This implies simply that in these countries there will be no possibility at this time for fully realizing the historical tasks of the national democratic revolution, and that even under the best of circumstances their realization will remain fragmentary, haphazard, and distorted. Of course, this is not a reason for abandoning the revolutionary struggle against imperialism, neocolonialism, and oppression, even in the most backward countries.

2. *The conquest of political power by the working class in less developed countries is impossible without the proletariat (and its party or parties) gaining national hegemony through becoming the recognized political leader of the nation, that is, without carrying out the "reconstruction of the nation under the leadership of the proletariat" (Trotsky).*

This thesis is based on the following propositions:

2.1. The national and democratic tasks of the revolution—as specified above—represent a real central priority during the first stages of the revolutionary process. All the exploited and the oppressed generally recognize this priority and act accordingly. This does not mean that *all* of these tasks have the same weight in determining mass mobilizations, or that all sectors of the mass movement adopt the same central preoccupations. Nor does it imply that no tasks other than the national-democratic ones can come to the fore during the mass struggle in that first stage of the revolutionary process. Nevertheless, the centrality of the national democratic tasks corresponds to such political realities as the struggle to overthrow reactionary or repressive dictatorships, the fight to realize national independence when this banner is broadly raised, or the agrarian revolution when an important sector of the peasantry is already rising to conquer the land.

2.2. The proletariat is not the only social class engaged in mass struggles, and certainly not the only class politically supporting the central national-democratic goals in the first stages of the revolutionary process. Essentially the peasantry, the urban poor (semi-proletariat), and urban petty-bourgeoisie will be its natural allies in the struggle. This process can and should find its expression in political united fronts or other alliances in which the proletariat and its party (or parties) fight for political hegemony. This is the concrete way in which the "reconstruction of the nation under the leadership of the proletariat" develops, as these social classes, taken together, represent the overwhelming majority of the popular masses of any country.

2.3. The concrete process of the formation of such alliances and fronts—above all that of the worker-peasant alliance—cannot be predetermined by purely objective criteria. It depends on the concrete political alignments in each country—themselves a function of its past history, of the varying levels of consciousness of the working class and other social forces engaged in the liberation struggle, of the weight of the revolutionary vanguard party of the working class and its ability to organize and lead broad masses, including the peasantry. But while many variants of such alliances have occurred, there is no example in history of the "national" or "liberal" bourgeoisie accepting the political leadership of the proletariat and its party (or parties). Therefore, a successful struggle for the full implementation of the national-democratic revolution implies a systematic education of the workers, peasants, and urban poor in opposition to the bourgeoisie and its political parties, a systematic education of the masses in the spirit that the bourgeoisie is both unwilling and unable to realize a complete break with imperialism, a radical agrarian reform, and complete political democratization of the country.

2.4. Wherever strong bourgeois-national or petty-bourgeois nationalist parties have broad popular support, a successful struggle for proletarian hegemony in the revolutionary process is impossible unless this systematic education and denunciation is combined with a united front approach. This policy should include critical support to all proposals and practical steps which these parties might take in the direction of realizing popular national-democratic demands. There is nothing opportunist or class collaborationist in such a united front approach, provided the proletariat:

- keeps its organizational and political class independence;
- is not miseducated by propaganda which presents these bourgeois or middle-class political forces as "socialist" or "anti-capitalist";
- is not called upon to put a systematic brake upon mass mobilizations and self-organization, whenever these correspond to the real mood and aspirations of the toiling masses;
- is not led to subordinate the realization and consolidation of the worker-peasant alliance to the aim of avoiding a conflict with the "national" bourgeoisie or the petty-bourgeois nationalists;
- does not envisage any participation in a coalition government or any external support to such a government, or in any other way maintains or props up the bourgeois state and bourgeois class rule.

3. *The proletariat cannot conquer state power, even in the less developed countries, without defending its own class interests. This means that after having conquered state power, fighting first of all for national and democratic demands, it will, from the start, implement at least some socialist, anti-capitalist measures, for which it will have generally started to fight before the victory of the revolution. From these initial measures to the full scale realization of the socialist tasks there will be some delay, but not an indefinite one. The length of that delay depends on objective and subjective circumstances (the rhythm and concrete forms of the class struggle and its practical needs being the most important of these constraints). The permanent character of the revolution is expressed by the fact that there is no "stage" in which the proletariat will not fight or should not fight for its own specific anti-capitalist demands. There is likewise no "stage" in which the dictatorship of the proletariat can or will abstain from implementing at least some of its demands. The revolution "grows over" from the fight for national and democratic demands into a socialist revolution, without any interruption of continuity.*

This thesis is based on the following propositions:

3.1. The struggle of the workers for their own class demands, including anti-capitalist ones, is an aspect of the real class struggle, unfolding in less developed countries during the revolutionary crisis. It is not a "dogmatic prejudice" of "Trotskyists." The option is not whether to "prematurely unleash" that struggle or not. The option is whether to lead and consciously support the real emancipatory movement of the working class during the revolution or to actively oppose it, including by repression. Thereby the theory and strategy of permanent revolution are indissolubly intertwined with the Marxist theory of self-emancipation and self-organization of the working class. Revolutionists can and should try to lead the proletariat along the correct road to the conquest of state power by developing all the necessary tactics and alliances for achieving this goal. But they should never subordinate the defense of the class interests of the proletariat and the support of its independent mobilizations to alleged "political priorities" or "historical necessities." This has been the practical behavior of Marx, Engels, Lenin, Trotsky, and Rosa Luxemburg in *all* revolutions in which they participated or which they witnessed. A different attitude, as displayed by social democrats first and the proto-Stalinists, Stalinists, and post-Stalinists later, is one of the key aspects of a break with proletarian class politics, expressing the particular interests of labor bureaucracies.

3.2. There can be no break in continuity of state power, and therefore of the class nature of the government between the implementation of so-called "democratic" and so-called "socialist" tasks (of course, this does not mean of the actual composition of the government!). *It is the same state power which implements both.* The idea that a bourgeois state could implement even initial measures of socialist revolution is a monstrous caricature of Marxism, unsubstantiated by any historical fact. Like the idea that one could pass from a bourgeois to a proletarian state, from the class power of the bourgeoisie to the class power of the proletariat, without a real social and political revolution, it represents the quintessence of reformist revisionism. What *is* possible is the coexistence in a given country, for a certain time, of organs of power of two antagonistic classes, that is, *a situation of dual power* under different forms. But dual power always concerns *different* organs of *different* classes, not a single "combined" worker-bourgeois army or a single "combined" bourgeois-worker state apparatus.

3.3. The growing over of the revolution from fulfilling national and democratic tasks to fulfilling socialist tasks is a concrete historical process (the process of permanent revolution in its first aspect). It is impossible to determine the rhythm and scope of the combination of tasks of the revolution in advance in each country by "objective criteria" alone, such as the percentage of the proletariat in the active population, the degree of differentiation of the peasantry, the relative weight of the city *vis-à-vis* the countryside, and so on. Among the main actual determinants are the *realities of the class struggle*, which are both objective and subjective, and involve, among other elements, the internal logic of mass mobilization—the need to maintain and increase a high level of mass participation, mass self-activity, and class consciousness of the toilers and oppressed.

3.4. The strategy of permanent revolution also expresses the fact that a proletarian state power cannot pursue the road of building a capitalist economy, nor can it realize the utopia of a "non-capitalist and simultaneously non-socialized" road or economy. This is impossible in practice. It is also irreconcilable with a consistent defense of the day-to-day interests of the working class. While it is possible to have a rather large private sector in a socialized economy, as it is possible to have a rather large nationalized sector in a capitalist economy, in the final analysis either the proletarian state commands (including by despotic means against the bourgeoisie, which does not necessarily presuppose democracy for the working class) or the law of value commands. In the first case there is a break with capitalism. In the second case there is (re)integration in the capitalist world market. Some time can pass before the struggle between the two trends has come to fruition, but certainly not an unlimited period, or even decades.

3.5. The question of the gradual socialization of the economy, led either consciously by proletarian self-activity or by proletarian state power (even a bureaucratized one), or by various combinations of the two, as history has shown us, is completely distinct from that of a full-scale achievement of a socialist classless society. The first is a necessary but insufficient condition of the second. Likewise, as understood by all classical Marxists, the complete disappearance of private property, especially of the small peasants, hand-icraft workers, repair shops, small service businesses, and so on, can take decades if the proletariat is to avoid unnecessary social and political tension, conflicts, and internal divisions. This is provided that all the conditions for developing the socialized sector of the economy and for satisfying the basic material and moral needs of the toiling masses have been met. In and of itself the disappearance of private property does not automatically imply that a classless society already exists.

4. *The process of revolution in the 20th century begins on the national level, it unfolds in the international arena, and can only be completed by the world victory of the socialist revolution, or at least its victory in all the main countries of the world ("main" in both the sense of population and of concrete economic, military, and political weight).*

This thesis is based upon the following propositions:

4.1. The world character of the economy is decisive in the epoch of imperialism—the weight of the world market, the influence of that market on all countries, including those which have overthrown the national class power of the bourgeoisie. Workers' states can free themselves from the *domination* of the law of value and of the world market; they cannot free themselves from its *influence* except through establishing a qualitatively higher level of productivity of labor and satisfaction of consumer needs than the most advanced capitalist countries. It is absolutely utopian to believe that this could be achieved in one or a restricted number of countries, especially if these do not include the most developed ones from the point of view of industry, technology, skill, and the culture of the toilers, and the advantages these countries enjoy from the international division of labor.

4.2. The internationalization of the class struggle and of politics in the epoch of imperialism is nothing but the concentrated expression of the world character of the economy. This manifests itself both through the regular recurrence of international wars (two world wars and innumerable "local" wars) and through the tendency of all civil wars since 1917 to become international civil wars, with systematic intervention by foreign capitalist powers against the attempts of the proletariat to conquer, to consolidate, and to maintain its state power. The internationalization of the class struggle has an increasing tendency to assert itself even in "peaceful" times, including in "essentially" economic struggles, although this is not a mechanical tendency evident in all countries, in all moments and in all struggles to the same degree. In fact, the delay of the international proletariat to answer efficiently the high degree of internationalization of the capitalists' operations, designs, and projects is a growing obstacle on the road of successful workers' struggles even on a day-to-day trade union basis, let alone for the historical tasks of the proletarian revolution.

4.3. *It follows that it is impossible completely to achieve the building of a socialist classless society with the withering away of the state (the first stage of communism) in a single country or in a restricted number of countries, inasmuch as these do not include the most industrialized ones.* The pressure of the world market (including the pressure of new consumer demands and of "consumerism" in general), as well as the survival of the military-political threats and pressures from imperialism, implies that it is impossible to achieve a withering away of scarcity in one or a restricted number of countries, without which the withering away of social classes and of the state are unrealizable. Stalin's revisionist theory that it is possible to achieve the full building of socialism in one country is not only in opposition to the classical concept of Marx and Lenin, of the need for an international development of the proletarian revolution; it is above all opposed to their classical concept of a socialist society. It is an attempt to legitimize a society with growing social inequality and social tensions, a constantly strengthened state apparatus, and a monopoly of the exercise of power and control over the means of production and the social surplus by a privileged social layer (the bureaucracy) combined with a complete exclusion of the workers and the toiling peasants from the exercise of state power. This society is presented to the world working class as "socialist" or "really existing socialism." In fact, it is a rationalization of the dictatorship of the bureaucracy.

4.4. The impossibility of fully achieving the building of a socialist society in one country, or in a restricted number of countries, does not mean that once the proletariat has conquered state power it and other workers' states will have to wait for other victorious revolutions before new *advances* can be made *toward* socialism. A process of permanent revolution continues after the victory of the socialist revolution. It continues inside the workers' states as well as on the international arena. If the exercise of state power has been usurped by a privileged bureaucracy, this process passes of necessity through the phase of a new political, antibureaucratic revolution. If such a

usurpation has not occurred—if the working class can extend its exercise of
state power and its power to dispose of the social surplus product and the
decisive means of production by way of reforms—then this specific stage of
the permanent revolution will take essentially peaceful forms. There will be
a gradual restriction of the market and money economy, a gradual decline
of petty commodity production and ownership, a passage to successively
higher stages of a planned democratically centralized workers' management, and a gradual reduction of the state apparatus in favor of the direct
exercise of power by democratic self-administering bodies. The concrete
steps toward realization of these goals depend on a series of objective and
subjective conditions, among which the relative weight of the proletariat,
its level of culture and class consciousness, and the correct policies of the
vanguard party are of key importance.

4.5. The strategy of permanent revolution implies that under no circumstances should possible extensions of the proletarian revolution to new
countries be subordinated to the priority of "defending existing bastion(s)
of socialism." On the contrary, each new victorious revolution should be
seen as the most efficient way to defend the existing workers' state(s). No
contradictions can be construed between the interests of the proletariat (or
of the proletarian state) of any country and that of other countries. Such a
contradiction has no material foundation. What does have a material foundation is the contradiction between the interests of the labor bureaucracies
(including those of workers' states) and the interests of the working class,
both those of their own country and the world proletariat.

4.6. Counterposed to the dogma of "socialism in one country" is not the
absurd concept of "exporting the revolution" through "revolutionary
wars" or artificially "provoking" revolutionary uprisings which do not
enjoy the support of the majority of the toilers in other countries. Counterposed to it is a course of preparing the working class and its revolutionary
vanguard in other countries for the struggle for power under those favorable conditions when deep crises of bourgeois society coincide with rising
explosions of mass action, which make a conquest of power by the working
class objectively possible.

5. *The victory of the socialist revolution, not only in a single country or in a
restricted number of countries, but even on a world scale, is only the beginning and
not the end of the social revolution. While the conquest of power by the proletariat
and the abolition of private property are necessary prerequisites for the building of a
classless society, they are in and of themselves insufficient for assuring the establishment of social relations devoid of exploitation, oppression, and violence. The
revolution remains permanent after its political victory. A continuous revolutionary
transformation of the basic relations of production and of all basic superstructural*

relations (family, culture, ideology/religion, science, arts, ethics, modes of behavior, and so on) is indispensable for the final victory of socialism.

This thesis is based on the following propositions:

5.1. A socialist society presupposes a high level of development of the productive forces and a qualitative leap forward in the satisfaction of all rational needs for material goods (a saturation of these goods, which is the Marxist as opposed to idealist definition of plenty). But there is no mechanical correspondence between a development by leaps and bounds of basic consumer-needs satisfaction and the creation of basically socialist relations in all fields of social life. The second is not the automatic product of the first. It needs specific revolutionary transformations in each field of social life, sometimes simultaneously, sometimes in contradiction with each other, sometimes complementary to each other. It is in that sense also that the process of permanent revolution must continue, will continue, and actually already has continued after each victorious socialist revolution.

5.2. The desynchronization between the conquest of power by the proletariat and the disappearance of private property on the one hand and the establishment of really socialist relations of production and of distribution on the other is the most important source of the necessity of a permanent revolution in social life in the transition period between capitalism and socialism. It creates the material basis of all other contradictions. One of the main reasons for this desynchronization, even in rich, developed countries, is the delay of consciousness in relation to actual existence—the fact that the level of consciousness is to a certain extent the product of the past. A deep psychological revolution is necessary for work to be performed as the expression of individual needs, as the self-realization of the individual, as the rich unfolding of each personality, rather than in expectation of reward or fear of penalties. Likewise, a deep psychological revolution is needed for the individual to understand that it is a waste of time and an actual threat to the health and physical survival of humankind to remain obsessed with the continual accumulation of material goods, once a threshold of saturation of basic needs has been passed. Pure indoctrination will not achieve any lasting result in these fields. Material preconditions—a high level of self-management in production and a high degree of consumer satisfaction—are indispensable, as well as radical transformations of technology subordinating machinery to the needs of the producers. But real revolutionary experimentation, practice, debate, as well as deep conflicts, will occur before these psychological revolutions can be thoroughly realized.

5.3. Real exercise of power by the mass of the toilers (increasingly the mass of citizens) in the economy and the state presupposes high levels of socialist democracy, real power for democratically elected workers, and popular councils and political pluralism. But in order for these freedoms and these powers to become substantial and not purely formal, the mass of the toilers (citizens) must enjoy material and social conditions for the actual exercise of power. This implies a withering away of the social division of labor between producers and administrators, which in turn hinges on two preconditions above all: a radical shortening of the working day and a revolutionary breaking down of all barriers to culture and information. In that sense *a continuous cultural revolution*, the abolition of all monopolies of culture and communication, not only in the field of consumption but also in the field of production, is a necessary prerequisite for socialism. A radical revolution of the forms and content of education is closely interrelated with the cultural revolution.

5.4. In the same way as the full achievement of a socialist classless society is impossible in one or a small number of countries, so is the withering away of the state—the complete disappearance of all bureaucratic apparatuses. But this does not imply that under conditions of isolation of the victorious revolution—especially under relatively underdeveloped economic, social, and cultural conditions—that it is impossible to avoid a growing bureaucratization or bureaucratic degeneration of the workers' state and of society in its totality. While underdevelopment undoubtedly favors bureaucratization, growing bureaucratization is not predestined, especially once a certain threshold of industrialization and education of the toilers has been passed. Much depends on subjective factors, the experience and reality of the self-organization of the workers and the poor peasants, and the conscious understanding of the nature and dangers of bureaucracy by the revolutionary vanguard (especially its party) and its deep commitment to socialist democracy and workers' self-organization.

5.5. In no other field is the desynchronization between the victorious socialist revolution and the establishment of real socialist relations more obvious than in the relation between nations, incipient nationalities, and ethnic and racial groups. National prejudices, chauvinism, and racism in all its forms will survive long after the bourgeoisie has lost power and property. As a result, forms of national inequality and thus of oppression, as well as the inevitable nationalist reactions they provoke among the oppressed, will survive too. Without a revolution in inter-nation relations, a constant radical struggle against chauvinism, racism, and national inequality, a constant endeavor to demonstrate international solidarity and cooperation, especially to the oppressed and the poorer nationalities, these obstacles on the road to world socialism cannot be overcome. The need to free humankind from the threat of nuclear and other weapons of mass destruction, through the total and definitive banning of their production, means also a necessary restriction of national sovereignty, especially of the richest and most developed nations, in the interests of all humanity.

5.6. The oppression of women is the oldest form of social oppression, anterior to the establishment of class society. It will also unfortunately survive a long time after the abolition of capitalism, in the transition period between capitalism and socialism. Its radical disappearance is a necessary precondition for the victory of really socialist relations. This disappearance demands both the conscious development of "affirmative action" by the workers' states, that is, measures which make it easier to overcome in practice the consequences of thousands of years of sexist discrimination, violence, and inequality suffered by women, and the vigorous activity of an independent women's movement. Without a growing self-activity, self-realization, and exercise of power by women themselves it is impossible to achieve equality between the sexes.

6. *The theory and strategy of permanent revolution are also characterized by what they do not claim.*

That theory does *not* include any idea that:

6.1. The socialist *revolution* can only triumph simultaneously in all or many countries.

6.2. The proletariat (and the toiling masses) should not fight for power in backward countries when that conquest of power is possible, lest it becomes trapped in an impasse, is inevitably crushed by world imperialism, or becomes inevitably oppressed by a totalitarian bureaucracy.

6.3. The victorious workers' state has the duty to extend world revolution through revolutionary wars.

6.4. Progress of any kind, especially advances in industrialization, is impossible in a less developed country without the establishment of the dictatorship of the proletariat.

6.5. In the epoch of imperialism, under no circumstances and in no country could the "national" bourgeoisie move in any way against imperialism.

6.6. Even if the "national" bourgeoisie does make such moves, however hesitantly and temporarily against imperialism, the working class should give no support to these moves, lest it thereby automatically lose its class independence.

6.7. The working class of any country should subordinate its class interests to the alleged needs of defending or extending the revolution in other countries.

6.8. The impossibility of fully achieving the building of a socialist society in a single country (or a restricted number of countries) implies that before the victory of world revolution, no important progress can be made in the direction of the withering away of scarcity, of market economy, of social inequality, of restriction of bureaucracy, and of internal repression, independently of the level of development of the productive forces, the relative weight of the proletariat, its level of class consciousness, and the quality of the revolutionary leadership already achieved.

6.9. The inevitable survival of the state during the period of transition between capitalism and fully achieved socialism implies severe restrictions of political democracy (socialist democracy) in the field of freedom of organization, of freedom of expression, of free access to the mass media for opposition or dissenting tendencies, or the need for a single party system.

All these ideas are thoroughly mistaken, have never been formulated by Trotsky or serious adherents to his theory of permanent revolution, and in no way form any part of that theory.

Note

1. See, for example: the exchange between Doug Jenness and Ernest Mandel in *International Viewpoint*, Special Supplement, no. 32, 1983; the article by Jack Barnes, "Their Trotsky and Ours: Communist Continuity Today," in *New International*, 1, no. 1 (Fall 1983); and the document "The Present Stage of Building the Fourth International," in *Resolutions of the Twelfth World Congress of the Fourth International, International Viewpoint*, Special Issue, 1985.

8

Reasons for Founding the Fourth International and Why They Remain Valid Today

It has been alleged that the founding of the Fourth International was based on two predictions of Trotsky which turned out to be wrong. First, that the Second World War, which was then imminent, would lead to a huge revolutionary upsurge by the international working class, and that this upsurge would be greater than the one after the First World War, largely bypassing the traditional working–class organizations and giving a genuinely revolutionary current the historical opportunity for a decisive breakthrough. Second, that the Stalinist bureaucracy would come out of the war greatly weakened, if not overthrown, thereby losing its political stranglehold over the more militant sections of the international working class and anti-imperialist movement.

CONJUNCTURE AND STRUCTURE

Undoubtedly these perspectives kept different groups of Trotskyist cadres in various countries motivated in the late 1930s and early 1940s. When they turned out to be wrong there were important consequences. Many cadres broke with the Fourth International and often even with the workers' movement.

Others tried to adjust their continuing revolutionary commitment to a world which looked quite different from the way they had expected it to

---

This article appeared in the *International Marxist Review*, Vol. 3, no. 2 (London, Autumn 1988), p. 80.

look a few years earlier. In order to achieve that revolutionary goal, they thought it essential to revise essential parts of the Fourth International's program, with respect both to capitalism's further perspectives and the nature of the Soviet Union.

In any case the 1949–53 period saw the biggest crisis in the history of the Fourth International, which led to a disastrous split. It took the movement 10 to 15 years to overcome the negative results of the crisis, first through the 1962–63 reunification and then through May 1968 and the subsequent radicalization. Today the Fourth International, while still far too weak, is much stronger than it was in 1938, 1949–53, or 1963.

This fact alone would already be sufficient to prove that all those who believe the founding of the Fourth International to have somehow been connected with the short-term prognoses mentioned above are very much mistaken. History has proved again and again that any working-class or revolutionary organization, be it national or international, is built on quicksand if it comes out of a judgment about conjunctural circumstances or any other sort of analytical idiosyncrasies. Only those organizations with a program and activities corresponding to the historical needs of the proletariat, as expressed in many struggles for decades if not generations, are built on firm foundations. Such organizations will ultimately have a real influence if they also learn how to exploit opportunities and avoid disastrous mistakes.

The First and Second Internationals corresponded to the need for wage earners' class independence. This remains a key task of the class struggle as long as capitalism exists, as vital today as it was 125 or 90 years ago. The Third International combined that need with the aim of a revolutionary overthrow of international capitalism in the imperialist epoch. Today this is as burning a task as it was in 1914 or 1919.

The founding of the Fourth International corresponds to historical reality on an international scale of similar nature. We have to examine in a scientific way, without personal or "generational" impatience, disappointment, or discouragement, whether these historic needs are as real today as they were 50 years ago.

Trotsky's conjunctural articles—especially the more polemical ones— contain incomplete, imprecise, or even mistaken short-term perspectives— just like similar writings by Marx, Engels, and Lenin, not to speak of their later co-thinkers, even the most gifted ones. However, such errors are by and large absent from his main programmatic writings of that period, especially three key ones: *The Transitional Program, The Manifesto of the Emergency Conference of the Fourth International* of May 1940 (his political testament), and *The Revolution Betrayed*. The same is true of his three previous key programmatic works: his *Critique of the Comintern Program*, his

Permanent Revolution, and his thesis *The Fourth International and the War*, which is too little read and studied today.[1]

This point can be easily confirmed by the following paragraph of the 1940 *Manifesto* regarding the historical schedule for Trotskyist perspectives:

> The capitalist world has no way out, unless a prolonged death agony is so considered. It is necessary to prepare for long years, if not decades of war, uprisings, brief interludes of truce, new wars and new uprisings. A young revolutionary party must base itself on this perspective. . . . The question of tempos and time intervals is of enormous importance; but it alters neither the general historical perspective nor the direction of our policy.[2]

The same remark applies to the use of the word "period" throughout the initial chapter of *The Transitional Program*.[3] At that time war was not imminent and the European revolution had not suffered major defeats (with the exception of the Nazi victory in Germany). In fact, revolutionary victory was still possible in Spain and France. It would probably have prevented the outbreak of the Second World War. The huge Stalinist purges of 1936–38 could also have been prevented.

We also have reliable information that the decision to found the Fourth International was taken as early as 1933, with the Comintern's final demise as a revolutionary organization, in the same way as Lenin's call for the Third International was made as early as 1914, when the Social Democratic parties capitulated.[4]

THE BASIC CONTRADICTIONS OF OUR EPOCH

The need to found the Fourth International derives from the fundamental contradictions which have determined the history of the 20th century. They can be summarized in the following points:

- Since 1914, the capitalist mode of production has entered its period of historic decline. The huge productive forces built up by that system periodically enter into contradiction with the capitalist relations of production, the private mode of appropriation, and the nation-state. This has led to a succession of grave economic depressions, of wars, and of social explosions (crisis of all the basic social relations propping up bourgeois society). The longer the decaying capitalist system survives, the more these successive crises threaten to destroy the basis of material civilization and even the physical survival of humanity. Periodically, the productive forces are transformed into terrifying forces of destruction. While capitalism in the 20th century undermines the fruits of past progress in parts of the world, it blocks progress in other parts. The polarization of haves and have-nots in each capitalist country, in spite of the resources available, is interconnected with a worldwide polarization between relatively rich and relatively poor nations.

- The periodically explosive nature of the contradiction between the productive forces and the capitalist relations of production is also expressed through periodic rebellions of the *human* forces of production, that is, huge outbreaks of working-class struggles which paralyze the functioning of the capitalist system and objectively put socialist revolution on the agenda. These types of struggles are much more than the normal attempts of workers to fight for their immediate interests. They represent an instinctive attempt by the proletariat to reorganize society upon a new socialist basis. The basic crises produced by decaying capitalism/ imperialism can only be solved in a positive way, through the working class conquering power, destroying the bourgeois repressive apparatus, and building a workers' state. In imperialist countries this implies the radical elimination of capitalist property relations, and in the less developed countries at least the beginning of such elimination.

  But, contrary to all previous social revolutions in history, a socialist revolution can only achieve its goals *consciously*. So the outcome of the successive waves of explosive mass struggles does not depend only on the objective social relationship of forces between the capitalists and wage earners. It also depends on the relative level of proletarian class consciousness and the revolutionary quality of its leadership. These have proved to be inadequate in most cases. Therefore, most 20th-century revolutions have ended in partial or total defeat: "The crisis of humankind is the crisis of proletarian-revolutionary leadership." The 20th century thus unfolds as a century of crises and wars, revolutions and counter-revolutions.

- The first nationwide, victorious socialist revolution occurred in October 1917 in Russia. It was victorious because, under the leadership of the Bolshevik Party, soviet power, the building of a workers' state, the establishment of the dictatorship of the proletariat, solved the most burning political problems of the day—peace—and the key tasks of the national-democratic revolution. But the working class could not accomplish all these tasks and consolidate them (through a costly civil war) without at the same time trying to eliminate its own exploitation, in other words, without starting to build a socialist economy and society.

  While the U.S.S.R.'s modernization and industrialization led to spectacular successes, progress toward building a classless society was by and large stopped and actually reversed. The political counter-revolution triumphed in the U.S.S.R. through Stalinism, resulting in a monopoly of political power being held by a bureaucratic caste. This led to a growing social inequality. Workers have lost all control over their working conditions and the appropriation of their production. These conditions create the material basis for a mass rebellion against Stalinism, for a new anti-bureaucratic political revolution. This revolution is part and parcel of the world socialist revolution.

- The mistaken policies of the social democratic and Communist mass parties and the trade union leaderships prevented the successive waves of explosive mass struggles of the 1920s and 1930s from leading to victorious socialist revolutions. Their mistaken policies reflected major theoretical shortcomings, but in the last analysis they express specific material interests, those of the privileged workers' bureaucracies. Reformists and Stalinists (including post-Stalinist bureaucratized C.P.s) subordinate the interests of the majority of workers to the defense of their own privileges, which in the best cases are camouflaged as the defense of the working class's historic conquests (which obviously have to be defended). While the bureaucrats claim to defend the workers' "strongholds" and gains won through struggle, in practice they undermine them. Defending gains must not be counterposed to the struggle for new radical advances of the socialist revolution wherever and whenever they become possible. Hence the need to build new working-class parties. A real process of differentiation within the working class reflects this objective need. In each wave of explosive class struggle new natural leaders emerge in the factories, offices, neighborhoods, countryside, the unions, and inside and outside the mass parties. But this potential new leadership for the working class becomes dissipated if it does not create the nucleus of new political parties. Their potential as new *revolutionary* parties is likewise at risk if the lessons of more than a century of workers' struggles are not assimilated or if easily avoidable mistakes are made. So it is necessary for revolutionary Marxists to root themselves firmly in the working class, especially its vanguard layers, and to fight for their program, which embodies the whole historical experience of the world proletariat. New revolutionary parties need to be built on that basis.

• The growing internationalization of the productive forces in the imperialist epoch and the no less pronounced internationalization of capital and the class struggle means that the achievement of socialism in a single country or a small group of countries is impossible. This does not mean that socialist revolution is impossible in a single country, even a relatively backward one, or that these countries cannot *begin* to build a socialist society. But in this process they will be subjected to international capitalism's economic, military, and ideological pressure. This will be reflected, to varying degrees, in the internal splits which will at times block the road to socialism. The socialist revolution will begin with a victory in one country, it will be extended internationally, linking up with the international class struggle, and it will finally culminate in the construction of socialism on a world scale. The achievement of "socialism in a single country" is a reactionary utopia.

Just as "national-communism" is the organizational consequence of the "socialism in one country" theory, so the building of a new International is the consequence of the theoretical understanding of the world character of the class struggle in the imperialist epoch. Without the international organization of the proletariat, national workers' organizations will sink even more easily into the morass of national-reformism and national-communism. Without the international organization of the proletariat, the coordination and indeed the understanding of the international process of class struggle and the revolution will be infinitely more difficult, the defeats heavier, the victories more costly and more often immediately put into question.

We are convinced these five key problems of the 20th century show the necessity for the Fourth International, for a new revolutionary international of the proletariat. Finding a solution to these five problems is just as crucial today as it was 50 years ago.

There Is No Perspective for Capitalism

The main objection made against the theoretical analysis justifying the Fourth International—the objective necessity for the world socialist revolution to resolve humanity's crisis—is that it supposedly underestimates the capitalist system's adaptive capacities (and therefore the at least partial capacity it has for further progress). How can one talk about the "agony" of the system that has gone through exceptional economic growth from 1948 to 1968 (even up to 1973)? How is it possible to deny that in the main imperialist countries, as well as in quite a lot of so-called third world countries, during the same period there has been an unquestionable increase in living standards, skills, and culture of broad proletarian layers?[5]

Our reply is that it is the critics of revolutionary Marxism and not Marxists who have only a partial and incomplete view of world reality since 1938 or 1948. It is they who are guilty of subjectivism, utopianism, even blind dogmatism.

Let us accept that Marxists may have indeed underestimated the international capitalist system's adaptive resources.[6] But a question immediately arises: What was the price of such adaptability? How can one draw the balance sheet of the last 50 years without including the 100 million dead of the Second World War, without bringing in Auschwitz, Hiroshima, the millions killed in the colonial war since 1945, the holocaust of children dying of hunger and curable diseases in the third world since 1945 (a figure much higher than those killed in the Second World War)? Is it a secondary problem, this enormous mass of human suffering; is the concept of "agony" so misplaced when we survey this overall reality?

True, the decline of civilization is not linear or total. Unlike some infantile leftists, serious Marxists have never claimed that. Shouldn't we remember Lenin's famous phrase about there not being a situation where there is no way out for capitalism? Capitalism has to be overthrown. If it is not, then it can always sort itself out for a certain period at the expense of the exploited masses.

The delay in the world revolution has held back the tremendous contribution the human mind and human creativity could make to progress in the widest sense. But it has not stopped the human mind from functioning. Science and our understanding of reality proceed apace. The fruits of such endeavors are as yet only partially diverted to ends that are destructive of humanity and nature. We continue partially to benefit from such progress as proved by the lengthening of life expectancy and the fall in infant mortality worldwide over the last 50 years.

But this progress in production and consumption, paid for by the infinite suffering which preceded it or which still accompanies it, can only be temporary, precisely because it has taken place within the framework of an economic and social regime racked by insoluble contradictions. The postwar "boom" was followed by a new, long depression.[7] Marxists were not surprised by that, unlike the reformist, neo-reformist (post-Stalinist), and neo-Keynesian acolytes of the capitalists. We said this reversal of tendency was inevitable even before it took place.[8]

What remains today of the dreams of "guaranteed economic growth, full employment, and social progress"! Where are the real utopians if not in the camp of those who assumed that capitalism (sorry, the "mixed economy") was capable of ensuring all that? They have egg on their faces now with 40 million people unemployed in the imperialist countries, hundreds of millions unemployed in the third world, a fall in the real income of at least 10 percent of the Western proletariat (the emergence of the "new poor" is part and parcel of this), and a fall ranging from 30 to 50 percent in real wages in most dependent semi-colonial and semi-industrialized countries.

Finally, while capitalism may have been able to more or less adapt itself to a world marked by the crisis of the decline of its civilization, the threshold of inadaptability is gradually approaching. Few lucid men and women doubt that a new "adaptation" by world war, by the irresponsible development of technology, by the super-exploitation of the third world, by the erosion of civil liberties (torture is already institutionalized in more than 50 countries), would threaten not only civilization but the physical survival of the human race.

Formerly, the alternative was presented as "socialism or barbarism." Today it has taken the form "socialism or death." For it is impossible in the long term to avoid these disasters without ending the egotistical and competitive behavior that flows from the regime of private property and competition, which inspires double moral standards and the incapacity of extending real solidarity to the whole of the human race.

More "nuanced" critics of Marxism label this line of reasoning "excessive catastrophism." They do not deny the tendency for crises to multiply (social, economic, political, moral, military), which in any case would be a bit difficult since 1968. But they argue that these crises do not necessarily result in "final" catastrophes. Up to now they have been "absorbed" below the threshold mentioned above. There is mass unemployment, but it is proportionally less serious than during the 1930s. There is a "new poverty," but the unemployed and other marginalized people are not forced to sell their beds to buy bread. There is hunger in the third world, but the population there is still growing and not declining, which proves that the great majority are not dying of hunger. The economic depression is continuing and getting worse, but a "soft landing" for capitalism is nonetheless not ruled out. The working class is still capable of resisting the most provocative attacks the capitalists throw at it, but it is said to be sufficiently weakened for the bourgeois restructuring plans to go through. The tendency toward a strong state is deepening, but it will not necessarily take the extreme form of fascism. "Local" wars are increasing in number, but they do not necessarily lead to the world war, etc., etc. . . . .

ONLY THE WORKING CLASS IS CAPABLE OF OVERTHROWING CAPITALISM AND ESTABLISHING A SOCIALIST WORLD

There is no other social force but the working class anywhere in the world capable of overthrowing international capitalism and establishing a social order founded on universal cooperation and solidarity. Here we are talking about the working class in the classic definition of the term (already mentioned earlier)[9]—all those wage earners economically obliged to sell their labor power in order to obtain their means of consumption, since they lack access to the means of production and do not own capital. Far from declining in numbers or becoming heterogeneous or having a greater segmentation than in 1914, 1939, or in 1954, the working class is today stronger and less heterogeneous than at those times.[10] It is true that the billion-strong army of wage earners throughout the world is not growing at the same rate in every country at all times, nor are their living standards and working conditions bringing them closer together than they were at all times in the past. The development of the working class does not progress in a linear way. It declines (and becomes de-skilled) in certain sectors, regions, or even countries while progressing and becoming more skilled in others. But there are no data which prove that the long-term, worldwide tendency is one of decline, far from it.

The number of wage earners in the capitalist countries is already higher than the number of peasants, even if we include the most populous third world countries (India, Pakistan, Indonesia). Furthermore, this historic transformation has only taken place in the recent past. Just to put things in context, we should remember that when the October revolution took place wage earners were scarcely 20 percent of Russia's working population. Worldwide at that time peasants constituted 75 percent of the working population. Even in Europe, the United States, and Japan the proportion of wage earners was much smaller than it is today.

The fact that only the proletariat has the potential to overthrow capitalism and replace it with a social order based on solidarity and cooperation does not mean in any way that in the dependent semi-industrialized countries, and particularly in the most important semi-colonial countries, there is no need of allies in order to conquer and hold onto power. Even if they have become a minority in those countries, the poor peasants still represent an important social force. Peasants can engage in socially explosive struggles, and their main demands cannot be satisfied by the existing regimes. The worker-peasant alliance is still the main motor force for successfully carrying through a strategy of permanent revolution, the *sine qua non* for solving problems of underdevelopment.

Furthermore, the specific combination of development and underdevelopment which characterizes the emerging dependent semi-industrialized countries over the past two decades has led to the growth of a particular social layer—the marginalized, semi-proletarian urban population, the shantytown dwellers surviving without proper jobs through irregular work in the "informal" economy. This social layer, often a majority in third world metropolises (including the semi-colonial countries), are often arbiters of political struggles in the short term. It can and must also be won as an ally of the proletariat through a permanent revolution strategy which takes up the fight for urban reform, an indispensable complement to the agrarian revolution.

Sometimes the impact of "new social movements" is brought up to cast doubt on the proletariat's role as the main potential revolutionary subject in the world today. Concerning the definition of "revolutionary subject" we should note the confusion of those who blindly worship the "new social movements" or those who systematically denigrate them by defining them as petty-bourgeois.

One of Marxism's seminal ideas, without which historical materialism loses all its potential to explain history, is precisely the *concept of "social class" having an objective character*. Social classes exist and struggle against one another independently of the consciousness they have of their own class and of their own historic interests (this obviously does not mean the level of consciousness does not influence the development and end result of these struggles). A good proportion of American wage earners see themselves as being middle class. This does not prevent them leading tough strikes against the bosses, sometimes in a harder way than the wage earners of other countries, who have a much higher level of class consciousness. They behave like wage earners because they *are* wage earners, even if they do not see themselves as such.

Viewed from this perspective the great majority of the people involved in the "new social movements" are wage earners, at least in the imperialist and dependent semi-industrialized countries. This is a quasi-automatic consequence of the social structure of these countries, given the very size of the "social movements." The only social groups outside the proletariat from which they could recruit in a mass way would be housewives or school and college students. But these groups are a long way from being a majority either in the antiwar, ecologist, anti-imperialist, or antiracist movements. Only the student or school students' movement—as a mobilized mass movement—has up to now been the exception.

Confusion arises because the "new social movements" are organizationally, and often ideologically, not really connected to the organized labor movement. In fact, in most cases it is the labor movement's fault, since it has been slow or simply refused to take up the defense of the objectives of these struggles. Hence we have fragmented and tangential movements. As single-issue movements they often mobilize big numbers. But at the same time their fragmentation facilitates their diversion into reformist dead-ends. It is not possible seriously to defend the idea that students, housewives, or even third world peasants have sufficient economic and social power to *overthrow* bourgeois states in the main centers. They can weaken this power. They are vital allies of the socialist revolution. This is especially the case with the feminist movement. Its liberating potential concerns more than half the human race, and its independent effectiveness is considerable. It mobilizes an important sector of wage earners and a growing proportion of the proletariat as a whole. However, these social movements cannot on their own bring about the socialist revolution. This victory is necessary if humanity wants to survive. Only the proletariat is socially capable of making sure this comes about. Any other project of overthrowing international capitalism is unrealistic.

Just as unrealistic is the idea that used to be quite popular on the left, but which practically nobody supports today anymore, that imperialism could be overthrown through a combination of strengthening the "socialist camp" and victorious revolutions in the third world. To the extent this hypothesis implied a world nuclear war "won" by the "socialist camp" it was criminally irresponsible. It presupposed you could "build socialism" with atomic dust instead of with living men and women. Once this hypothesis was dropped the general approach was limited to the idea that a monstrous giant could be killed by cutting off a leg, an arm, and a few toes. Given the monster's vast resources for equipping itself with very effective artificial limbs it is a remarkably silly position to hold.

Other critics reply that if the proletariat is the only potentially revolutionary subject capable of overthrowing international capitalism, then the world socialist revolution becomes a utopian project, since the proletariat has shown itself incapable of carrying out any such revolution in any sort of advanced industrial country. In fact, throughout the history of the international workers' movement a refusal to recognize the *potential* revolutionary role of the proletariat has nearly always led to giving up any revolutionary perspectives or activity.[11]

But is it really correct, on the basis of the concrete experience of the last 50 years, to assert that the proletariat has ceased to be the revolutionary subject as Marx predicted? Merely to list all the defeats in successive revolutionary crises is not sufficient to prove this argument. Not only is the historical period much too short to draw definitive historical conclusions,[12] *but Marx's very analysis of the proletarian situation implied that the first wave of proletarian revolutions would be almost inevitably defeated.*[13]

The correct approach to this question is quite different. We must not start from the metaphysical norms which reflect idealized visions of the proletariat and the proletarian revolution, but from the real movement of the actual proletariat in history. We should ask: Is it the case that millions of wage earners have continued *periodically* (not every year or in every country) to mobilize in struggles of such scope that the possibility of working-class, popular counter-power is put on the agenda—in other words a generalization of dual power, of struggles that *can* lead to the overthrow of the bourgeois state and to the establishment of the dictatorship of the proletariat in the classic Marxist sense of the term? Have these struggles a tendency to broaden or to get smaller in the long term? Have they a tendency to paralyze bourgeois power more than in the past, or has the latter increased its ability to technically and materially defeat them? Do wage earners have a perspective of taking over the factories and centers of communication, or is this less so than before? Do they tend more or less than in the past to move toward self-administration and self-management?

We just have to compare the 10 million strikers of May 1968 with the 3 million of June 1936 in France, the 10 million Polish workers in Solidarnosc in 1979–80 with the ½ million who were involved in the general strikes of 1905–06 or the 1918–20 revolutionary movements in Poland, and those involved in the 1974–75 Portuguese revolution with the numbers of participating in previous struggles there. We can see that at least in a number of countries (we do not say all countries) there is a clear tendency for the numbers involved to increase significantly.

It is certainly true that the scope of these explosive mass struggles is not enough in itself to bring about victorious proletarian revolutions. But it is enough to make them *possible*. Once you accept that these revolutions, the only chance to ensure the survival of the human race, are possible, then a refusal to fight to bring about the conditions for their victory appears unreasonable. It means literally playing Russian roulette with the physical survival of humanity. Never was the equivalent of the "Pascalian gamble" in relation to revolutionary political commitment as valid as it is today. By not committing oneself everything is lost in advance. How can one not make that choice even if the chance of success is only 1 percent? In fact, the odds are much better than that.

WITHOUT ANTI-CAPITALIST THEORY AND PRACTICE NO ANTI-CAPITALIST VICTORY IS POSSIBLE

The fact that broadly based mass struggles strong enough to put on the agenda the objective possibility of overthrowing the capitalist regime only break out *periodically* presents Marxists with the problem of day-to-day activity. In the long term you cannot be involved in revolutionary activity cut off from mass actions and activity having at least objectively revolutionary effects. Any attempt at revolutionary activity isolated from the masses, incomprehensible to them, even has, by and large, counterproductive consequences. Furthermore, any activity exclusively focused on reforms, limited to what is immediately achievable (if not brazenly reformist, limited to what is acceptable to the bourgeoisie)[14] has three disastrous effects.

It tends to miseducate the masses, not preparing them for sharp turns in the situation, inevitable in our epoch.[15] So it means the masses approach prerevolutionary and revolutionary crises without understanding what is necessary and possible. In the same way it tends to objectively hold back and fragment, even consciously break up, mass struggles which threaten the consensus with the bourgeoisie, which go beyond the framework of the bourgeois state. It also tends to deform those organizations which follow such a line, making them less and less capable of understanding the future of capitalism[16] and of moving to revolutionary action when this becomes possible.

Various solutions have been proposed to this real difficulty. Retreating into (revolutionary) propaganda activity alone is obviously not a solution. An organization which abandons any intervention into the real class struggle other than a propagandist one degenerates almost automatically into a Jehovah's Witness-type sect.

Retreating into an exclusive identification with actual, ongoing revolution elsewhere in the world—following the practice of the Comintern, when it was controlled by the Stalinist faction, or of the Maoists—is also counterproductive. Such identification is useful and necessary as an indispensable feature of proletarian internationalism. But in no way can it replace an intervention into the class struggle of each country, starting from the objective needs and the real concerns of the masses, independently of what is happening in other countries.

Systematic and prioritized activity in the mass organizations and in the working class does not provide an adequate answer to the question. Certainly it is indispensable. But we come back to our starting point— intervention to do what, to carry out what activity?

If we combine everything that is positive about these three approaches (which are insufficient precisely because they are partial), we get closer to a satisfactory solution. It is summarized in what Trotsky and the Fourth International called the *strategy of transitional demands*.

Starting from the immediate concerns of the masses, which in nonrevolutionary situations remain by the force of things focused on economic, social, political, democratic, and cultural reforms and on opposition to war and the tendency toward a strong, repressive state, revolutionaries show in practice that they are the best organizers of these struggles, both in formulating their objectives and in action and organizational proposals. They try to ensure the maximum of success. But they combine this activity with systematic anti-capitalist propaganda, which constantly puts the masses on their guard against the illusion of continuous progress within the framework of the system. They warn them of the inevitable risk that these partial conquests will be canceled out totally or principally, and prepare them for the crises and inevitable reactions of the capitalists and their "democratic" state. Finally, they outline the necessary responses to these reactions and crises. These alternative responses are crowned with proposals about power, working-class power against that of the bourgeoisie.

This is not a purely pedagogical/literary task, although that aspect of the overall strategy must not be underestimated in any way. It has an impact on the real class struggle insofar as it tends to *constantly promote mass self-organization*, strike committees, neighborhood committees, committees centralizing these organs, and national coordinating structures in the mass movements. These are the indispensable *schools of experience* for the masses, without which no overall transformation of these struggles into generalized dual power and (this is even more the case) toward the seizure of power is possible in the industrialized countries. These are possible and necessary experiences even before the outbreak of prerevolutionary crises.

Here is where the reformist conception and the revolutionary conception of politics constantly come into conflict, at least in the framework of bourgeois-parliamentary democracy and independently of the precise conjuncture. For the reformists (and the neo-reformists of all shades) politics equals elections and activity inside the institutions of the bourgeois state. Strikes are considered to be fundamentally "economic" and therefore outside politics, indeed, apolitical. The same comment applies to their attitude to other forms of direct mass action (to the extent that the reformists and neo-reformists do not reject them entirely). So they have to be subordinated to electoral and parliamentary needs. This is the fundamental basis of reformist electoralism.

For revolutionaries, on the other hand, however important electoral-parliamentary activity may be,[17] it remains subordinated to the self-activity and self-organization of the masses, which is the real practice preparing the emancipation of working people. The emancipation of the workers can only be the work of the workers themselves and not that of parties or trade unions, whatever their indispensable role in this—not to mention that of parliaments or local councils. That is what Marxism is all about.

Reformist strategy and revolutionary strategy are opposed to each other not only because the first writes off the inevitability, indeed even the possibility, of revolutionary crises. They are in opposite corners when it comes to day-to-day activity in the class struggle even in a nonrevolutionary conjuncture. Reformists more and more subordinate the defense of workers' interests to "safeguarding the institutions" and "social equilibrium," in other words, to class collaboration. Revolutionaries defend at all times and against all forces the interests of working people and the political independence of the proletariat, not only from bourgeois parties but also with respect to the institutions of the bourgeois state.

The intransigent defense of socialist revolutions underway anywhere in the world is an integral part of the strategy of transitional demands. Above all it is a practical task, since these revolutions generally are subject to many forms of aggression by imperialism. Their resistance and survival as well as their later trajectory depends in good part on the size of the international solidarity movement which responds to this aggression. Ernesto "Che" Guevara was even more right than we understood at the time when he lamented the insufficient solidarity given to the Vietnamese revolution when it was under such severe pressure from imperialism in the 1960s (and this continued to be the case in the 1970s after Che's assassination). Even if the Vietnamese revolution finally ended in victory it did so in such conditions and at such a price that its whole future was heavily "mortgaged." The understandable psychological/ideological reactions from people on the left, faced with the Cambodian catastrophe and the way things turned out in Vietnam, would have been much more sober if the world workers' and anti-imperialist movements' co-responsibility in the Indochinese tragedy had been included in their understanding of these events.

It is also one aspect of the general struggle to raise the level of class consciousness. Internationalism cannot be learned in books (except for a

relative minority of individuals). For the masses it is gained through repeated activity. Solidarity action with unfolding revolutions is not the only
practical form of proletarian internationalism. But as long as the masses are
not deeply involved in revolutionary activity in their own country it is the
only way of raising consciousness to the understanding of revolution as a
fundamental historical reality for the broadest layers. It is of key importance
for their own future.

Given the enormous political experience of the bourgeoisie of the imperialist countries and the economic reserves available to them, it seems
ruled out that the proletariat can seize power without a level of class consciousness and a leadership that has been prepared years beforehand. So the
anti-capitalist component in the activity of the workers' movement is vital
for the future. If there is no coherent anti-capitalist theory, no systematic
anti-capitalist education, and no anti-capitalist activity by revolutionary
organizations, then no victorious proletarian victory is possible in the
imperialist countries, and therefore there will be no solution to humanity's
crisis, no future.

THE BUREAUCRACY CANNOT INTRODUCE
INSTITUTIONALIZED SOCIALIST DEMOCRACY

The inevitability of antibureaucratic revolutions predicted in the Fourth
International's program has been historically confirmed since the Second
World War. It has ceased to be a speculative idea. The explosive events of
June 1953 in the G.D.R., of Hungary and Poland in 1956, of Czechoslovakia in 1968–69, of Poland in 1980–81, and partially in China during the
1966–86 period give the concept of political revolution an increasingly
concrete form and content.

In fact, an adequate perception of the future of bureaucratized societies in
transition between capitalism and socialism is an integral part of the Marxist
political armory today. No correct international proletarian political activity is possible without such a perception. Also, the perspective of the antibureaucratic political revolution and the consequent political strategy is
opposed to:

• The ideology of "totalitarianism" and its allied anticommunist and anti-
  socialist analyses and political positions. Presenting the U.S.S.R., Eastern
  Europe, and China as countries where the revolution has not brought any
  progress, or in any case has brought more reaction and human misery
  than progress, is just not a tenable position given material reality and its
  consequences for the masses' activity and attitudes. Painting a picture of
  the masses as either totally terrorized or totally "integrated" by the

regime and therefore in both cases incapable of reacting and defending their interests, whatever the circumstances, can be seen to be quite false in the light of historical experience, including in the U.S.S.R.

- The idea of a strict parallel between the antibureaucratic political revolution and the socialist revolution in the capitalist countries, a parallel which is the corollary of any theory defining the U.S.S.R. as a capitalist country. The events listed above have all shown the ease and rapidity with which the masses were able to dominate the bureaucracy, precisely because the latter is not a class, neither a capitalist class nor a "new ruling class." On each occasion the intervention of an external military force was necessary to prevent a rapid triumph of the developing political revolution, almost without serious cost in human terms. It is difficult to see what would be the military force "external" to the revolutionary process in the event of political revolution in the U.S.S.R., certainly not the Soviet Army.

- The idea that bureaucracy—or (and this comes down to the same thing) healthy forces inside the ruling Communist parties—would, "under the pressure of the masses" or from their own perception of an unhealthy reality, or from a combination of both these reasons, radically abolish their own dictatorship, fundamentally democratize society and the state, and establish a workers' regime of self-management and self-administration—that is, a regime in which real power belongs to and is exercised by the sovereign and democratically elected mass workers' councils—has proved to be wrong. For revolutionary Marxists such councils must allow a plurality of political parties, the right of workers and peasants to elect whomever they want to the soviets, and the right of those elected to join together around different platforms in tendencies, factions, and groupings of their choice. All experience since the coming to power of the Stalinist faction in the U.S.S.R. confirms the incorrectness of the self-reform hypothesis—whatever the growing diversity of forms of bureaucratic power and domination in those bureaucratized societies that are in transition between capitalism and socialism (the bureaucratized workers' states). In no way does this mean the bureaucracy is incapable of carrying out any reforms, sometimes even very bold ones, when this is the price it has to pay for its survival. The imperialist bourgeoisie and even the bourgeoisie of several semi-colonial or dependent semi-industrialized countries have incidentally shown a similar capability. Just think a moment of the workers' self-management set up by the Yugoslav C.P. in 1950, the concessions the Nagy faction made to the masses in Hungary in 1956, the reforms implemented by the Dubcek leadership in summer 1968 in Czechoslovakia. Today's *glasnost* policy in the U.S.S.R. is along the same lines. But these reforms come up against an insurmountable barrier of social interests when they endanger the material privileges of the bureaucracy. Any real sovereignty of workers' and people's councils, indeed, any restoration of unrestricted democratic rights for the broad masses, will tend to have the same effect. This is why the reform movement will stop before these thresholds are breached (generally defined also by any challenge to the C.P.'s monopoly of power). Even if it is initiated by a wing of the bureaucracy, it can only break these thresholds if it is transformed into a genuine "revolution" from below, with powerful mass mobilizations and the emergence of various forms of self-organization by the proletariat and other working people.

The interaction between layers within the bureaucracy, triggered by internal contradictions of the system as well as by the first signs of popular opposition, *and* the subsequent development of an autonomous mass movement is part of the real process toward the antibureaucratic political revolution since 1948. The role played in this by de-Stalinization (de-Maoization) initiatives, such as the spectacular one taken by Khrushchev from 1955 to 1956, comprising not only the famous "secret report" to the C.P.S.U.'s 20th Congress but also the release of millions of prisoners, must also be understood.

The Fourth International was almost alone among the tendencies of the international workers' movements to have had a generally correct approach to this vast historic movement, although it has been mistaken sometimes on conjunctural judgments. This meant it had a more correct analysis of the evolution of these countries and the international situation as a whole (particularly during the Korean war, the Vietnam war, and when there was hysteria about the "imminent danger of war and extermination" at the beginning of the 1980s). This also permitted the Fourth International to assign the proper importance to solidarity with the antibureaucratic mass movements in the bureaucratized workers' states (specifically Hungary in 1956, Czechoslovakia in 1968, Poland in 1980–81) within a framework of trying to reconstitute the continuous unity of the world proletariat in line with the old maxim: one for all and all for one.

Above all it is a practical and political task, a duty all workers' organizations and in any case all international currents outside our own have failed to carry out. But more than that is involved. We need to understand that the antibureaucratic political revolution is an integral and an extremely important part of the world proletarian revolution, due to the fact (far from a secondary one) that a third of the world proletariat lives today in these countries and will participate in these revolutions.

Its importance for the world revolution is even greater today, owing to the profound discredit Stalinism and the post-Stalinist bureaucratic regimes have cast on communism, socialism, and Marxism in general. Today this is the main subjective obstacle preventing the masses of the industrialized capitalist countries from committing themselves to socialist alternatives.

Consequently, there is an objective dialectic between progress toward the antibureaucratic political revolution on the one hand and progress to the proletarian socialist revolution in the imperialist countries on the other. This dialectic operates in both directions. In today's world no decisive progress of the world revolution is even thinkable without the unfolding of this dual dialectic. Without this victorious political revolution there will be no solution to the crisis in the U.S.S.R., Eastern Europe, or China.

EXTENT AND LIMITS OF THE NEW REVOLUTIONARY GAINS

Trotsky's prediction that the Second World War would end in a revolutionary upsurge even greater than the one after the First World War, and that it would generally escape from the control of the traditional organizations (especially the Stalinist parties), turned out to be inaccurate. But it was not totally contradicted by what actually happened. There was a revolutionary upsurge, but more limited than expected, in Italy and France. There were new revolutionary victories but not in predominantly industrial/proletarian countries. These revolutions were led by parties of Stalinist origin (except for Cuba), but they had to break with Stalinism in order to lead the revolutions. These revolutionary victories have deepened the crisis both of the international imperialist system and of Stalinism but they have not led to the overthrow of either. This was the general historical context of the period stretching roughly from the end of the Second World War to May 1968.

The most infantile way of responding to the unforeseen turn of events was to deny it ever took place at all. Some comrades even went so far as to deny there had been a social revolution of unparalleled magnitude in China. Others, when pushed on it, accept that there had been something like "a revolution." But since it was not "the" pure proletarian revolution we had been waiting for, it was not a "true" social revolution that broke with the imperialist/capitalist system. Instead we were dealing with the seizure of power by "petty-bourgeois" nationalists or even by a "new ruling class" (which did not apparently exist until the moment it seized power!).

There is no point here in dwelling too long on the idealistic/normative character of these circumstantial analyses, which depart from Marxist methodology, or on the sectarian self-justification underpinning them. A social revolution is characterized by a fundamental change in property and production relations. Can one seriously deny that such a change took place in Yugoslavia, China, or Vietnam? A social revolution is also defined by the destruction of ruling-class power. Can one seriously assert that in Yugoslavia, China, or Vietnam power is held by the same social class that held it in 1940? On what facts can one base the proposition that the petty bourgeoisie, that is, the peasants, artisans, and "petty-bourgeois intellectuals," are in power *as a class* in these countries?

But once you recognize these revolutions are authentically social and anti-capitalist ones leading to the development of new transitional societies between capitalism and socialism, albeit bureaucratized, and the creation of new bureaucratized workers' states (these two concepts are synonymous for us), another theoretical difficulty arises. Trotsky said that Stalinism had definitively gone over to the side of bourgeois order in the capitalist countries. Now, here we had three authentic popular revolutions involving the mobilization of millions of men and women (tens of millions in China), which had certainly been led by parties of Stalinist origin.[18] Was Trotsky therefore mistaken on this question? Should all the traditional analyses of Stalinism by the Fourth International be revised?

Your answer to a large extent depends on the very definition given to Stalinism. This has to be materialist and not ideological.[19] Stalinism is the subordination of the interests of the masses to those of a privileged bureaucracy. Clearly, with their line of the revolutionary overthrow of the ruling classes the Yugoslav, Chinese, and Vietnamese C.P.s did not subordinate the interests of the revolution and the proletariat of their countries to those of the Soviet bureaucracy. It is also clear that neither did they subordinate these interests to those of some privileged Yugoslav, Chinese, or Vietnamese bureaucracy that did not exist at that time. Consequently, these parties ceased to be Stalinist parties from the moment they decided to take a line of working toward the revolutionary conquest of power at the head of a powerful mass movement.

Furthermore, they were only able to seize power because they had broken in theory and practice with Stalinism. They had refused to subordinate the revolutionary struggle to the interests, the injunctions, and "theories" of the Kremlin, and they did this years before the seizure of power. Saying that these changes were only due to the "pressure of the masses" reduces the decisive role of the subjective factor in the victory of a revolution to nothing. Indeed, such a line of reasoning leads to a paradoxical conclusion: Was it, then, the insufficient pressure of the masses which lay behind the defeat of the revolution in Greece, Indonesia, and Chile, as opposed to victory in Yugoslavia, China, and Cuba? Responsibility would then fall on the shoulders of the masses and not on the traitorous leaderships.

Reality is quite different. There was not less pressure from the masses (nor less severe counter-revolutionary threats) in Greece than in Yugoslavia, in Indonesia than in Indochina or China, in Chile than in Cuba. There were parties which acted differently. On one side they consciously worked toward the revolutionary seizure of power, and on the other (including the Stalinist Cuban C.P., as opposed to the July 26th Movement) they deliberately refused to do so, invoking the theory of revolution by stages.

The fact that the Yugoslav, Chinese, and Vietnamese C.P.s broke with Stalinism to lead the revolution in their countries *without becoming revolutionary Marxist parties* must not be blotted out of the analysis on the pretext that the only thing that counts is the seizure of power. The partial and not total break with their Stalinist past meant the leadership of these parties still held bureaucratic organizational positions in terms both of their internal regime and their relations with the masses. Consequently, these revolutionary victories were not accompanied by the institutionalization of direct (soviet) workers' and people's power. From the beginning the party apparatus was identified with the state. The bureaucratization and depoliticization of the masses—both reinforced by the rapid emergence of the exorbitant material privileges of a new bureaucracy—become more and more firmly established. We can legitimately speak of socialist revolutions bureaucratically manipulated and deformed from the start. True, such definitions are unwieldy and a little complex but they do give a better account of a real historical process in all its complexity.

The reality that these parties were not revolutionary Marxist has gradually become an obstacle to further progress of the revolution both domestically and internationally. While the victory of the Chinese revolution severely upset the relationship of forces on a world scale—dealing a mortal blow to the colonial system as it existed in 1940 and as imperialism still wanted it restored in 1945—the actual political/ideological forms the victory took contributed a great deal to the defeat of the Indonesian revolution and to the paralysis of the revolutionary movement in India. On a more modest scale the pole of attraction represented by China, combined with the political/ideological confusion produced by Maoism (including its final form of the Cultural Revolution), helped divide and weaken the revolutionary forces emerging in the imperialist countries out of the 1960s' youth radicalization, particularly after May 1968. In the same way these things lessened the possibilities opened in this period for a broader recomposition of the international workers' movement and politically destroyed dozens of thousands of revolutionary (or potentially revolutionary) cadres in Europe, Japan, and North America.

Later in Cuba, Grenada, and Nicaragua authentic socialist popular revolutions took place that are clearly distinguished from the Yugoslav, Chinese, and Vietnamese revolutions because they were led by revolutionary parties coming not out of Stalinism but from differentiations and developments of anti-imperialist and socialist currents within their own countries. Consequently, the processes of bureaucratization of power have been much less in these countries compared to the others. Also, limited and still insufficient steps have been taken toward an institutionalization of workers' and people's power, more locally than nationally. As a result of these real differences, the Cuban revolution and the Cuban workers' state have continued to make revolutionary progress a long time after the seizure of power, a progress which has had a real influence on a part of the anti-imperialist and workers' movement in Latin America.

But here again, the non-assimilation of the essential tenets of revolutionary Marxism has had serious political consequences. The absence of authentic socialist democracy in Cuba becomes increasingly a brake on further economic progress. The paternalist conception of the party involves serious risks of political and social conflicts.[20] The subsequent identification of the party with the state greatly limits the internal influence of the Cuban leadership for promoting the revolution in Latin America. Inevitable diplomatic maneuvers of the Cuban state tend to influence if not dictate the tactical, even strategic, advice given to revolutionary forces in the rest of the continent. The lack of revolutionary victories up to now in Latin America weakens in turn the position of the Cuban state against imperialism, increases its material dependence on the Soviet bureaucracy, and deepens the dynamic of crises in Cuba itself. The question of supporting the revolutionary Marxist program as a whole is not, therefore, an insignificant or secondary detail even in the case of Cuba and Nicaragua.

Given the qualitatively different character of the Cuban and Nicaraguan leaderships, one question is raised: Could these cases be repeated and thereby pose in quite new terms the question of a new revolutionary leadership of the proletariat on a world scale?

It is not serious to assert that in no country of the world can a revolution ever triumph without a revolutionary Marxist leadership. Revolutionary forces can emerge here or there within an essentially national or "regional" framework of differentiation, as occurred in Cuba, Grenada, and Nicaragua. In order to assess this possibility you have to drop any dogmatic predispositions—either "positive" or "negative"—and concretely study in practice the choices, activities, and dynamics of such and such a revolutionary organization (for example, in El Salvador, Guatemala, or the Philippines). There is no ready-made answer. It depends on the concrete practice of such organizations over a long period. *But we are convinced we are talking here of only a few exceptions.* To grasp this exceptional character we need to recall the particular conditions of the victories in Cuba and Nicaragua:

- The genuinely independent character of the revolutionary leaderships, above all, from the bourgeoisie and the Soviet bureaucracy.
- The weakness, demoralization, and extreme decomposition of the ruling classes.
- The weak tradition of proletarian self-organization.
- The relative paralysis of imperialism, given the unforeseen turn in the

revolutionary process and the failure of its political maneuvers.
- The superior political quality of the revolutionary leadership, acquired through long activity and growing authority among the masses, a precondition for successfully countering imperialism's political maneuvers.

If we examine the situation in all the imperialist countries, in the dependent semi-industrialized ones, and in most semi-colonial countries, we can see that nowhere are all the factors enumerated above to be found nor even a majority of them, which explains how the Cuban and Nicaraguan victories came under a nonrevolutionary Marxist leadership.

EXTENT AND LIMITS OF THE RECOMPOSITION OF THE WORKERS' MOVEMENT

The case of the Castroist and Sandinista leaderships must be placed in a larger context: the ongoing recomposition of the workers' movement in a growing number of countries. Historically this process began with the victory of the Cuban revolution, was brought to a brutal halt in Latin America with the defeats of the revolution in Venezuela, Brazil, Bolivia, and Chile, was relaunched with May 1968, the Italian "Hot Autumn" and the Portuguese revolution, and has continued since then, albeit at an uneven and spasmodic pace. It is the reflection of a rise in struggles partially escaping from the control of the traditional leaderships.

The most spectacular expressions of this are: the emergence of the Workers Party in Brazil, a mass-based, class-based socialist party with a programmatic orientation to the socialist revolution; the mass trade unionization of Black workers in South Africa; and the rallying of the majority of the Polish proletariat for a time within the ranks of the independent trade union Solidarnosc (and then, after the illegalization of Solidarnosc by the Jaruzelski dictatorship, identifying with it). These three formations already influence millions of workers. One of their features is support for internal democracy and self-organization qualitatively superior to that of the S.P.s and C.P.s. On a more modest scale a similar process is taking place in several Central American countries, in Mexico, the Philippines, Peru, and Denmark. Although regroupments of the still small far-left forces, which have a certain weight in the trade union movement and in the "new social movements" in certain European countries, do not come into the same category, they do indicate that something comparable is becoming possible in several countries. Everything indicates that countries like South Korea, several Eastern European countries, even Argentina, could go through similar developments. Of course, in most imperialist countries and in several dependent semi-industrialized countries the traditional bureaucratic apparatuses—whether political (reformist, neo-reformist, post-Stalinist) or trade union (particularly in the U.S.A., Argentina, and Mexico)—continue to be the main obstacles blocking mass struggles and the conquest of working-class political independence. Historical experience over the last 50 years confirms the lesson drawn from the revolutionary upsurge of 1917 to 1921—this obstacle cannot be removed simply through denunciation of the successive capitulations of these apparatuses to the bourgeoisie. These capitulations led to serious defeats of the working class. While denunciation is correct and necessary it must be combined with a *united front tactic* intelligently applied by the revolutionary forces. In this way the revolutionaries will be seen as a political tendency standing resolutely for unity on all the questions and objectives of the masses' central struggles—in fact, it must be *the most pro-unity of all currents*.

We should understand that the continued control of the reformist apparatuses over the workers' movements, not to speak of the working class, in the main imperialist countries is relative and not absolute. It is above all an electoral influence. Even here it is not as absolute as in the past, that is, in 1945 or even in 1968 (apart from Britain, where it has been maintained).[21] Furthermore, this electoral influence is rather a reflection of lesser-evil options than a systematic opposition to fundamental social changes. Alongside this there is a growing skepticism, seen particularly in the massive abstentionism of the American working-class electorate, despite calls from the trade union bureaucrats each time for a vote for the Democratic Party presidential candidate. At the same time there is a real erosion in the traditional apparatuses' control inside the trade unions. The most spectacular example is in France. In this country the Social Democrats have received the most votes in their history and yet their presence in the workplaces is marginal (sometimes even less in absolute figures than the revolutionary activists). They are a minority in most of the trade unions.

In fact, if we look more closely we can detect a complex process of recomposition of the workers' movement (the relations between working people and its old and new organizations) underway in practically all countries even if it does not have the same form in every case. You have developments inside the trade unions, inside the traditional political parties, the emergence of new currents and formations, and progressive differentiations inside these formations. These processes join together in different proportions in the various countries and change from stage to stage.

Once again, we need to understand and approach this real movement without pre-established schemas that are claimed to be valid for every country. We should look at what develops in each concrete case in terms of the real forces and opportunities to go forward in the building of new revolutionary leaderships of the proletariat. We have to take into account the specificity of the workers' movement, the mass movement, and the class struggle in each country. No particular tactic should be rejected in advance—as long as the tactic does not disarm revolutionaries in their historic task of winning the majority of the working class for the fight to overthrow the bourgeois state and capitalism.[22]

While the level of real control of the traditional apparatuses over the working class and the mass movement is in the process of changing, compared to the state of affairs after the Second World War, in the 1950s, and even in 1968, there are as yet no authentic mass revolutionary parties being built, parties consciously for the socialist revolution and preparing the masses for that end (the case of the Brazilian P.T. is probably the closest to that stage, but even here the decisive test is still to come). This situation is *an intermediary one characterized by a predominantly half-way political class-consciousness.* Broad vanguards have emerged, having more advanced positions than the reformists and neo-reformists on a whole series of political questions, but they do not yet have an overall anti-capitalist political project.

There are many reasons for this intermediary class consciousness of the (new) working-class vanguards:

- The great disillusionment caused by the classic Stalinist (post-Stalinist) and social-democratic political projects which for decades have failed and led to repugnant capitulations.
- The lamentable situation in the U.S.S.R. and China, which is by and large recognized as such by these vanguards.
- The disastrous military interventions in Czechoslovakia, Poland, and Afghanistan, as well as the horrific Pol Pot experience.

All this burden of negative experiences is not yet compensated by pilot experiences comparable to the October revolution or even the 1936 Spanish revolution, which could really sustain hope on a historic scale for the world proletariat.

But underlying this explanation, which emphasizes the weight of the subjective factor, there is also an objective materialist explanation. *The building of mass revolutionary parties can in the last analysis only result from a real working-class movement, combined with an adequate intervention by revolutionaries.* Now, while there have been big class-struggle movements at different times over the last decades, involving the key sectors of the working class of some important countries (France, Italy, Great Britain, Brazil, Spain, Poland, Argentina, partially Mexico, just to list the main ones), some of the main armies of the world working class are absent from the political scene: in the U.S.A., U.S.S.R., China, India, and to a large extent Germany and Japan. If the proletariat of these key countries either developed an independent political movement or even engaged in strong mass struggles—which in present conditions could scarcely be safely channeled by the traditional apparatuses—it would turn upside down the scope, pace, and content of the process of recomposition of the international workers' movement.

Meanwhile, revolutionary Marxists must continue to act while recognizing the fact that the crisis of the revolutionary leadership of the proletariat is not yet resolved in any of the imperialist or dependent semi-industrialized countries. Mass revolutionary parties still have to be built—especially as the conditions for their construction have become clearer and more realistic—and as real progress has been made in several of these countries.

Revolutionary Marxists take their full place in the ongoing process of recomposition, where it is happening and in ways relating to the specific situation of each country, with all the enthusiasm and loyalty that such a renewal requires. But nowhere in carrying out such tasks do they sacrifice the intransigent defense of their program. This refusal to drop their program is not sentimental faith or routinism and even less sectarian self-assertion. It reflects their deep conviction that if essential elements of the program are not assimilated then it certainly will lead the workers' movement into disastrous defeats. This does not mean in any way that this program should be considered already finished or that it does not require periodic enrichment in the light of new objective demands and new experiences of the mass movement.

In the same way, while participating in the tasks required for the recomposition of the workers' movement, revolutionary Marxists do not sacrifice the building of their own current as a specific political-organizational task at all levels:

- forming a leadership and achieving its continuity;
- educating cadres;
- intervening in struggles;
- implanting the current as a priority in the workers and trade union milieu;
- creating an identity with a long-term political project;
- taking political initiatives in a flexible way.

This sort of approach is in turn justified by our opinion that a revolutionary leadership will only be built over a long period—at least in the industrialized countries and especially where the bourgeoisie and the proletariat have a long political experience.

Paradoxically, it is during nonrevolutionary situations and phases that the essential contribution to building revolutionary leaderships and parties must be made. When the revolution starts there is too little time to go through certain stages of party-building. These tasks have to be well on the way to completion in the previous period.

THE CHALLENGE OF INTERNATIONALIZATION

The main weakness of the new organizations that have emerged or are emerging within the present process of recomposition of the workers' movement is their refusal to build simultaneously a national and an international organization. In the best of cases this leads to a new version of "national-communism." In the worst of cases it combines a misunderstanding of key aspects of the world class struggle with political positions that abandon or even betray the defense of the interests of whole sections of the international proletariat.

This deficiency is particularly striking since at the same time there is a literally dramatic "internationalization" of crises and decisive problems of the survival of the human race. To a qualitatively greater extent than in 1914, 1939, or 1945, these problems can no longer be resolved except on a world scale. The three main ones are: avoiding nuclear catastrophe; avoiding ecological disaster; and solving the problem of hunger and underdevelopment in the third world.

Given the present level of our knowledge it has been established that a nuclear war (or a biological/chemical one), even if only a part of today's arsenal of massive destruction were used, would mean the destruction not only of civilization but of the human race itself. *In these conditions, preventing a world war (nuclear, biological, chemical) becomes the central strategic objective of the international workers' movement.* If we fail in this objective, any project of world revolution or building socialism loses all meaning. You cannot build socialism on a lifeless planet.

Our differences with the radical pacifists do not relate to the objectives we need to achieve. We agree with them wholeheartedly on this. We recognize the vital contribution they have made to a new scientific, rational, and non-sentimental consciousness about new conditions for the class struggle and revolutionary struggle today, given the permanent threat of humanity's collective extermination.

Our differences with the pacifists turn on the necessary conditions for the definite elimination of this mortal threat. Revolutionary Marxists are convinced that it is an illusion to think we can ensure peace in the world and avoid the nuclear (biological/chemical) holocaust without the overthrow of capitalism and the sovereign national state in the countries holding or potentially holding arms of mass destruction. It is a particular illusion to think partial arms agreements—however worthwhile and positive they may be—combined with a growing pressure from the mass anti-imperialist, antiwar movements will be enough to avoid the nuclear (biological/chemical) holocaust. We criticize the pacifists in the end not for exaggerating but for underestimating the gravity of the danger, at least in the long term.

The bourgeoisie has also become conscious of the implications of the suicidal threat involved in the massive use of such arms of extermination. Consequently, it does not see a world war as a "solution," however perverse and inhumane, to its crisis (starting with its economic crisis), as was still the case in 1914 or 1939. A dead bourgeoisie will not resolve the capitalist crisis by "selling" destroyed "commodities" to atomized "customers." So it is unlikely that any fairly rational leadership of a bourgeois state will deliberately unleash a nuclear world war.

But unfortunately, this statement of facts is not the end of the question.

First, as long as significant stocks of nuclear weapons remain spread about the world there is a permanent risk they might be detonated by accident, a risk that increases with the shortening of the operational responses and automation of the systems. The precondition for a first threshold of guarantees against the threat of nuclear destruction is consequently not partial nuclear disarmament but total nuclear disarmament, the *complete* destruction of all nuclear, biological, and chemical weapons and a *definitive and guaranteed* ban on their manufacture. It seems ruled out that this can be achieved while capitalism survives. Prevalent military strategy in the imperialist countries and all the logic of the market/profit economy invalidates any hypothesis of real disarmament under capitalism.

Second, even if there were a total elimination of nuclear weapons the mere fact that there are hundreds of nuclear reactors in the world would transform a "classic" world war, or even a large-scale "regional" war in several key zones, into a nuclear holocaust, since each of these reactors could turn into a sort of "nuclear warhead" under the effect of a conventional bombing raid. Since 1945, local and regional wars, caused nearly always by imperialism, have resulted in millions of deaths and have continued practically without interruption. It is an illusion to think the coming decades will be any different in this respect. As long as capitalism survives, the threat of exterminating the human race will remain—whatever the level of consciousness about this threat worldwide, even among the bourgeoisie.

It should be also understood that as the arms race continues, driven especially by the "long depression,"[23] more and more devastating conventional weapons are being produced. Already, "ordinary" artillery shells can have a destructive capability equal to the atomic bombs that destroyed Hiroshima and Nagasaki. Tomorrow this capability could be even greater. The distinction between a nuclear world war and a conventional world war is shrinking. Total (not only nuclear) disarmament is therefore a condition for the survival of the human race. Expecting this total disarmament without the abolition of capitalism is even more illusory than expecting nuclear disarmament without a victorious socialist revolution.

Finally, while it is true that rational representatives of capitalism would doubtless not deliberately commit nuclear hari-kari, it has been in no way proved that the bourgeois state is always and everywhere led by rational politicians. History has given us the example of at least one great imperialist power—Nazi Germany—led by a fanatical adventurer, behaving more and more irrationally at the end of his career, who firmly opted for his own suicide and that of his class, state, and nation. It would be imprudent, to say the least, to claim such an extreme case would not repeat itself in similar historical conditions of economic, social, and political crisis of the system and during an ideological/moral crisis of the bourgeoisie (just think of the American far-right with its "better dead than red" mentality).

So it is the outcome of the class struggle in the U.S.A., France, Britain, and tomorrow surely in West Germany and Japan which will decide what form of government and political personnel will lead these countries—as was the case in Germany 1929–33—and which will resolve the question of whether the nuclear holocaust becomes a tangible threat in the short term if the workers' movement and the "new social movements" are crushed.

In the long term there is no possibility of avoiding the destruction of civilization and humanity through external pressure, the "balance of forces," the strengthening of the "socialist camp," the growing consciousness of the nuclear danger, and so forth. Only the takeover of all factories capable of producing weapons of mass destruction by the producers themselves, and their collective resolution to destroy all the existing stocks of arms and definitively prevent new production, can guarantee the survival of the human race. This cannot be guaranteed either nationally or on a continental scale. The establishment of the World Socialist Federation is the only conceivable solution for lifting the threat of extermination forever. This can only be the result of the proletariat winning the class struggle in each of the key countries.

A "new reality" of recent decades has to be brought into consideration here. While most of the continuous wars we have seen since 1945 are the responsibility of imperialism and the international bourgeoisie, not all fall into this category. There have been several military conflicts between post-capitalist states (bureaucratized workers' states): the Soviet-Chinese military conflict, the Vietnam-Cambodian war, the military conflict between China and Vietnam (the intervention of Warsaw Pact troops in Czechoslovakia has to be added here, although this did not lead to a military confrontation).

Trotsky himself could not foresee this final and terrifying logic of the bureaucratic ideology of "socialism in a single country" and of "national communism." The importance for the future of the human race of consistent internationalist education and activity—without regional restrictions or "messianic national communism" of any sort—only becomes more vital. Once and for all we must finish with the idea that there can be some sort of "bastion" to be defended over and above the need to ensure the survival of humanity worldwide. We have to work to turn the working class as a whole towards a consistent internationalism.

It is not necessary to repeat the detailed arguments concerning the problem of extermination by war when we refer to the threat of ecological catastrophe or of hunger in the third world. Our differences with the ecologists or "third worldists" in no way centers on the extent of these threats. We totally share their concern on this. As for the pacifists, we acknowledge their merit in having raised people's consciousness on a question that is inherent in Marxism but which has been insufficiently articulated, concretized, and taken up by the organized workers' movement (including sometimes by its revolutionary wing).

Our differences are all to do with the conditions for eliminating these dramatic threats. While supporting all struggles for immediate, partial, transitory solutions we think that "pure" ecologists and "third worldists"—those who are not socialist, anti-capitalist, and revolutionary—seriously underestimate the structural links between these growing threats and the maintenance of an economy based on private enrichment, competition, profit, capital accumulation, the market economy, and the consequent social behavior and mentalities. These problems will only be solved by a radical break with this logic. These problems can always re-emerge as long as things remain within the framework of the capitalist system and bourgeois society.

Faced with this "internationalization" of humanity's crisis, "campism" loses all credibility. This is particularly true when, under Gorbachev (we cannot foresee his future either), the Kremlin masters are increasingly challenging such a position themselves.

The Kremlin bureaucrats have taken a step forward in dropping criminal and inhuman utopias, like the one they used to promise of "winning a nuclear war." But they are not replacing this line with a much better alternative.

In fact, there are only two coherent responses to the challenge of internationalization. One consists in thinking that, given the threats confronting the whole human race, imperialism and large-scale capital (what the post-Stalinists reduce unscientifically to "the monopolies") will gradually change their character. This argument suggests they will abandon their most aggressive and competitive practices, will stop behaving as imperialists, and will accept progressive cooperative relations with post-capitalist societies, the third-world peoples, and their own working classes. It is supposedly necessary to "encourage" them in this development, carefully avoiding anything that could exacerbate any contradictions, especially dropping any revolutionary activity.

The other response starts from the conclusion that in the present stage of the crisis of bourgeois society the exacerbation of these contradictions is periodically inevitable whatever politicians, ideologists, economists, or workers' organizations do. Consequently, the only adequate answer to the challenge of globalization is to accept the seriousness of the threats and to adopt an orientation toward the only possible solution of the crisis—the creation of the World Socialist Federation by the successive victories of the proletarian revolutions in the main countries of the world (socialist revolution in the capitalist countries, antibureaucratic political revolution in the main bureaucratized workers' states, and permanent revolution in the major third-world countries).

The first response is based on a serious underestimation of the crisis of the system and of its terrifying dynamic. It is utterly unrealistic and illusory. The second is undoubtedly more difficult to get accepted in the short term by the broad masses. But it is the only realistic way forward. To the extent that the second tends to fit better with the real march forward of history it will also be increasingly better understood.

WITHOUT INTERNATIONAL THEORY, PRACTICE, AND ORGANIZATION THERE WILL BE NO BUILDING OF THE WORLD SOCIALIST FEDERATION

The delay shown by the main groups emerging today from the recomposition of the international workers' movement in taking up a consistent internationalist commitment has a great many causes. Among the subjective causes we can mention in particular the bad experiences of the manipulative bureaucratic-administrative "centers," which go right back to the Zinovievist deformation of the Comintern.[24] The culminating point was reached with the Stalinized Comintern; then there was the Cominform, the attempts by the Kremlin to maintain control over the "international communist movement," the Chinese efforts to align Maoist groups on the twists and turns of Chinese diplomacy, and so on. Skepticism certainly exists about the possibility of combining international policies valid for all countries with the specific state of the class struggle in each country—a skepticism that has been particularly fostered by the bankruptcy of the Second International in 1914 in failing to hold a common world front against the war, despite all the solemn commitment entered into beforehand. But objective causes, which are in the final analysis more important, must be added to these subjective reasons.

For parties already in power, the unavoidable obligations of diplomatic maneuvers make it impossible to take completely into account the interests of the world proletariat, since at certain times and for certain countries there is a contradiction between these interests and the immediate consequences of the maneuver. This does not imply that revolutionary Marxists have to condemn the necessity of such maeuvers. It does imply the need for a clear separation between any state policies and the class policy of the world proletariat. It is impossible to achieve this separation if it is not organizationally institutionalized.

Lenin understood this. This was one of the reasons why he pushed for the rapid creation (some said at the time it was premature) of the Communist International, not to give Soviet Russia a supplementary instrument to manipulate but, on the contrary, to counterbalance the obligation of Russian communists to maneuver as a state on the world political scene.

For Lenin, Trotsky, Zinoviev, Bukharin, and all the Comintern leaders it was quite straightforward that when Soviet Russia concluded the Brest-Litovsk peace accords with Germany and Austro-Hungary, the duty of revolutionary socialists in the three countries and elsewhere was not to defend this treaty but to denounce it as a *diktat* imposed on Russia by imperialism. When Soviet Russia later concluded an agreement with capitalist Germany at Rapallo, which even included the beginnings of military collaboration, the German communists did not suspend for one day their struggle to overthrow the German government and bourgeoisie.

But if one begins by refusing to distinguish between the state apparatus and the party, if the latter is generally identified with the former, if it follows that the international policy of the state and the party is not quite separated, then the objective implications of what the state requires and the objective results of the state's maneuvers become an insurmountable obstacle to the creation of an international revolutionary organization.

Another objective reality weighs down over parties and currents emerging from the process of recomposition of the workers' movement (elsewhere than in Cuba and Nicaragua), and this is that the identity of interest between the three sectors of the world revolution, which is a historic reality, is not yet part of the day-to-day experience of significant sectors of the vanguard, not to speak of the broad masses. The desynchronization and largely autonomous development of mass struggles in these three sectors is an important obstacle.

At a given moment in 1968 it was possible to hope that the "Prague Spring" would have a unifying role, multiplying the combined effects of May 1968 and the Tet Offensive in Vietnam. The suppression of the "Prague Spring" is thus the political crime with the most unhealthy long-term effects in the long list of crimes committed by the Soviet bureaucracy since the Second World War.

Since then it is a fact that—just to take a few examples—the experiences of the masses and the revolutionaries in Central America are generally cut off from those of the Polish workers in Solidarnosc and from those of the British miners, the Fiat workers in Italy, the French railworkers, or the West German steelworkers. Attempts to build bridges can be made by propaganda and solidarity activities. But that does not really replace a common mass experience or one simultaneously transmitted internationally. The very fragmented and partial character of the mass struggles and of the political progress of the vanguard in a number of countries contributes to the same effect.

Finally, as we said above, the fact that some of the biggest national working-class battalions are still absent from the scene of the battle has a big influence on the credibility of the project of rebuilding a mass revolutionary International.

In these conditions only the Fourth International and a few small groups, equivalent in size to its strongest sections, are fully behind a really universal class solidarity. Only the Fourth International has drawn the corresponding organizational conclusion—simultaneously to build national revolutionary parties and a world revolutionary party.

These obstacles will only be overcome as a result of new explosive developments of the class struggle in the key countries, of new differentiations inside the developing revolutionary organizations, and by new events, splits, regroupments, and unifications affecting the traditional mass organizations.

But any idea that all these processes can lead spontaneously and automatically to the re-emergence of a real universal internationalism of the sort seen in the first years of the Comintern (minus hypercentralization and tactical errors) has to be rejected as woolly-minded and spontaneist. There will be no new mass revolutionary international without a tireless battle for the building of an international here and now. There will be no new mass revolutionary international without the continued building of the Fourth International, even if the former will not be a simple outgrowth of the latter but will come out of wide-ranging regroupments.

We can extend the argument further: there will be no World Socialist Federation in the foreseeable future—and therefore no salvation for humanity—without the prior experience of important sectors of the working masses with a mass revolutionary international functioning as such, that is, as a real world organization, bound by statutes (rules of functioning) freely accepted by all and involving at least a partial limiting of sovereignty by its member parties (sections).

But you would have to believe in Father Christmas to think that after thousands of years of exploitation, oppression, and violence by the strongest states against other ethnic groups, peoples, states, or weaker classes; after a century of imperialist super-exploitation and oppression against colonial and semi-colonial peoples; after centuries of racial discrimination, violence, and even extermination; after a half-century of oppression and discrimination by the Soviet bureaucracy against various foreign nations and nationalities inside the U.S.S.R. . . . that all peoples, oppressed minority groups, working classes, and revolutionary parties will automatically and freely accept, without any afterthoughts, such a limitation of sovereignty as something quite logical.

It seems indispensable that they first have to go through an experience teaching them that worldwide collaboration is possible on a strict basis of equality, where the "small" forces will not have fewer rights and powers than the "big" ones, where limits on sovereignty are applied first of all on the "powerful" before being placed on the "weaker," where all discrimination on the grounds of gender, race, nationality, and ethnic group is strictly forbidden.

Everything points to participation inside a mass revolutionary international as a place where this experience could be acquired. The functioning of such an international—as is already the case with the Fourth International today—must be founded on a twofold principle: total autonomy for national parties in the selection of their leaderships and national tactics but international discipline based on the principle of majority rule (democratic centralism in the original Leninist sense of the term and not its Stalinist perversion into bureaucratic centralism) when it comes to international political policies.

If the first principle is abandoned it leads to Zinovievist manipulation or blatantly Stalinist-bureaucratic methods that stifle internal democracy, and to a completely wrong process of selecting national leaderships whereby only the most servile followers of the "international center" survive. But if the second principle is rejected, there is a risk of ending up with the terrible result, admirably defined by Rosa Luxemburg, "Workers of the world unite in times of peace but cut yourselves to pieces in times of war!"

So the reasons behind the foundation of the Fourth International in 1938 all remain valid today. Let us summarize the results of our analysis. The survival of capitalism implies more than ever the risk of a succession of catastrophes threatening to destroy not just civilization but the physical existence of the human race. Salvation can only come from the revolutionary overthrow of the capitalist regime—its gradual disappearance by reforms is an inconsistent utopia—and its replacement by the reign of freely associated producers, federated on a world scale. Only the international working class is able to overthrow capitalism. But to do this it needs an adequate level of class consciousness and revolutionary leadership.

The working class's periodic upsurges into direct action create at the same time the conditions for resolving the crisis of the subjective factor, on condition that revolutionaries have been active in the movement for long enough, effectively enough, and on a sufficiently wide enough scale. They must simultaneously aim to build new national revolutionary parties and a new International.

On a historic scale the dilemma is therefore identical to what it was in 1938.

Either the international proletariat remains generally fragmented into national sectors, fighting separate battles and essentially limited, defensive ones, not breaking except in a few countries with the framework of the bourgeois state and bourgeois society. In this case building a mass revolutionary international will fail, but building new mass national revolutionary parties will also necessarily fail. Humanity will be condemned.

Or the proletariat of the main countries will act as the French and Italian workers did in 1968–69, the Portuguese workers in 1974–75, the Czech and Polish workers in 1968 and 1980–81, and the Brazilian and Black African proletariats have done in recent years. On condition that a sufficient number of cadres, solidly rooted in the working class, equipped with a correct program and strategic vision, and able to take appropriate political actions and initiatives, are grouped together in those situations, then the political, organizational, and geographical limits of the ongoing process of recomposition of the workers' movement will be progressively overcome. The building of new national revolutionary leaderships and a new mass revolutionary international will become possible.

Since we do not doubt for one second that the second eventuality will become reality, we do not doubt for an instant the future of humanity, the development of a mass revolutionary international, and the victory of the Fourth International.

Notes

1. This document is especially important because it projected a dual tactic (combined tactic) in the event of world war: in the imperialist countries allied to the U.S.S.R. and then in the imperialist countries attacking the U.S.S.R. The realism and necessity of this combined tactic was largely confirmed by the experience of the Second World War. Trotsky was practically the only one who thought through this tactic in such a way as to avoid any renunciation of the class interests and political independence of the proletariat in the imperialist countries allied to the U.S.S.R.
2. Trotsky, *Writings of Leon Trotsky 1939–40* (New York: Pathfinder Press, 1973), p. 218.
3. See "The Rocky Road to the Fourth International," by George Breitman, (New York: Fourth Internationalist Tendency, 1988).
4. See Lenin's article of November 1, 1914: "The Position and Tasks of the Socialist International." (Collected Works, Vol. 21 [Moscow: Progress Publishers, 1977], p. 35.)

5. Presenting the considerable increase in the production and mass consumption of foodstuffs, textile products, consumer durables, medical services, education, etc., as "a development of the destructive forces" is obviously to invite justifiable ridicule.

6. In his report to the Third Congress of the Communist International in 1921 Trotsky outlined the hypothesis of renewed sustained capitalist growth in 25 years after the historic defeats of the working class and terrible slaughter and destruction: 1921 + 25 = 1946. . . .

7. I have tried to develop a systematic theory of "long conjunctural waves" (inspired by Trotsky's writings on this) in my book *Late Capitalism* (London: Verso, 1987) and especially in a little ad hoc book. *The Long Waves of Capitalist Development* (Cambridge: Cambridge University Press, 1980).

8. This is the historical role played by inflation and the soaring debt in recent decades.

9. This is the definition used by Lenin in the first program of the Russian Social Democratic Workers Party, which he drew up with Plekhanov.

10. See our article on the future of labor published in *Quatrième Internationale, 20* (May 1986).

11. This is what happened to the most gifted intellectual collaborator of Trotsky, Jean Van Heijenoort, who broke with Trotskyism and Marxism on this basis in 1948.

12. Do we need to remind our readers that 200 years passed between the first bourgeois revolution (in Holland) and its victory in France in a "mature" and definitive form, consolidated by the industrial revolution?

13. "Now and then the workers are victorious, but only for a time. The real fruit of their battles lies not in the immediate result, but in the ever expanding union of the workers." *Communist Manifesto (Marx and Engels, Basic Writings on Politics and Philosophy*, ed. L. Feuer [New York: Doubleday 1959], p. 58.) Also see the famous last paragraph of the preface to Marx's *18th Brumaire of Louis Bonaparte*, on the long-term provisional and self-critical character of proletarian revolutions.

14. This is indeed the infernal logic of reformism: taking the dangerous step between what is immediately *obtainable* (cf. Bernstein: "the movement is everything, the end is nothing") and what is *compatible* with the institutions of the bourgeois–parliamentary state, that is, with the maintenance of a basic consensus with the bourgeoisie.

15. "The revolutionary character of the epoch does not lie in being able at every moment to achieve the revolution, that is, to take power. This revolutionary character is ensured by deep, sharp turns and frequent, unexpected changes in the situation. . . ." Trotsky, "Criticism of the Comintern Program," in *The Communist International after Lenin*, Vol. 1 (Paris: Presses Universitaires de France 1969), p. 179 (translated from the French).

16. Here are two classic examples: Kautsky claimed in an article written for *Die Neue Zeit* that ultra-imperialism would make wars impossible. The article was published just after the outbreak of the First World War. The unfortunate Rudolf Hilferding stated in an article written for the S.P.D. magazine *Die Gesellschaft* that, thanks to an intelligent and wise tactic, this party had prevented the alliance between the state apparatus and the Nazis and thereby stopped Hitler from coming to power. The article was published just after President von Hindenberg had chosen Hitler as Chancellor.

17. Following Karl Marx's approach, revolutionaries assess the precise value of any

social legislation in terms of how far it extends to the whole of the working class and notably to its weakest sectors, the less well organized, the most exploited layers, those conquests which only the best organized and generally the best paid can win through direct action.

18. As for Albania and North Korea, we still do not have enough information to judge to what extent the C.P.'s seizure of power resulted from an authentic popular revolution or from a foreign military intervention as in Eastern Europe.

19. Defining Stalinism as parties founded on the theory of socialism in a single country is essentially idealist. It is also a source of obvious confusion. A great number of social democratic parties were supporters of "socialism in one country" without for all that being Stalinist.

20. Significantly, Fidel Castro assigns the responsibility for the disaster in Grenada to the "division" of the revolutionary forces. In reality differentiations within any victorious revolutionary movement faced with new problems and new choices are inevitable. Avoiding such differences ending up in degeneration like that of the Coard faction could hardly be the result of stifling differences inside the apparatus and the leadership. The remedy lies in the widest internal democracy, with tendency rights. It also lies in the working masses, organized in their democratically elected councils, being able to exert sovereign power.

21. Even if we leave aside West Germany, where the Green Party gets 7 percent of the vote and is generally seen as being to the left of the social democracy, we can look at Denmark where the S.F. party, clearly to the left of the social democracy, has just won 13 percent of the votes nationally. In the proletarian capital of Copenhagen it gets nearly 25 percent, which, added to the votes of the two smaller far-left parties, is more than the S.P. gets. We can also mention that even in France the three far-left presidential candidates, according to a poll in *Le Monde*, received together (despite their division) 7 percent of the workers' votes. This is a new phenomenon.

22. Under the heading "The new epoch requires a new International" the "Open Letter for the Fourth International," drawn up by Trotsky in 1935, includes the following passage: "It would be a fatal mistake to prescribe a single path forward for all countries. In function of the national conditions, of the degree of decomposition of the old workers' organizations and finally of the state of their own forces at any given moment, Marxists (revolutionary socialists, internationalists, Bolshevik-Leninists) can operate sometimes as an independent organization, sometimes as a faction inside one of the old parties or trade unions. Of course in every place this faction work is never anything else but a stage towards the creation of new parties of the Fourth International, parties which can be formed either as a regroupment of revolutionary elements from the old organizations or from the action of independent political groups." Leon Trotsky, *Oeuvres*, Vol. 5 (p. 355).

23. This does not at all contradict what we said above. While nuclear world war is obviously not a solution to the capitalist economic crisis, the arms race is certainly a "market of substitution" for large-scale capital in a climate of crisis. It will continue, then, independently of any considerations on the suicidal character of a nuclear war.

24. The Zinovievist regime which flourished in the Comintern after 1923 in particular involved changing national leaderships by brutal interventions (sometimes purely administratively) of the international leadership inside the Comintern sections.

9

The Marxist Case for Revolution Today

I. WHAT IS A REVOLUTION?

Revolutions are historical facts of life. Almost all major states in today's world are born from revolutions. Whether one likes it or not, our century has seen something like three dozen revolutions—some victorious, others defeated—and there is no sign that we have come to the end of the revolutionary experience.

Revolutions have been, and will remain, facts of life because of the structural nature of prevailing relations of production and relations of political power. Precisely because such relations are *structural*, because they do not just "fade away"—as well as because ruling classes resist the gradual elimination of these relations to the very end—revolutions emerge as the means to overthrow these relations.

From the nature of a revolution as a sudden, radical overthrow of prevailing social and (or) political structures—leaps in the historical process—one should not draw the conclusion that an impenetrable Chinese wall separates evolution (or reforms) from revolution. Quantitative gradual social changes do occur in history, as do qualitative revolutionary ones. Very often the former prepare for the latter, especially in epochs of decay of a given mode of production. Prevailing economic and political power relations can be eroded, undermined, and increasingly challenged—or they can even slowly disintegrate—as a result of new relations of production and the political strength of revolutionary classes (or major class fractions) rising in their midst. This is what generally characterizes periods of prerevolutionary crises. But the erosion and decay of a given social or political order remains basically different from its overthrow. Evolution is not identical with

This article appeared in *The Socialist Register*, eds. Ralph Miliband, Leo Panitch, and John Saville (London: Merlin Press, 1989), p. 159.

revolution. It transforms dialectics into sophism when, from the fact that there is no rigid absolute distinction between evolution and revolution, the conclusion is drawn that there is no basic difference between them at all.

The sudden overthrow of ruling structures is, however, only one key characteristic of that social phenomenon. The other one is their overthrow through huge popular mobilization, through the sudden, massive, active intervention of ordinary people in political life and political struggle.[1]

One of the great mysteries of class society, based upon exploitation and oppression of the mass of direct producers by relatively small minorities, is why that mass in "normal" times by and large tolerates these conditions, be it with all kinds of periodic but limited reactions. Historical materialism tries, not without success, to explain that mystery. The explanation is many-dimensional, drawing upon a combination of economic compulsion, ideological manipulation, cultural socialization, political-juridical repression (including occasionally violence), and psychological processes (internalization, identification).

Generally, as one revolutionary newspaper wrote at the beginning of the French revolution of 1789, oppressed people feel weak before their oppressors, in spite of their numerical superiority, because they are on their knees.[2] A revolution can occur precisely when that feeling of weakness and helplessness is overcome, when the mass of the people suddenly thinks, "We won't take it any longer," and acts accordingly. In his interesting book, *The Social Bases of Obedience and Revolt*, Barrington Moore has tried to prove that suffering and consciousness of injustice are not sufficient to induce large-scale revolts (revolutions) in broader masses. In his opinion a decisive role is played by the conviction that suffered injustice is neither inevitable nor a "lesser evil," that is, that a better social set-up could be realized.[3] A concomitant brake upon direct challenges to a given social and/or political order, however, is the locally or regionally fragmented nature of revolts pure and simple. Revolts generally become revolutions when they are unified nationwide.

Such challenges can be explained, among other things, by that basic truth about class societies formulated by Abraham Lincoln, empirically confirmed throughout history, and which is at least one reason for historical optimism (belief in the possibility of human progress) when all is said and done: "You can fool all of the people some of the time and some of the people all the time. But you can't fool all of the people all of the time."

When the majority of the people refuse to be fooled and intimidated any longer; when they refuse to stay on their knees; when they recognize the fundamental weakness of their oppressors, they can become transformed overnight from seemingly meek, subdued, and helpless sheep into mighty lions. They strike, congregate, organize, and especially demonstrate in the streets in increasing numbers, even in the face of massive, gruesome, bloody repression by the rulers, who still have a powerful armed apparatus at their disposal. They often show unheard-of forms of heroism, self-sacrifice, and obstinate endurance.[4] This may end in their getting the better of the repressive apparatus, which starts to disintegrate. The first victory of every revolution is precisely such a disintegration. Its final victory calls for the substitution of the armed power of the revolutionary class (or of a major class fraction) for that of the former rulers.[5]

Such a descriptive definition of revolutions has to be integrated into an analytical/causal one. *Social revolutions* occur when prevailing relations of production can no longer contain the development of the productive forces, when they increasingly act as fetters upon them, when they cause a cancerous growth of destructiveness accompanying that development. *Political revolutions* occur when prevailing relations of political power (*forms* of state power) have likewise become fetters upon a further development of the productive forces within the framework of the prevailing relations of production, a development which is, however, still historically possible. That is why they generally consolidate a given social order instead of undermining it.

This materialist explanation of revolutions offered by Marxism seems indispensable for answering the question: "Why, and why just at the moment?" Revolutions have occurred in all types of class societies but not in a uniform way. It appears clearly illogical to attribute them either to permanently operating psychological factors (humanity's allegedly inborn aggression, "destructiveness," "envy," "greed," or "stupidity") or to accidental quirks of the political power structure: particularly inept, stupid, blind rulers meeting increasingly self-confident and active opponents. According to the particular school of history concerned, one can see that blind ineptitude in the excessive recourse to repression, in the excessive amplitude of suddenly introduced reforms, or in a peculiar explosive combination of both.[6]

There are, of course, kernels of truth in such psychological and political analyses. But they cannot explain in a satisfying way the regular and discontinuous occurrence of revolutions, their cyclical nature so to speak. *Why* do "inept" rulers at regular intervals succeed "adequate" ones, so many times in so many countries? This can surely not be caused by some mysterious genetic mutation cycle. The big advantage of the materialist interpretation of history is to explain that occurrence by deeper socioeconomic causes. It is not the ineptness of the rulers which produces the prerevolutionary crisis. It is the paralysis engendered by an underlying social-structural crisis which make rulers increasingly inept. In that sense Trotsky was absolutely right when he stressed that "revolutions are nothing but the final blow and *coup de grace* given to a paralytic."

Lenin summarized the underlying analysis in a classical way by stating that revolutions occur when those below no longer accept being ruled as before and those above cannot rule any longer as before. The inability of a ruling class or major fraction to continue to rule has basically objective causes. These reflect themselves in increasingly paralyzing internal divisions among the rulers, especially around the question about how to get out of the mess visible to the naked eye. It intertwines with growing self-doubt, a loss of faith in its own future, or an irrational search for peculiar culprits ("conspiracy theories") as a substitute for a realistic objective analysis of social contradictions. It is this combination which produces political ineptitude and counterproductive actions and reactions, if not sheer passivity. The basic cause always remains the rotting away of the system, not the peculiar psychology of a group of rulers.

One has obviously to distinguish the basic historical causes of revolutions from the factors (events) triggering them. The first ones are structural, the second ones conjunctural.[7]

But it is important to emphasize that, even as regards the structural causes, the Marxist understanding of revolutions is by no means monocausally "economistic." The conflict between the productive forces and the prevailing relations of production and/or political power relations isn't all purely economic. It is basically socioeconomic. It involves all main spheres of social relations. It even eventually finds its concentrated expression in the political and not in the economic sphere. The refusal of soldiers to shoot at demonstrators is a political-moral and not an economic act. It is only by digging deeper below the surface of that refusal that one discovers its material roots. These roots don't transform the political-moral decision into a pure "appearance" or a manifestation of mere shadowboxing. It has a clear reality of its own. But that substantial reality in its turn doesn't make the digging for the deeper material roots irrelevant, an exercise in "dogmatism," or an "abstract" analysis of only secondary interest.[8]

In any case the inability of the rulers to continue to rule is not only a socio-political fact, with its inevitable concomitant of an ideological moral crisis (a crisis of the prevailing "social values system"). It has also a precise technical-material aspect. To rule also means to control a material network of communications and a centralized repressive apparatus. When that network breaks down, the rule collapses in the immediate sense of the word.[9] We must never, therefore, underestimate the technical aspect of successful revolutions. But the Marxist theory of revolution also supersedes a peculiar variant of the conspiracy theory of history, which tends to substitute for an explanation of victorious revolutions an exclusive reference to the technical mechanism of successful insurrections or coups d'état.[10] Instead, it is the material interests of key social forces and their self-perception which provide the basic explanation of turning points of history.

II. REVOLUTIONS AND COUNTER-REVOLUTIONS

While revolutions are historical facts of life, counter-revolutions are likewise undeniable realities. Indeed, counter-revolutions seem regularly to follow revolutions as night follows day. Etymology confirms this paradox. The very concept of "revolution" originates from the science of astronomy. The planets move in an orbital manner, returning to the point of departure. Hence the suggested analogical conclusion: the role of revolutions as great accelerators, as locomotives of history, is just an optical illusion of short-sighted and superficial observers, not to say utopian daydreamers. Such an interpretation (denigration) of revolutions is compatible with the great Italian historian Vico's cyclical conception of world history.

Under the influence of the victorious counter-revolution in England in 1660, the great political philosophers of the 17th century, above all Hobbes and Spinoza, developed a basically pessimistic view of human destiny. Revolutions are doomed to fail: "Plus ça change, plus ça reste la même chose." ("The more things change, the more they remain the same.") Two thousand years earlier, Greek and Chinese political philosophers had arrived at similar conclusions. There is supposedly no way out for human destiny but the search for individual happiness under inevitably bad social conditions, be it happiness through self-discipline (Stoics, Confucians, Spinoza) or through hedonism (the Epicureans).[11]

In the 18th century the Enlightenment questioned both the empirical and the theoretical roots of dogmatic skeptical pessimism.[12] A belief re-emerged in the perfectibility of humankind (only sophists or dishonest critics identify perfectibility with attaining a final state of perfection, be it said in passing), in historical progress, and thus likewise in the progressive role of revolutions. Revolution, indeed, looked beautiful in times of reaction. But already, before the outbreak of the revolution of 1789, the camp of the Enlightenment had split between the basically skeptical and socially cautious, if not outright conservative, bourgeois like Voltaire ("cultivez votre jardin")[13] and the more radical petty-bourgeois ideologues like Rousseau, who would inspire the Jacobin revolutionists. This split deepened in the revolution itself. After the successive stages of counter-revolution (Thermidor, the Bonapartist Consulate, the Empire, the Bourbon restoration) the reversal to 17th-century skepticism became general, including erstwhile enthusiasts for revolution exemplified by the English poet Wordsworth (but not Shelley). Only a tiny minority continued to pin their hopes on future revolutions and to work for them.[14] The near consensus was: the overhead of revolutions is too large, especially given the fact that they achieve very little.[15]

The Russian revolution's Thermidor and its tragic aftermath, the horrors of Stalinism, reproduced the same revulsion toward revolutions, first in the late 1930s and 1940s, then, after a temporary reprieve in the 1960s and the early 1970s, on a generalized scale from the middle '70s on. The Soviet military intervention in Czechoslovakia, and especially Cambodia and Afghanistan, but more generally the reflux of the revolutionary wave from 1968 to 1975 in Europe, from France through Czechoslovakia, Italy, and Portugal, strengthened this political retreat. The near consensus can again be summarized in the formula: revolutions are both useless and harmful from every point of view, including that of progress toward a more humane society. Indeed, this is one of the key platitudes of today's prevailing neo-conservative, neo-liberal, and neo-reformist ideologies.

It is, however, based upon obvious half-truths, if not outright mystifications. The idea that revolutions revert to their historical points of departure, if not to situations worse than the prerevolutionary ones, is generally based upon a confusion between social and political counter-revolution. While a few social counter-revolutions have indeed occurred, they are the exception, not the rule. Neither Napoleon nor Louis XVIII restored semi-feudal socioeconomic conditions in the French countryside, nor the political rule of a semi-feudal nobility. Stalin did not restore capitalism in Russia, nor did Deng Hsiao-ping in China.[16] The restoration in England was quickly followed by the Glorious Revolution. The compromise of the American Constitution did not lead eventually to the generalization of slave labor but to its suppression, after the Civil War. The list can be extended *ad libitum*.

To this objective balance-sheet the problems of subjective choice are closely related. They confront the skeptics and the pessimists with a real dilemma. Counter-revolutions are not simply "natural" reactions to revolutions, the products of an inevitable mechanical yo-yo movement, so to speak. They originate from the same exacerbation of a system's inner contradictions which give rise to the revolution, but with a specific shift in socio-political relations of forces. They reflect the relative decline of political mass activity and efficiency. There is indeed a "natural law" operating here. As genuine popular revolutions generally imply a qualitatively increased level of political mass activity, this cannot be sustained indefinitely, for obvious material and psychological reasons. You have to produce in order to eat, and when you demonstrate and participate in mass meetings, you don't produce. Also, great masses of people cannot live permanently at a high level of excitement and expenditure of nervous energy.[17]

To this relative decline of mass activity there corresponds a relative rise of activity and efficiency of the old ruling classes or strata and their various supporters and hangers-on. The initiative shifts from the "left" to the "right," at least momentarily (and not necessarily with total success: there have been defeated counter-revolutions as there have been defeated revolutions).[18] There are likewise preventive counter-revolutions: Indonesia 1965 and Chile 1973 may be taken as examples. But these preventive counter-revolutions clearly reveal the skeptic's dilemma. They are generally very costly in human lives and human happiness—much more costly than revolutions. It stands to reason that much more repression, much more bloodletting, much more cruelty, including torture, is needed to suppress a highly active, broad mass of ordinary people than to neutralize a small group of rulers. So, by abstaining from intervention against a rising counter-revolution—on the pretext that revolution itself is useless and bad—one actually becomes a passive if not active accomplice of bloody counter-revolution and large-scale mass suffering.

This is morally revolting, as it means tolerating, aiding, and abetting the violence and exploitation of the oppressors, while finding all kinds of rationalizations for refusing to assist the oppressed in their self-defense and attempted emancipation. And it is politically counter-productive as well as obnoxious. In the end it often proves to be suicidal from the point of view of the skeptics' alleged devotion to the defense of democratic institutions and reforms.

The most tragic example in that respect was of German social democracy at the end of World War One. Under the alleged motive of "saving democracy," Ebert and Noske kept the Imperial Army's hierarchy and the Prussian officer corps intact. They conspired with it against the workers—first in Berlin itself, then in the whole country. They made the generals of the *Reichswehr* into the political arbiters of the Weimer Republic. They permitted them to create and consolidate the *Freikorps* from which a good part of the later S.A. and S.S. cadres were recruited. They thereby paved the way for the rise and eventual conquest of power by the Nazis, which in turn led to the social democracts' destruction. They thought they could contain regression and reaction in the framework of a democratic counter-revolution.[19] History taught the bitter lesson that democratic counter-revolutions in the end often lead to much more authoritarian and violent ones, when the sharpening of the socioeconomic contradictions makes a total instead of a partial suppression of the mass movement into an immediate goal of the ruling class.

This again is not accidental but corresponds to a deeper historical logic. The essence of revolution is often identified with a widespread explosion of violence and mass killings. This is, of course, a false picture. The essence of revolution is not the use of violence in politics but a radical, qualitative challenge—and eventually the overthrow—of prevailing economic or political power structures. The larger the number of people involved in mass actions targeting these structures, the more favorable the relationship of forces between revolution and reaction, the greater the self-confidence of the first and the moral-ideological paralysis of the second, and the less the masses are inclined to use violence. Indeed, widespread use of violence is counter-productive for the revolution at that precise phase of the historical process.

But what does occur most often, if not always, at some point of the revolutionary process is the desperate recourse to violence by the most radical and the most resolute sectors of the rulers' camp, intent on risking everything before it is too late, while they still have human and material resources left to act in that way. At some culminating point, the confrontation between revolution and counter-revolution thus generally *does* assume a violent character, although the degree of violence depends largely upon the overall relationship of forces. In answer to reaction's violence, the masses will tend toward armed self-defense. Disintegration, paralysis, and the disarming of the counter-revolution paves the way toward revolutionary victory. The victory of the counter-revolution depends upon a disarming of the mass.[20]

When the chips are down, when power relations are stripped of all mediations and are nakedly reduced to bare essentials, Friedrich Engels's formula is then borne out by empirical evidence: in the final analysis, the state *is*, indeed, a gang of armed people. The class or layer which has the monopoly of armed force possesses (either keeps or conquers) state power. And that again is what revolution and counter-revolution are all about. Sitting on the sidelines cannot prevent this confrontation. Nor can it help delay forever the day of reckoning. In the last analysis the skeptics' and reformists' revulsion against revolution covers an implicit choice: the conservation of the status quo is a lesser evil compared to the costs and consequences of its revolutionary overthrow. This choice reflects social conservatism. It is not a rational judgment of the empirically verifiable balance-sheets of the "costs" of historical, that is, real, revolutions and counter-revolutions.

No normal human being prefers to achieve social goals through the use of violence. To reduce violence to the utmost in political life should be a common endeavor for all progressive and socialist currents. Only profoundly sick persons—totally unable to contribute to the building of a real classless society—can actually enjoy advocating and practicing violence on a significant scale. Indeed, the increasing rejection of violence in a growing number of countries is a clear indicator that at least some moral-ideological progress has occurred in the last 70 to 75 years. One only has to compare the wild and brazen justification of war by nearly all the leading Western intellectuals and politicians in the 1914–18 period to the near universal revulsion toward war today in the same milieu to note that progress.

Double moral standards still reign supreme in inter-class and interstate relations, but the legitimacy of the widespread use of violence by rulers is at least increasingly questioned in a systematic and consistent way by a much greater number of people than in 1914–18 or 1939–45. The future, indeed the very physical survival of humankind, depends upon the outcome of this race between increasing consciousness about the necessary rejection of armed confrontation on the one hand and the increasing de facto destructiveness of existing and future weapons on the other. If the first does not eliminate the second through successful political action, the second will eventually destroy not only the first but all human life.

But such a political action can only be revolutionary and thus implies the use of at least limited armed force. To believe otherwise is to believe that the rulers will let themselves be disarmed peacefully, without using the arms they still control. This is to deny the threat of any violent counter-revolution, which is utterly utopian in the light of historical experience. It is to assume that ruling classes and strata are exclusively and always represented by mild, well-meaning liberals. Go tell that to the prisoners of the Warsaw ghetto and of Auschwitz, to the million victims of Djakarta, to the oppressed non-white population of South Africa, to the Indochinese peoples, to the Chilean and Salvadoran workers and peasants, to the murdered participants of the *Intifada*, to the millions and millions of victims of reaction and counter-revolution throughout the world since the colonial wars of the 19th century and the Paris Commune.

The elementary human-moral duty in the face of that terrifying record is to refuse any retreat into (re)privatization and to assist the oppressed, the exploited, the humiliated, and downtrodden to struggle for their emancipation by any means necessary. In the long run this also makes the individual participant a more human, happier person, provided he does not make any pseudo-*Realpolitik* concessions and observes unrestrictedly the rule: fight everywhere and always against any and every social and political conditions which exploits and oppresses human beings.

III. THE POSSIBILITY OF REVOLUTION IN THE WEST

Revolutions and counter-revolutions, being real historical processes, always occur in actual social-economic conditions, which are always specific. No two countries in the world are exactly alike, if only because their basic social classes and the major fractions of these classes are products of the specific history of each of these countries. Hence the character of each revolution reflects a unique combination of the general and the specific. The first derives from the logic of revolutions as sketched above. The second derives from the specificity of each particular set of prevailing relations of production and relations of political power in a given country, at a given moment, with its own inner contradictions and a specific dynamic of their exacerbation.

A revolutionary strategy[21] represents the conscious attempt by revolutionists to influence, through their political actions, the outcome of objectively revolutionary processes in favor of a victory of the exploited and the oppressed—in today's world essentially the wage-earning proletariat, its allies, and the poor peasantry. In turn, it must therefore be specific to have a minimum chance of success. It has to be attuned to the differentiated social reality which prevails in today's world. We can use the formula of the "three sectors of world revolution" to designate significantly different strategic tasks, that is, roughly: the proletarian revolution in the imperialist countries; the combined national-democratic, anti-imperialist, and socialist revolution in the "third world" countries; and the political revolution in the post-capitalist social formations.[22] We shall consider each of these in turn.

Regarding the industrialized metropolises of capitalism, a formidable objection is raised with regard to the possible effectiveness of revolutionary strategy. Many skeptics and reformists do not limit themselves to alleging that revolutions are useless and harmful. They add that revolutions are impossible in these countries, that they won't occur anyway, that to hope for them or expect them is utterly utopian; that to try to prepare for them or to further them is a total waste of time and energy.

This line of reasoning is based on two different—and basically contradictory—assumptions. The first one (which is still true) states that no *victorious* revolution has ever occurred in a purely imperialist country. The case of Russia in 1917 is seen as exceptional, a unique combination of underdevelopment and imperialism. But it is irrational, even childish, to recognize as revolutions only those that have been successful. Once one accepts that revolutionary processes did occur in 20th-century imperialist countries, surely the logical conclusion for a revolutionist is to study them carefully so as to be able to map out a course which will make defeat unlikely when they occur again.

The second assumption is that whatever triggered past revolutions (revolutionary crises and processes)[23] will never happen again. Bourgeois society—the capitalist economy and parliamentary democracy—are supposed to have achieved such a degree of stability, and "integrated" the mass of wage earners to such an extent, that they won't be seriously challenged in the foreseeable future.[24] This assumption, which already prevailed during the postwar boom (as an obvious result of the undeniable increase in living standards and social security which was its by-product for the Western proletariat), was seriously challenged in May 1968 and its immediate aftermath, at least in Southern Europe (and partially in Britain in the early 1970s). It regained a powerful credibility in the wake of the retreat of the proletariat in the metropolitan countries toward essentially defensive struggles after 1974–75.

We should understand the nub of the question. The seemingly a-prioristic assumption is in reality a prediction which will be historically either verified or falsified. It is in no way a final truth. It is nothing but a working hypothesis. It assumes a given variant of the basic trends of development of capitalism in the latter part of the 20th century: the variant of *declining contradictions*, of the ability of the system to avoid explosive crises, not to say catastrophes.

In that sense it is strikingly similar to the working hypothesis of the classical version of reformism in its rejection of a revolutionary perspective and revolutionary strategy: that of Eduard Bernstein. In his book which launched the famous "revisionism debate," he clearly posited a growing objective decline in acuity of inner contradictions of the system as the premise for his reformist conclusions: fewer and fewer capitalist crises; fewer and fewer tendencies toward war; fewer and fewer authoritarian governments; fewer and fewer violent conflicts in the world.[25] Rosa Luxemburg answered him succinctly that precisely the opposite would be the case. Under the influence of the Russian revolution of 1905, Kautsky came the nearest to revolutionary Marxism and was the undisputed mentor of Lenin, Rosa Luxemburg, and Trotsky.[26] He also explicitly identified the perspective of *inevitable catastrophes* to which capitalism was leading as one of the main pillars of Marxism's revolutionary perspectives.[27] When he moved away from revolutionary Marxism, he started to consider these catastrophes as becoming more and more unlikely, that is, he started to share Bernstein's euphoric working hypothesis.[28]

What does the historical record reveal? Two world wars, the economic crisis of 1929 and onwards, fascism, Hiroshima, innumerable colonial wars, hunger and disease in the third world, the ongoing ecological catastrophe, and the new long economic depression. It is Rosa Luxemburg who has been proven more right than Bernstein; and it is the Kautsky of 1907 who has been proven right by history and not the Kautsky of the 1914 "ultra-imperialism" theory. Today it seems truer than ever, to paraphrase a famous formula of Jean Jaures, that late capitalism carries within itself a succession of grave crises and catastrophes, as clouds carry storms.[29]

One transforms that obvious truth—obvious in the sense that is borne out by solid historical evidence for three-quarters of a century—into a meaningless caricature when one insinuates that revolutionary Marxists expect or predict *permanent* catastrophes every year in every imperialist country, so to speak. Leaving aside the lunatic fringe, serious Marxists have never taken that stand, which doesn't mean that they have never been guilty of false analysis and erroneous evaluations regarding particular countries. If one soberly analyzes the ups and downs of economic, social, and political crisis in the West and Japan since 1914, what emerges is a pattern of *periodic* upsurges of mass struggles in *some* metropolitan countries, which have at times put revolutionary processes on the agenda. In our view the mechanisms leading in that direction remain operative today as they were since the period of the historical decline of the capitalist mode of production was first posited by Marxists. The burden of proving that this is no longer the case rests upon those who argue that today's bourgeois society is somehow *basically* different from that of 1936, not to say that of 1968. We haven't yet seen any persuasive argumentation of that nature.

The concept of *periodically and not permanently* possible revolutionary explosions in imperialist countries logically leads to a *topology of possible revolutions in the West*, which sees these revolutions essentially as a qualitative "transcroissance" of the mass struggles and mass experiences of nonrevolutionary times. We have often sketched this process of "overgrowing," based not upon speculation or wishful thinking but on the experience of prerevolutionary and revolutionary explosions which have really occurred in the West.[30] We can therefore limit ourselves to summarizing the process in the following chain of events: mass strikes; political mass strikes; a general strike; a general sit-down strike; coordination and centralization of democratically elected strike committees; and transformation of the "passive" into an "active" general strike, in which strike committees assume a beginning of state functions, beginning with the public and the financial sectors. (Public-transport regulation, access to telecommunications, access to savings and bank accounts limited to strikers, free hospital services under that same authority, and "parallel" teaching in schools by teachers under strikers' authority are examples of such inroads into the realm of the exercise of quasi-state functions growing out of an "active" general strike.) This leads to the emergence of a de facto generalized dual power situation with emerging self-defense bodies of the masses.

Such a chain of events generalizes trends already visible at high points of mass struggles in the West: 1920 in northern Italy; July 1927 in Austria; June 1936 in France; July 1948 in Italy; May 1968 in France; the "hot autumn" of 1969 in Italy; and the high points of the Portuguese revolution 1974–75. Other general strike experiences[31] involving a similar chain of events were those of Germany 1920 and Spain (especially Catalonia) in 1936–37. (Albeit in a very different social context, the tendency of the industrial proletariat to operate in the same general sense in revolutionary situations can also be seen in Hungary in 1956, Czechoslovakia in 1968–69, and Poland in 1980–81).

Such a view of proletarian revolutionary behavior in the imperialist countries makes it easier to solve a problem which has haunted revolutionary Marxists since the beginning of the 20th century: the relation between the struggle for reforms (economic as well as political-democratic) and the preparation for revolution. The answer given to that problem by Rosa

Luxemburg in the beginning of the debate remains as valid today as it was then.[32] The difference between reformists and revolutionists does not lie in the rejection of reforms by the latter and the struggle for reforms by the former. On the contrary: serious revolutionists will be the most resolute and efficient fighters for all reforms which correspond to the needs and the recognizable preoccupations of the masses. The real difference between reformists and revolutionary Marxists can be thus summarized:

1. Without rejecting or marginalizing legislative initiatives, revolutionary socialists prioritize the struggle for reforms through broad, direct, extra-parliamentary mass actions.
2. Without negating the need to take into consideration real social-political relations of forces, revolutionary socialists refuse to limit the struggle for reforms to those which are acceptable to the bourgeoisie or, worse, which don't upset the basic social and political relations of power. For that reason reformists tend to fight less and less for serious reforms whenever the system is in crisis, because, like the capitalists, they understand the "destabilizing" tendency of these struggles. For the revolutionists the priority is the struggle for the masses' needs and interests and not the defense of the system's needs or logic nor the conservation of any consensus with capitalists.
3. Reformists see the limitation or elimination of capitalism's ills as a process of gradual progress. Revolutionists, on the contrary, educate the masses in the inevitability of crises that will interrupt the gradual accumulation of reforms and will periodically threaten the suppression of past conquests.
4. Reformists will tend to brake, oppose, or even repress all forms of direct mass actions which transcend or threaten bourgeois state institutions. Revolutionists, on the contrary, will systematically favor and try to develop self-activity and self-organization of the masses, even in daily struggles for immediate reforms, regardless of "destabilizing" consequences, thereby creating a tradition, an experience of broader and broader mass struggle, which facilitates the emergence of a dual power situation when generalized mass struggles—a general strike—occur. Thereby, proletarian revolutions of the type sketched above can be seen as an organic product—or climax—of broader and broader mass struggles for reforms in prerevolutionary or even nonrevolutionary times.
5. Reformists will generally limit themselves to propagating reform. Revolutionary Marxists will combine a struggle for reforms with constant and systematic anti-capitalist propaganda. They will educate the masses in the system's ills and advocate its revolutionary overthrow. The formulation and struggle for transitional demands (which, while corresponding to the masses' needs, cannot be realized within the framework of the system) plays a key role here.

Doesn't such a view of "really feasible revolution" in the West seriously underestimate the obstacle posed by the Western proletariat's obvious attachment to parliamentary democracy? Doesn't this block the overthrow of bourgeois institutions, without which no victorious revolution is possible? We don't think so.

In the first place, many aspects of the legitimate attachment of the masses to democratic rights and freedom are not attachments to bourgeois state institutions. To use a clarifying formula of Trotsky, they express the presence of nuclei of proletarian democracy inside the bourgeois state.[33] The larger the masses' self-activity, self-mobilization, and self-organization, the more the butterfly of democratic workers' power tends to appear out of its "bourgeois" chrysalis. The fundamental issue will be growing confrontation between the "naked core" of bourgeois state power (the central government, the repressive apparatus, etc.) and the masses' attachment to democratic institutions *which they themselves control*.

In the second place, there is no reason to counterpose, in an absolute and dogmatic way, organs of direct workers' and popular power and organs resulting from undifferentiated universal franchise. Workers and popular councils and their centralized coordination (local, regional, national, international council congresses) can be more efficient and democratic forms, making possible the direct exercise of political, economic, and social power by millions of toilers. But if it is necessary to reject parliamentary cretinism, it is likewise necessary to reject anti-parliamentary cretinism. Whenever and wherever the masses clearly express their wish to have parliamentary-type power organs elected by universal franchise—the cases of Hungary, Poland, and Nicaragua are clear—revolutionists should accept that verdict. These organs need not supersede the power of soviets, insofar as the masses have learned through their own experiences that their councils can give them more democratic rights and more real power than the broadest parliamentary democracy alone; and insofar as the precise functional division of labor between soviet-type and parliamentary-type organs is elaborated into a constitution under conditions of workers' power.

Of course, soviet institutions can and should also be elected on the basis of universal franchise. The fundamental difference between parliamentary and soviet democracy is not the mode of election but the mode of functioning. Parliamentary democracy is essentially representative, that is, indirect, democracy and to a large extent limited to the legislative field. Soviet democracy contains much higher doses of direct democracy, including the instrument of "binding mandates" of the electors for their representative and the right to instant recall of these representatives by their electors. In addition, it implies a large-scale unification of legislative and executive functions, which, combined with the principle of rotation, actually enables the majority of the citizens to exercise state functions.

The multiplication of functional assemblies with a division of competence serves the same purpose. A key specificity of soviet democracy is also that it is a producers' democracy, that is, that it ties economic decision-taking to work places and federated work places (at local, regional, and branch levels etc.), giving those who work the right to decide on their workload and the allocation of their products and services. Why should workers make sacrifices in spending time, nerves, and physical strength for increasing output, when they generally feel that the results of these additional efforts don't benefit them and they have no way of deciding about the distribution of its fruits? Producers' democracy appears more and more as the only way to overcome the declining motivation (sense of responsibility) for production, not to say the economy in its totality, which characterizes both the capitalist market economy and the bureaucratic command economy.

IV. THE LESSONS OF THIRD-WORLD REVOLUTIONS

The revolutionary processes in the third world since World War II have confirmed the validity of the strategy of permanent revolution. Wherever these processes have climaxed in a full break with the old ruling classes and with international capital, the historical tasks of the national-democratic revolution (national unification, independence from imperialism) have been realized. This was the case of Yugoslavia, Indochina, China, Cuba, and Nicaragua. Wherever the revolutionary process did not culminate in such a full break, key tasks of the national-democratic revolution remain unfulfilled. This was the case of Indonesia, Bolivia, Egypt, Algeria, Chile, and Iran.

The theory (strategy) of permanent revolution is counterposed to the traditional Comintern/C.P. strategy since the middle 1920s, to wit the "revolution by stages," in which a first phase of "bloc of four classes" (the "national" bourgeoisie, the peasantry, the urban petty-bourgeoisie, and the proletariat) is supposed to eliminate by a common political struggle the semi-feudal and oligarchic power structures, including foreign imperialist ones. Only in a second phase is the proletarian struggle for power supposed to come to the forefront. This strategy first led to disaster in China in 1927. It has led to grave defeats ever since. It is increasingly challenged inside many C.P.s.

It is of no avail to avoid making this fundamental choice by the use of abstract formulas. The formulas, "workers' and farmers' government" or, worse, "people's power" or "broad popular alliance under the hegemony of the working class," just evade the issue. What revolutions are all about is state power. The class nature of state power—and the question of which major fraction of a given class exercises state power—is decisive. Either the formulas are synonymous with the overthrow of the bourgeois-oligarchic state, its army, and its repressive apparatus, and with the establishment of a workers' state, or the formulas imply that the state apparatus is not to be "immediately" destroyed—in which case the class nature of the state remains bourgeois-oligarchic and the revolution will be defeated.

When it is said that without the conquest of power by the working class, without the overthrow of the state of the former ruling classes, the historical tasks of the national-democratic revolution will not be fully realized, this does not mean that *none* of these tasks can be initiated under bourgeois or petty-bourgeois governments. After World War II, most of the previously colonial countries did, after all, achieve political national independence without overthrowing the capitalist order. In some cases, at least, India being the most striking one, this was not purely formal but also implied a degree of economic autonomy from imperialism, which made at least initial industrialization under national bourgeois ownership possible. Starting with the late 1960s, a series of semi-colonial countries succeeded in launching a process of semi-industrialization that went much farther (South Korea, Taiwan, Brazil, Mexico, Singapore, and Hong Kong are the most important cases), often supported by substantial land reforms as indispensable launching pads. The famous controversy of the 1950s and 1960s on the "dependencia" theory—the impossibility of any serious degree of industrialization without a total break with imperialism—has thus been settled by history.

It is likewise incorrect to interpret the theory of the permanent revolution as implying that the overthrow of the old state order and the radical agrarian revolution must perforce *coincide with* the complete destruction of capitalist private property in industry. It is true that the working class can hardly be supposed to tolerate its own exploitation at the factory level while it is busy, or has already succeeded in, disarming the capitalists and eliminating their political power. But from this it flows only that the victorious socialist revolution in underdeveloped countries will start making "despotic inroads" into the realm of capitalist private property, to quote a famous sentence of the *Communist Manifesto*. The rhythm and the extent of these inroads will depend on the political and social correlation of forces and on the pressure of economic priorities. No general formula is applicable here for all countries at all moments.

The question of the rhythm and the extent of the expropriation of the bourgeoisie is in turn tied to the question of the worker-peasant alliance, a key question of political strategy in most of the third-world countries. Keeping capitalist property intact to the extent of not fulfilling the poor peasants' thirst for land is obviously counter-productive. Hitting private property to the extent of arousing fear among the middle peasants that they too will lose their property is counter-productive from an economic point of view (it could become also counter-productive politically).

On balance, however, experience confirms what the theory suggests. It is impossible to achieve genuine independence from imperialism and genuinely motivate the working class for the socialist reconstruction of the nation without the expropriation of big capital in industry, banking, agriculture, trade, and transportation—be it international or national capital. The real difficulties only arise when the borderline between that expropriation and the tolerance of small and medium-sized capital (with all its implications for economic growth, social equality, and direct producers' motivation) has to be determined.

The historical record shows that a peculiar form of dual power, of confrontation between the old and the new state order, has appeared during all victorious socialist revolutions in underdeveloped countries: dual power reflecting a territorial division of the country into liberated zones, in which the new state is emerging, and the rest of the country, where the old state still reigns. This peculiar form of dual power expresses in turn the peculiar form of the revolutionary (and counter-revolutionary) processes themselves, in which armed struggle (guerrilla warfare, people's war) occupied a central place. In the cases of China, Yugoslavia, and Vietnam, this resulted from the fact that the revolution started as a movement of national liberation against a foreign imperialist aggressor/invader, while becoming increasingly intertwined with civil war between the poor and the well-to-do, that is, with social revolution. In the cases of Cuba and Nicaragua, the revolution started likewise as armed struggle against a viciously repressive and universally hated and despised dictatorship, again growing over into a social revolution.

One should, of course, not simplify the pattern emerging from these experiences. At least in Cuba and in Nicaragua (to some extent also in the beginning of the Indochinese revolution and in several stages of the Yugoslav revolution) urban insurrections played an important role. A successful general strike and a successful urban insurrection decided the outcome of the Cuban and the Nicaraguan revolutions. The proponents of the strategy of armed struggle today generally adopt a more sophisticated and complex strategy than in the 1960s, combining guerrilla warfare, the creation of liberated zones, and the mobilization of mass organizations in urban zones (including forms of armed self-defense) in order to lead the revolution to victory. This combination seems reasonable in many semi-colonial countries, where state repression under prerevolutionary conditions leaves no alternative to revolutionary strategy. We believe, however, that this pattern should not be considered unavoidable in all third-world countries, regardless of specific circumstances and particular social-political relationships of forces at given moments.

V. POLITICAL REVOLUTION IN SO-CALLED SOCIALIST SOCIETIES

The concept of political (antibureaucratic) revolution in the bureaucratized societies in transition between capitalism and socialism (bureaucratized workers' states) was first formulated by Trotsky in 1933. It resulted from the diagnosis of the growing contradictions of Soviet society, and the prediction that these contradictions could no longer be removed through reforms; and it was related, therefore, to the prediction that a self-reform of the bureaucracy was impossible.[34] Most left tendencies considered this concept, and the premises on which it was based, as either a fantasy or objectively a call for counter-revolution. The overthrow of the bureaucratic dictatorship could only lead to a restoration of capitalism: that was the assumption.

These objections were unfounded. Trotsky's prognosis of political revolution, like his analysis of the contradictions of Soviet society, appear as one of his most brilliant contributions to Marxism. Since 1953 we have witnessed a chain of revolutionary crises in Eastern Europe: the G.D.R. in June 1953; Hungary in 1956; Czechoslovakia in 1968; Poland in 1980–81. One can discuss whether similar crises didn't also occur in China, in the 1960s and 1970s. (Mikhail Gorbachev himself calls his *perestroika* a revolution and compares it with the political revolutions which occurred in France in 1830, 1848, and 1870.)[35] In all these concrete revolutionary processes there was no prevalent tendency to restore capitalism. This did not result only from the objective fact that the overwhelming majority of the combatants were workers, who have no interest in restoring capitalism. It was subjectively determined by the very demands of these combatants, who in Hungary set up workers' councils, with the Central Workers Council of Budapest leading the struggle. Similar developments occurred in Czechoslovakia and in Poland. The line of march of the political revolution in the U.S.S.R. will be quite similar.

On the other hand it cannot be denied that attempts at self-reform of the bureaucracy have been many—the most spectacular of them being the introduction of workers' self-management at the factory level in Yugoslavia in 1950. While often instrumental in triggering a "thaw" of the bureaucracy's stranglehold on society and enabling a revival of mass activity and mass politization at various degrees, these attempts have always failed to solve the basic ills of these societies. This was especially true for the historically most important attempt, the one initiated by Khrushcheve in the U.S.S.R. Indeed, most "liberal" and "left" Soviet historians and intellectuals today agree that the reason for the failure of Khrushchev was insufficent activity from below. This, incidentally, is also Gorbachev's official version of the Khrushchev experience.

So the historical balance-sheet is again clear: attempts at self-reform can start a movement of change in the bureaucratized workers' states. They can even facilitate the beginning of a genuine mass movement. But they cannot bring about a successful culmination of such change and movement. For this, a genuine popular revolution is indispensable. Self-reform of the enlightened wing of the bureaucracy cannot be a substitute for such a revolution.

The bureaucracy is a hardened *social* layer, enjoying huge material privileges which depend fundamentally on its monopoly of the exercise of political power. But that same bureaucracy does not play any indispensable or useful role in society. Its role is essentially parasitic. Hence its rule is more and more wasteful. It tends to become the source of a succession of specific economic, social, political, and ideological-moral crises. The need to remove it from its ruling position is an objective necessity for unblocking the march toward socialism. For this, a revival of mass activity, in the first place political activity of the working class, is needed. While a revolution will have many implications in the field of the economy, it will basically consolidate and strengthen the system of collective ownership of the means of production and of socialized planning—far from overthrowing it. That is why we speak of a "political revolution" instead of "social revolution."[36]

To a large extent the bureaucracy rules as a result of the political passivity of the working class; Trotsky even said through passive "tolerance" by the working class. The historical-social origins of that passivity are well-known: the defeats of the international revolution; the pressure of the scarcity of consumer goods and of a lack of culture born from the relative backwardness of Russia; the consequences of the Stalinist terror; and a disappointment of historical dimensions, leading to a lack of historical alternatives to the bureaucracy's rule. But the very progress of Soviet society during the last half-century, achieved on the basis of the remaining conquests of the October revolution and in spite of the bureaucracy's misrule, slowly undermines the basis of that passivity. The stronger, more skilled, and more cultivated the working class becomes, the greater its resentments and expectations clash with the slow-down of economic growth and the manifold social crises which the bureaucracy's misrule and waste provoke. Conditions emerge which tend to revive the activity of the working class.

Timothy Garton Ash quotes a remarkable memorandum by the new Polish Prime Minister, Mieczyslaw F. Rakowski, which concludes with the prediction that if the "socialist formation" does not find the strength to reform itself, "the further history of our formation will be marked by shocks and revolutionary explosions, initiated by an increasingly enlightened people." Indeed. But as Ash himself clearly indicates, in spite of Rakowski's favoring reforms moving toward a restoration of capitalism tempered by a "liberal" democracy, the difficulty lies precisely in the social correlation of forces: the working class is not ready to pay the price for a return to capitalism, that is, massive unemployment and inequality. So you can't have a generalized market economy plus political democracy. You can only have a partial market economy plus partial repression. So you can't have radical reforms. So the likelihood that you'll have a political revolution is growing. Ash himself rather cynically concludes: "It seems reasonable to suggest that the reform has a rather higher chance of minimal success—that is, of averting revolution—if only because of the further diversification of social interests which it will promote. The freeing of the private sector, in particular, means that Hungary might yet have an entrepreneurial bourgeoisie that will go to the barricades—against the revolting workers. Capitalists and Communists, shoulder to shoulder against the proletariat: a suitably Central European outcome for socialism. To estimate the percentage chance of peaceful transformation, by contrast, requires only the fingers of one hand."[37]

Yet, precisely because the bureaucracy is not a new ruling class but a parasitic cancer on the working class and society as a whole, its removal through a political revolution by the workers does not require the type of armed conflict which until now has accompanied revolutions in class societies, including modern capitalist ones. It is more in the nature of a surgical operation. This was confirmed in the case of Hungary in 1956, which went the farthest toward a victorious political revolution. A significant part of the C.P. apparatus and practically the whole Army went over to the camp of the workers (of the people). Only a tiny handful of secret police agents opposed the victorious masses in open armed provocations, thereby provoking an overt conflict (and their own sad fate), which otherwise could have been avoided. In Czechoslovakia in 1968 a similar trend was set in motion. In fact, in all cases of such political revolutions witnessed up till now, only foreign military intervention could prevent it from becoming victorious nearly without bloodshed. One does not see what force could replace such a foreign military intervention in the case of the U.S.S.R., probably not the Soviet Army. And the capacity of the K.G.B. to repress 265 million people seems dubious, to say the least.

History has also confirmed the utopian character of the idea that the construction of socialism could be fully achieved in a single country or a small number of countries. It has confirmed that the U.S.S.R. (and the "socialist camp") cannot escape the pressure of the world market (of international capitalism), the pressure of wars and the permanent arms race, the pressure of constant technological innovations, and the pressure of changing consumption patterns for the mass of the producers. But, far from being an unavoidable result of that pressure, the bureaucratic dictatorship undermines the revolution's objective and subjective capacity of resistance. A victorious political revolution in the U.S.S.R. and Eastern Europe would considerably strengthen that resistance. It would make new advances toward socialism possible. But we should not fall into the illusion that it could actually achieve a classless society on its own, independently of revolutionary developments elsewhere.

VI. WORLD REVOLUTION TODAY

The concept of the three sectors of world revolution refers to the different strategic-historical tasks that confront the revolutionary process today. But this only represents the first step toward a full appreciation of the concept of world revolution. The question of these sectors and their interaction, and hence their growing unity, also has to be raised.

For decades the apologists of the Stalinist dictatorship used to say that revealing the dark side of the Soviet (the Eastern European, the Chinese) reality discourages the workers in the West from fighting to overthrow capitalism. But history has fully confirmed that it is impossible to conduct a fight for a good cause on the basis of lies, half-truths, or the hiding of truth. As it was impossible, in the long run, to hide the revolting aspects of Soviet reality, the mass of the workers in the West and Japan (including those adhering to or voting for the Communist parties) ended by assimilating them. What really discouraged and demoralized them was not the revelation of these facts but the facts themselves—including their decades-long suppression by the Communist parties and their fellow travellers. One of the biggest subjective obstacles to a new development of revolutionary consciousness among the Western working class is the repulsive mask which Stalinism has put on socialism (communism). By contributing to tearing off that mask, a victorious political revolution in the East greatly advances the cause of socialism the world over. It strengthens the struggle against capitalism and imperialism instead of weakening it.

The idea that, somehow, such a revolution would at least weaken the U.S.S.R. (or the "socialist camp") at the state level and thereby change the military relationship of forces worldwide in favor of imperialism is likewise unfounded. It is an undeniable fact that the existence of the U.S.S.R., in spite of the bureaucratic dictatorship with its policies of "peaceful coexistence," objectively contributed to the victory and especially the consolidation of the Chinese revolution and to the downfall of the colonial empires.

But parallel to that objective function is the fact that the Soviet bureaucracy tried to obstruct the victory of the Chinese revolution through the strategy it advocated, and that it played a key role in the post-World War II consolidation of capitalism in Western Europe.

Furthermore, it is impossible to disconnect military strength from its economic and social basis and from the political nature of governments. A Soviet Union, not to say a "socialist camp," governed through pluralistic socialist democracy and a broad consensus of the majority of the toilers would be much more efficient economically, far more influential in the world, and thereby much stronger militarily than the U.S.S.R. of today.[38]

The concept of unity between the three sectors of world revolution is supported by the fact that while victorious revolutions in third-world countries can weaken imperialism, they cannot overthrow it. In the epoch of nuclear weapons it is obvious that imperialism can only be overthrown inside the metropolis itself. But the main obstacle to that overthrow is not the objective strength of capitalism or the bourgeois state, nor the absence of periodically explosive contradictions inside the metropolis. The main obstacle is subjective: the level of Western (and Japanese) working-class consciousness and the political quality of its leadership. Precisely for that reason, new qualitative advances toward socialism in the U.S.S.R. and Eastern Europe, and the removal of the bureaucratic dictatorships, would greatly assist in the solution of the problem.

On the other hand, any leap toward a victorious proletarian revolution in the West or in the most advanced semi-industrialized third-world countries (like Brazil), which will occur under immeasurably more favorable objective and cultural conditions than the Russian October revolution, will usher in material and social changes which will operate as a powerful stimulant for the toilers of all countries, beginning with the Soviet toilers if they have not yet overthrown the bureaucracy's yoke. To mention just one key aspect of any future victorious proletarian revolution in an economically advanced country: the realization of the half workday would play the same role that the slogan "Land, Bread, Peace" played in the Russian revolution. If that were realized, what sector of the working class the world over could stay impervious to the conquest?

The potential interaction—we say potential because it is obviously not yet a fact—between the three sectors of world revolution is premised on the historical/social unity of the world working class and the strength of the forces operating toward the development of the conscious awareness of that unity. We know perfectly well how strong the obstacles are on the road toward that political consciousness. They have been enumerated and analyzed a thousand times. What we want to stress is that they can be overcome by the operation of still stronger objective trends.

The unity of the process of world revolution is related to the growing internationalization of the productive forces and of capital—exemplified in the emergence of the transnational corporation as the late-capitalist firm predominant in the world market—which leads unavoidably to a growing internationalization of the class struggle. Hard material reality will teach the international working class that retreating toward purely national defensive strategies (exemplified by protectionism) leaves all the advantages to capital and increasingly paralyzes even the defense of a given standard of living and of political rights. The only efficient answer to an internationalization of capital's strength and maneuvers is international coordination, solidarity, and the organization of the working class.

During recent decades the objective need for world revolution as a unity of the three world sectors of revolution has received a new and frightening dimension through the growth of the destructive potential of contemporary technological and economic trends, resulting from the survival of capitalism beyond the period of its historical legitimacy. The accumulation of huge arsenals of nuclear and chemical weapons; the extension of nuclear power; the destruction of tropical forests; the pollution of air and water the world over; the destruction of the ozone layer; the desertification of large tracts of Africa; the growing famine in the third world: all these trends threaten disasters which put a question mark on the physical survival of humankind. None of these disasters can be stopped or prevented at the national or even continental level. They all call for solutions on a worldwide scale. Consciousness about the global nature of humanity's crisis and the need for global solutions, largely overlapping nation-states, has been rapidly growing.

Mikhail Gorbachev and his main advisers and intellectual supporters, from a correct perception of the globalization of problems and of the absolute necessity to prevent a nuclear war, tend to draw the conclusion that, progressively, these global problems will be solved through an increased collaboration between imperialist and "socialist" states. They base themselves on two assumptions in that regard. First, they believe that a course toward world revolution would exacerbate interstate relations to the point where the outbreak of a world war would become more likely, if not unavoidable. Second, they tacitly presume that the inner contradictions of capitalism will tend to decrease, that the real class struggle will become less explosive, that trends toward increased class collaboration will prevail in the 21st century. Both these assumptions are utterly unrealistic. They are of the same type as the hope to achieve the building of a really socialist society in a single country, of which they represent in a certain sense the logical continuation.

The fact is that while victorious or even unfolding revolutions have undoubtedly led to counter-revolutionary interventions by imperialist powers, they have on several occasions prevented larger wars from occurring. Without the German revolution of 1918–19, the revolutionary general strike in that country in 1920, and the preparations for a general strike in Britain that same year, a major war of all imperialist powers against Soviet Russia would probably have occurred. Without the victory of the October revolution, World War I would probably have been prolonged. The revolutionary upsurge in Spain, France, and Czechoslovakia in 1936 significantly slowed the march toward World War II. If it had been victorious only in Spain, not to say in France and Czechoslovakia as well, World War II could have been prevented. So, to identify revolutions with unavoidable war is just a misreading of the historical record. In fact, a victorious revolution in France and Britain today, not to say in the U.S.A., would be the surest way to make world war impossible.

The real reasoning of the neo-reformist Gorbachev version of "globalization" is based on the classical reformist illusion of a decline in the explosiveness and intensity of the inner contradictions of capitalism and of bourgeois society. We have already dealt with the unrealistic character of that assumption. It errs especially by not taking into account the structural link between the destructive uses of technology and economic resources on the one hand and competitive attitudes, competitive strife, private property, and the market economy on the other hand. Bourgeois society can never lead and will never lead toward a world without weapons and without technological innovations applied, regardless of their costs, to the natural and human ecology. You need socialism to achieve these goals. And you have to achieve these goals if humanity is to survive. The strongest justification for world revolution today is that humankind is literally faced with the long-term dilemma: either a world socialist federation or death.

Notes

1. Precisely because the Marxist concept of revolution encompasses the necessary dimension of mass action, the concept of "revolution from above" is not strictly accurate, although it was used by Engels and has, of course, a well circumscribed significance. Joseph II's reforms in Austria, Tsar Alexander II's abolition of serfdom, Bismarck's unification of Germany, and the Meiji "revolution" in Japan were historical attempts to pre-empt revolutions from below through radical reforms from above. To what extent they were successful in that purpose must be analyzed in each specific case. The same applies *mutatis mutandis* to Gorbachev's reform course in the Soviet Union today.
2. This was the epigram of the weekly *Revolutions de Paris*, which started to appear from the end of August 1789 in Paris.
3. See Barrington Moore Jr., *The Social Bases of Obedience and Revolt* (White Plains, N.Y.: M.E. Sharpe, 1978).
4. This was the case during the days in 1979 preceding the downfall of the Shah of

Iran in the streets of Teheran, a spectacle largely forgotten because of the subsequent developments in that country.

5. This does not automatically flow from the disintegration and disarmament of the former army. The ruling class can attempt to substitute a new bourgeois army for the old one, as it did in Cuba after the downfall of Batista and in Nicaragua after the fall of Somoza, but without success.

6. This is the currently prevailing explanation of the reasons for the Shah's downfall: the combination of the "white revolution" destabilizing traditional Iranian society and the savagery of SAVAK.

7. In Russia the cause of the February–March 1917 revolution was the rottenness of tsarism and the tremendous parasitical weight of the peasants' exploitation upon the overall economic development of the country. The triggering factors of that revolution were hunger riots by the Petrograd women workers, which the Cossacks refused to repress. This expressed the emergence of de facto alliance between the working class and the peasantry, contrary to what had occurred in the repression of the 1905 revolution. There is, however, also a deeper dialectical mediation between structure and conjuncture. The specific social-political order in tsarist Russia determined both its participation in the First World War and its increasing incapacity to cope with the material and political prerequisites of successful warfare. This incapacity in turn deepened the social crisis in a dramatic way—leading to chronic food shortages, to hunger riots, and hence to the outbreak of the February–March 1917 revolution. A similarly multi-layered analysis is needed to understand contemporary revolutionary moments— including unsuccessful ones, such as May 1968 in France. What went on in France during the climax of the mass upsurge and the general strike deserves to be seen as a revolution, although it was defeated. The triggering factor of the student revolt in Paris must itself be seen in the context of a deeper structural crisis of social and political relations. Useful here is the remarkable study by the Soviet sociologist Alex D. Khlopin, *New Social Movements in the West: Their Causes and Prospects of Developments* which complements Western Marxist analyses.

8. In Russia the material interests of the Cossacks as sons of peasants, the connections of these interests to political awareness on the one hand and to the explosive crisis of the relations of production in the countryside on the other hand, all converge to explain the Cossacks' peculiar shift in behavior at a given moment in a given place.

9. It is, of course, possible that this breakdown is only temporary and only lasts some weeks or months. But this doesn't make the collapse less real. In Germany—not only but of course especially in Berlin—this is what occurred in November–December 1918. In France this is what occurred at the climax of May 1968. Indeed, it was recently confirmed that, at that moment, General de Gaulle couldn't phone General Massu, the commander of the French Army in Germany: he had lost control of the whole telecommunications system in Paris as a result of an effective general strike. An anonymous woman telephone operator, whom he finally succeeded in speaking to personally, refused to obey his order. The decision of the strike committee prevailed. These are the unknown heroines and heroes of revolution. This is the stuff proletarian revolutions are made of.

10. See Edward Luttwack, *Coup D'Etat: A Practical Handbook* (Cambridge: Harvard University Press, 1979); cf. interview with *Stampa-Sera*, August 8, 1988.

11. Nevertheless, Spinoza, who was himself skeptical about the outcome of revolutions, explicitly proclaimed the people's right to revolution, more than a century before that same right was ensconced in the Preamble of the American Declaration of Independence, and afterwards in the French Declaration of the Rights of Men and Citizens. To our knowledge the Yugoslav Constitution is today the only one which not only contains that right explicitly but even adds to it *the duty* to make a revolution under specific conditions.

12. The dogma of the basic "evil" of humankind is based in the West on the superstition of Original Sin. Of late it has received a pseudo-scientific veneer with the Konrad Lorenz school of the alleged universal aggressiveness of human beings, which some psychologists tend to generalize into a human trend toward self-destruction. Better psychologists, in the first place Sigmund Freud, pointed out that the human psyche combines both a trend toward cooperation and a trend toward self-destruction, Eros and Thanatos, to love and to kill. If only the second one had prevailed, humankind would have disappeared a long time ago instead of showing an impressive demographic-biological expansion.

13. Two thousand years ago the Jewish philosopher Hillel expressed the contradictions of individual skepticism in a succinct way: "If I am not for myself, who is for me? And if I am for myself alone, what then am I? And if not now, then when?" Kant tried to escape that dilemma through his categorical imperative, but failed to apply it convincingly to social conflicts (see his attitude toward the French Revolution). Marx found the solution in his categorical imperative to struggle against all social conditions in which human beings are debased, oppressed, and alienated.

14. Revolutionary continuity was maintained by a handful of followers of Babeuf, who, through the person of Buonarotti, helped to inspire Auguste Blanqui's *Societe des Pouvres*, which gave rise to a new revolutionary organization in the 1830s. But for nearly 40 years there were very few organized revolutionaries in the country, which witnessed five revolutions in a century.

15. The debate goes on, of course. Rene Sedillot (*Le coût de la revolution française* (Paris: Perrin, 1987) is the most brazen of the latter-day dragon-killers, who continue the good fight against the French Revolution after two centuries. The bases of his argumentation are revealed by the fact that he adds the victims of counter-revolution, in the first place of Napoleon's wars, to the cost of the revolution. But he does not compare these "costs" to those of the Ancien Regime's dynastic wars: the devastation of a quarter of Germany, the big famine in France at the beginning of the 18th century, etc.

16. The inclusion of Deng Hsiao-ping in this list is, of course, open to serious challenge. Mao was not Lenin; he was rather a unique combination of the traits of both Lenin and Stalin. Deng Hsiao-ping, in spite of many right-wing tendencies in his policies, cannot be considered the Chinese revolution's Thermidorian equivalent of Stalin.

17. Incidentally, this is one of the objective bases for the second "law of permanent revolution" formulated by Trotsky. For the revolutionary process to continue after it starts to recede in a given country, its center of gravity must shift to another one.

18. Classical examples of defeated counter-revolutionary coups are the Kornilov one in Russia, August 1917, the Kapp-von Luttwitz *putsch* in Germany in 1920, and the Spanish military-fascist uprising in July 1936 in Catalonia, Madrid, Valencia, Malaga, the Basque country, etc.

19. A democratic counter-revolution seeks to maintain the essential features of bourgeois democracy, including a legal mass labor movement, universal franchise, and a broadly free press, after having beaten back the workers' attempts to conquer power and to arm themselves. Of course, while engaged in suppressing the German revolution, Ebert, Noske, and Co. systematically curtailed democratic freedoms, forbade political parties, suspended newspapers, requisitioned strikers, and even outlawed strikes to preserve the bourgeois state. Moreover, Ebert cynically lied before the All-German Congress of Workers' and Soldiers' Councils (December 1918) when he denied having brought soldiers to Berlin for repressive purposes. He had actually done so, in direct connection with the Imperial Army's High Command, behind the back of his fellow "people's commissars" (ministers) of the Independent Socialist Party. The repression started a few days later.

20. This occurred in Germany throughout the country, starting with January 1919 in Berlin. It occurred in Barcelona after the May days in 1937, in Greece starting with December 1944, and in Indonesia in 1965, to quote some examples. Courageous left socialists like the prewar Austrian social democrats and Salvador Allende in Chile did not refuse to fight counter-revolution, arms in hand, but they refused to organize and prepare the masses systematically for this unavoidable showdown and deliberately left the initiative to the enemy, which meant courting disaster.

21. Revolutionists cannot "cause revolutions," nor can they "provoke" them artificially (this is the basic difference between a revolution and a *putsch*). Engels went even further: "Die Leute die sich ruhmen, eine Revolution *gemacht* zu haben, haben immer noch am Tage darauf gesehen, dass sie nicht wussten was sie taten, das die 'gemachte' Revolution, jener die sie hatten machen wollen, durchaus nicht ahnlich sah" (letter to Verra Sassulitch of April 23, 1885 [MEW], Berlin: Dietz-Verlag, Vol. 36, p. 307).

22. The concept of "combined revolution" also applies to some imperialist countries, but with a different weight of the combined elements from that of third-world countries: the combination of proletarian revolution and self-determination of oppressed national minorities in Spain; the combination of proletarian revolution and Black and Hispanic liberation in the United States.

23. For example, in Finland in 1917–18; in Austria in 1918–19, 1927, and 1934; in Germany in 1918–23; in Italy in 1919–20, 1944–45, and 1969; in Spain in 1931–37; in France in 1936 and 1968; and in Portugal in 1974–75.

24. Some argue that the impossibility of escaping "technology compulsion" (*technologischer Sachzwang*) constitutes an unsurpassable obstacle on the road to proletarian revolution and "Marxian socialism." This is an unproven assumption, based upon the *petitio principii* that technology somehow develops and is applied independently from the social interests of those who have the means (under large-scale commodity production: the capital) to apply it.

25. See Eduard Bernstein: *Die Voraussetzungen des Sozialismus und die Aufgaben der Sozialdemokratie* (Stuttgart, 1899).

26. On Kautsky's evolutions away from revolutionary Marxism in 1909–10, its turning point (his capitulation to the *Parteivorstand* on the censorship that body applied to his booklet *The Road to Power*), and its political outcome in his opposition to Rosa Luxemburg's campaign in favor of political mass strikes, see Massimo Salvadori, *Karl Kautsky and the Socialist Revolution* (London: NBL, 1979), pp. 123ff.

206   MARXIST PROGRAM AND THEORY

27. Karl Kautsky, *Les Trois Sources du Marxisme* (1907) (Paris: Spartacus, 1969), pp. 12–13.
28. Kautsky's articles on ultra-imperialism, in which he considered inter-imperialist wars more and more unlikely, started to appear in 1912. The final one had the unfortunate fate of appearing in *Die Neue Zeit* after the outbreak of World War I.
29. We have developed this idea further in our article "The Reasons for Founding the Fourth International and Why They Remain Valid Today," *International Marxist Review* (Summer-Autumn, 1988). (See pp. 143–78 of this volume.)
30. Ernest Mandel, *Revolutionary Marxism Today* (London: New Left Books, 1979).
31. The case of the German workers' answer to the Kapp-von Luttwitz coup of 1920 and of the Spanish workers' answer to the fascist-military uprising of July 1936—in a more limited way also the Italian workers' uprising of 1948—helps to integrate into this topology the question of the proletariat's capacity to answer massively counter-revolutionary initiatives by the bourgeoisie. This will remain on the agenda in the West in the future as it was in the past. But this does not justify any refusal to recognize that the process of proletarian revolutions likely to occur in the West and in Japan will most probably be quite different from these examples, as well as from the revolutionary processes which we witnessed in Yugoslavia, China, Indochina, Cuba, and Nicaragua during and after World War II.
32. See Norman Geras, *The Legacy of Rosa Luxemburg* (London: New Left Books, 1976), on this and on Luxemburg being one of the founders, together with Trotsky, of a theory of dual power emerging from workers' mass strikes.
33. Trotsky, "What Next? Vital Questions for the German Proletariat" (January 1932) *The Struggle Against Fascism in Germany* (New York: Pathfinder Press, 1972), p. 142.
34. Leon Trotsky first formulated that conclusion in 1933 in his article "The Class Nature of the Soviet State" (October 1, 1933) *Writings of Leon Trotsky 1933–1934* (New York: Pathfinder Press, 1975), p. 101f.
35. On the question of how far that characterization is legitimate, see Ernest Mandel, *Beyond Perestroika* (London: Verso, 1988).
36. On the theoretical foundations of the definition of "political revolution" and the analysis which leads to it, see Ernest Mandel, "Bureaucratie et production marchande," *Quatrieme Internationale*, 24 (April 1987).
37. *The New York Review of Books*, October 27, 1988.
38. The Mexican sociologist Pablo Gonzales Casanova has tried to refute the legitimacy of political revolution in the bureaucratized workers states on the basis of a hierarchy of revolutionary tasks on a world scale. As long as imperialism survives, revolutionists (socialists, anti-imperialists) everywhere in the world should give priority to the fight against that monster over and above all other struggles. (See his "La Penetraction metafisica en el Marxismo europeo," in *Sabado*, magazine supplement to the Mexican daily *Unomasuno*, 8/1/1983). Underlying that reasoning is the hypothesis that an ongoing, not to say a victorious, political revolution in a bureaucratized workers' state somehow weakens the fight against imperialism. But that supposition is completely unfounded, for the reason we have advanced.

Index